Fireworks, Brass Bands, and Elephants:

Promotional Events with Flair for Libraries and Other Nonprofit Organizations

Fireworks, Brass Bands, and Elephants:

Promotional Events with Flair for Libraries and Other Nonprofit Organizations

by Louise Condak Liebold

ORYX PRESS
1986

The rare Arabian Oryx is believed to have inspired the myth of the unicorn. This desert antelope became virtually extinct in the early 1960s. At that time several groups of international conservationists arranged to have 9 animals sent to the Phoenix Zoo to be the nucleus of a captive breeding herd. Today the Oryx population is over 400, and herds have been returned to reserves in Israel, Jordan, and Oman.

Copyright © 1986 by
The Oryx Press
2214 North Central at Encanto
Phoenix, AZ 85004-1483

Published simultaneously in Canada

All rights reserved
No part of this publication may be reproduced or transmitted in any form or by any means, electronic or mechanical, including photocopying, recording, or by any information storage and retrieval system, without permission in writing from The Oryx Press.

Printed and Bound in the United States of America

∞ The paper used in this publication meets the minimum requirements of American National Standard for Information Science—Permanence of Paper for Printed Library Materials, ANSI Z39.48, 1984.

Library of Congress Cataloging-in-Publication Data

Liebold, Louise Condak.
   Fireworks, brass bands, and elephants.

   Bibliography: p.
   Includes index.
   1. Public relations—Libraries. 2. Libraries-Cultural programs. 3. Libraries and community.
   4. Corporations, Nonprofit—Management. 5. Public relations—Endowments. 6. Promotion of special events.
   I. Title.
   Z716.3.L54   1986   021.7   85-43488
   ISBN 0-89774-249-4 (alk. paper)

Contents

Preface vii

Chapter 1: Guidelines for Success 1

Chapter 2: Special Events and Celebrations 9

Chapter 3: Cooperative Ventures 20

Chapter 4: Thematic Programing 30

Chapter 5: Special Events Fund-Raising 52

Chapter 6: Games, Contests, Festivals, and Fairs 66

Chapter 7: Publicity and the Media 86

Chapter 8: One More Time (Over 100 Additional Exciting Ideas) 113

Chapter 9: Quotable Quotes 126

Index 129

Preface

I still remember my first special event. My parents took me and my baby brother to the Memorial Day parade in our hometown of Haverhill, Massachusetts. This was followed a few months later by my first fireworks display in a neighbor's yard on the Fourth of July. Those were the special events of my early life—nothing to compare with the Macy's Thanksgiving Day Parade with all its hoopla or the fireworks celebration at the 100th birthday party of the Brooklyn Bridge in 1983—but special events all the same.

I have now been involved in creating and promoting special events for over 25 years. The craziest job I ever had was directing public relations for a season at Steeplechase Park in Coney Island. Gimmicks and stunts were an everyday happening. New York City fashion models and fledgeling actresses were always on call in the hopes that one of the gimmicky photo stories that we featured them in would make the wire services and they would be discovered. One summer's day, there was nary a model around. The staff photographer and Frank Tilyou, owner of Steeplechase and very much a promotional-minded individual, turned to me with "You're it." Before I knew it, I was in a bathing suit typing away in the swimming pool. It was a hot-weather story. The caption read, "It was so hot out at Coney Island's Steeplechase Park that Louise Condak, the Park's public relations director, took to writing her press releases in the Park's pool to cool off."

Relating all my on-the-job stories would fill another book. There have been plenty; I have worked as a fashion publicist, a newspaper reporter, a radio writer/commentator, and a public relations account executive handling a variety of clients. And now, doing public relations and programing for a public library is, I find, just as exciting and innovative as any of my other jobs have been.

Always seeking the ultimate special event or program has brought me in touch with many creative people. In this book, you will meet many movers and shakers. They have generously shared their ideas, creations, and thoughts; a few innovations come from my own bag of tricks. I must add, that in doing my research for the book, I was most impressed by the enthusiasm of the doers and the quality of their presentations. I know you will be too.

I would love to personally thank all of the wonderful people who helped me, but that would probably take another book! However, I would be remiss not to first thank the supportive staff at "my" library, the East Meadow Public Library, and the two terrific directors I have worked with, Tom Dutelle and Norman Seldes. Nothing could faze these two! Special thanks go to "my" printer, Ed Gianelli, and then to Jerry Goldman, Joan Johns, Fran Lewis, Marion Rothenberg, and Nancy Weinberg...and a large order of franks and beans to my husband Paul, who not only taught me more than I ever wanted to know about a personal computer but was my patient in-house editor. Thanks also to my Oryx editor, Jan Krygier. Oh, yes, one last thing. You will find recipes in this book besides all the good how-to ideas and show-and-tell examples. Enjoy them all...I did.

Chapter 1
Guidelines for Success

★ Creative Programing
★ Planning
★ Promotion
★ Doing It
★ After the Fact
★ You Gotta Have a Gimmick

You've got it. I've got it. Some have it more than others. Some of us have to work at developing it, but it is there to discover and use. I am not talking about money, charm, or chutzpah. Creativity is the name of this game.

You've heard people say, "Not me; I haven't a creative bone in my body." Pshaw. It may take searching and probing, but it will surface. You will be delighted to see what you can do. But be forewarned: Creativity can be habit-forming. Once the juices have been turned on, you may have trouble stopping the flow. But it'll be worth it. First, find the creative you and then join forces with other creative thinkers. The ideas, which are out there everywhere, are yours free for the taking. Once you start thinking, you'll formulate your own creative ideas. Now, you've got your confidence and know that you too can create, produce, and carry out programing and special events...for fun and profit. Why not both?

CREATIVE PROGRAMING

What makes an activity a creative program? Filling a calendar with lots and lots of programs is not necessarily creative programing, although it may make you look busy. There's nothing truly wrong with that, but what about the quality of the programing you are offering? Think about it. No one is suggesting that every day at your organization should be like a three-ring circus, but once in a while, it couldn't hurt! Quality, imagination, and that little something special make creative programing happen. Some simple examples. You do film programing. You conduct such programs often and people enjoy them. How about something different next time? Have a filmmaker present and talk about his/her film. Not possible? Then find an articulate film buff or film professor to speak instead. Choose a theme and show a series of films using a different speaker each time. If it's the right type of movie and the budget allows, serve free popcorn. Promote your series by printing the film information on brown paper popcorn bags.

It's spring, and your thoughts run to gardening programs. Certainly you could do one program and call it "Getting the Most Out of Your Garden" with a local horticulturist as the speaker. To be more creative, add another program, "Planting Herbs and Then Using Them." The speaker could be an amateur herbalist from a local garden club who would also demonstrate herbal cooking with a tasting session. Have dried herbs for people to touch and sniff. Print up some recipes and hand them out. You might even contact a local botanical garden and have some of their volunteers hold an herbal plant sale on a Saturday morning. Get a local garden center to donate a basket of garden tools for a door prize at your first program. Have a central area for displays? Plunk a bright red wheelbarrow loaded with gardening tools, packets of seeds, a bale of peat moss, and a sign announcing your gardening series. Got the idea? It's that added dimension that will draw a crowd and make whatever you do a creative program.

These are the simplest illustrations of creative programing. It takes a while, but once you get started, you won't think of doing it any other way. The results will be that impressive. Compliments from your community, your staff, and the media will be more satisfying than a super ice cream sundae and less fattening! You'll want more. And you'll be ready to deliver after you've examined the many ideas for exciting creative programs and special events presented in this book.

Special Events

Special events date back to the Romans and possibly earlier. They're nothing new, but more and more profit-making companies and nonprofit organizations are turning to the special event as a way to attract public interest and make money.

According to *Special Events Report*, (an international biweekly newsletter on events, festivals, and promotions), over 1,800 special events were held in this country in 1984. These 1,800 events were commercial ventures. Companies spend big bucks to sponsor and create them. General Foods spends approximately $1 billion a year on advertising and promotion; part of that money is used to fund such events. Companies have inaugurated special events/marketing departments within their corporate public relations/advertising divisions. Others hire public relations firms and advertising agencies, and now there's a whole new creative professional operating and ready for hire: the special events maker or coordinator. There's a reason. They pay off. Maybe you're not ready or big enough to hire a professional special events maker, and you might not be able to budget $5,000 for a special event (I can't), but there is a place in the special events arena for you...and me.

As each special event is unique, so is each organization, company, or group. What may work well for one may not be good for the other. But who's to say you cannot change your image? Maybe it's time for a change. In his book *Communication by Objective*, L. Robert Oaks writes, "A good image attracts people and resources. It is recognized within the community an organization serves...." Have you an identity? When the name of your organization is mentioned, what picture or thought comes to mind? What is the central purpose of your organization? Why do you plan and execute special events? Is it to better your image? To get your story across in a more palatable manner? Do you consider it another form of communication? Do you have guidelines, and what are the long-range objectives for your organization? If you don't have guidelines and objectives, sit down, think about them, and write them all down on paper. Then, go over the list with your staff, trustees, or friends of your organization. Develop an image, formulate long-range plans, and then explore and create special events which may, in turn, help favorably change or enhance your image.

Why should you have a special event? Here are a few reasons: to celebrate a birthday or anniversary of an organization or company...a building dedication...an open house...a festival.... There are at least 1,001 ways to celebrate with a special event. Again, I've only just skimmed the surface. There'll be plenty more later.

First and foremost, know your community. Look around. What's happening where you live and work? Right now. What's coming up? Be a part of it. Better still, be the instigator/creator. If you're enthusiastic, others will join in. Creativity can trigger more creativity and so on and so on. Look for the offbeat. One of my colleagues who loves quotations offered this wonderful one from G.K. Chesterton: "Look at the familiar until it seems strange."

It's there. Be resourceful. Take advantage of what's immediately around you: people, companies, professionals, academics, recreation centers, arts councils, museums, parks, town councils, celebrities, and most important, noncelebrities...just plain folks. Keep a people file. Keep an idea file—better make it a large filing cabinet! You will find that, through the years of researching, you'll run out of space before you run out of ideas! Watch television talk and news shows, listen to radio talk shows, and keep your pad and pencil handy. Of course, you certainly can't be glued to your radio or television 24 hours a day, but there are people and friends in your community who can serve as your talent scouts. Insomniacs in our community report back to me with handwritten notes containing some good ideas after listening to all-night radio talk shows. You're in a public service business, so it should be easier for you to ask people you know if they know of someone who would be good for a series of programs you are planning. Or where you can hire a good country and western band real cheap. Share ideas and resources with others. It's called networking. It pays. Remember, a special event is designed to dramatize and/or promote an idea, cause, image, or program. No two special events are alike. All are different and should be treated so.

Cooperative Ventures

There are many ways to create programming. You may feel you want to reach out and work with other agencies or organizations in your community. The idea will probably come from you. If you know your community well, and you have a good handle on the idea, then the quickest way to go would be phone calls. I always like everything in writing, so I would recommend follow-up letters with detailed information and plans. This is a must if you are also looking for monetary support from a local bank, service organization, or company. Working with community groups certainly will strengthen your community relations. So, do think of cooperative ventures as another method of programming. There are some interesting examples of such events and programs in Chapter 3, "Cooperative Ventures."

Thematic Programing

Another fun way to do programming is to find a theme. I find this kind of programming offers endless opportunities. For example, early in 1986 I began working on an idea tentatively called "Memories of Movies and Movie Palaces." The idea began at the Cooper-Hewitt Museum in New York City where I saw an exhibit, "American Picture Palaces." Much of the material came from a book, *American Picture Palaces* by David Naylor. I bought a few pieces of movie memorabilia display materials from the museum knowing I would use them eventually. In 1983, the New York Historical Society had a very interesting exhibit, "Lights, Camera, Action," in conjunction with the showings of some classic silent films. The exhibit was presented at the Historical Society by the Astoria Motion Picture and Television Foundation. My sources were growing. I was still looking for a more local connection and I found it one Sunday in 1984 in the Long Island section of *The New York Times*. Under the auspices of the Wantagh Historical Society, a Warren Hiltonsmith was to present a slide/talk show, "The Golden Age of the Movie Palace," at a public library on Long Island. I found Mr. Hiltonsmith's address and phone number in the phone book and wrote him of my idea. Delighted, he phoned me back immediately and said he would be happy to participate in the program series. He also gave me the name of another movie-palaces buff who might have some memorabilia for display. I plan to take a busload of people to the American Museum of the Moving Image on a Friday or Saturday evening so they can see the movie artifacts and also enjoy a classic film. I hope to be able to take another busload of people for a tour of a few "preserved" movie palaces in the nearby county of Queens. At least two more items are in my movie plans: showing of a silent film with a live piano player accompaniment with some free popcorn as the added attraction and, since we're a public library, publishing a bibliography of reading materials about movie stars, past and present. And, if I can work it out, I would like to have a movie night when everyone who attends gets a free dish, just the way the movie houses did it in the thirties! You will find some excellent theme ideas in Chapter 4, "Thematic Programing."

Special Events Fund Raising

Every once in a while you might want to plan a fund-raiser. There are many ways you can have a creative and fun event and make money at the same time. This is where knowing your community pays off. You get to know who the doers are; be certain to get them on a working committee. A certain type of event may do well in one community and not arouse a sleeping dog in another. Remember, you can always adapt a good idea and fashion it to your needs. More than ever, you should strive for careful planning with every minute detail attended to. Chapter 5, "Special Events Fund-Raising," is devoted to a myriad of fund-raiser events.

Games, Contests, Festivals, and Fairs

People love contests. Just look at the popularity of game shows on television. The media respond enthusiastically to an onion-eating contest or watermelon seed-spitting contest, and the thousand and more such contests held weekly throughout the world. Festivals and fairs can also be part of your creative efforts. You'll find plenty of such fun-filled and varied events in Chapter 6, "Games, Contests, Festivals, and Fairs."

Once you've gone to all this effort, you will certainly want more than you and your committee present at your event or program. To me, what comes next is just as important as the event itself in making the event successful. Promotion. Promotion is more than just spreading the word. Yes, it is sending the news releases out to the media in plenty of time. But promotion is also looking good graphically. Your brochures, fliers, and newsletters should all reflect your image. They should not be left to chance. All should be carefully planned and designed, to the best of your ability and budget. In Chapter 7, "Publicity and the Media," you will find a wealth of ideas and suggestions on public relations, image building, and graphics.

You'll find at least 100 more exciting ideas in Chapter 8, "One More Time (Over 100 Additional Exciting Ideas)." And, in Chapter 9, "Quotable Quotes," you will find further inspiration in the form of quotable quotes from many of the people who are doing it right.

PLANNING

Plan carefully and well in advance. Some events or programs may take as long as two or three years to plan. Think of a wedding. So much time and effort go into such an event and then, before you know it, it's over! If you're putting that much time and effort into it, do a little more. Look for a little twist or gimmick to make your special event truly special and more appealing to your community, your audience, and the media.

Strive for quality. If you cannot give an event the time it needs, don't do it. Save it for another time. You cannot make it with an idea alone, no matter how great it is. The event or program must be worked out in detail. Put everything down on paper, and review it carefully. Sometimes novices don't realize the work required in planning and executing events and find themselves shorthanded and in a frazzle when the day arrives. It can happen, and it's better to face the facts in the beginning. Be well organized. Creativity is the fun part. Organizing all the details is a must. Nothing should be left to chance.

Read, read, and research everything you can about the subject/theme you are creating. Develop a special events folder for each project. Save everything, including correspondence, for this one project. The folder should be bulging by the time you are ready for the launching.

Form a committee. You'll need help. But you should still be the one who is in charge, the one responsible for the coordination, etc. Involve trustees or friends of your organization. Assign each a definite task.

Have you checked the local calendars? Be certain there are no conflicts with other special events. There will never be a totally clear community calendar, but be sure there is nothing else "really big" going on at the same time as your big event.

If it's really a big show, be certain to be in touch with your local police department; you may need assistance with traffic and crowd control.

Need more ideas? Look to the commercial world, which daily inundates us with their attention-getting material. Check 'em out. Borrow and adapt what you like for your situation. I have gotten many ideas from *Advertising Age*, which is published twice weekly. It's filled with what's new and what's doing in the advertising world. I also check out *Public Relations Journal* each month for ideas. These are just two publications. There are many more, and don't forget your daily newspaper.

By this time, you have everything down on paper and find you could use some more help. Money? Even if you do have a special events/programs budget, there are times when you could use additional funding. Try for sponsorship from a state or local agency or for a mini-grant from a local bank, Rotary, Kiwanis, or Lions group. If you're planning something truly big, you may need a special grant. A note of caution: Grantsmanship takes time, talent, and know-how.

Just about every state has an "arts council" which may provide funding for your worthwhile projects. In your area, you may even have a regional arts council. Each council has guidelines. Write to the one in your area for information. If you want to learn about grant writing, check with "The Grantsmanship Center" listed in the "Resources" section at the end of this chapter. The center conducts grant writing workshops throughout the country. The National Endowment for the Arts, an independent agency of the federal government, is another funding source. Your public library is probably the best place for seeking grant information. I have found, from talking to some who have succeeded in obtaining grants, that writing grant proposals can be a full-time job. Personally, I find when you are juggling many hats on your job, it is difficult enough to find the time to plan, create, promote, and execute an event. I have attended several grant writing workshops and was overwhelmed by the paperwork required. But, on the other hand, I have succeeded several times in obtaining mini-grants from Poets & Writers for thematic events I had planned. Poets & Writers is interested in cosponsoring literary-related programs involving poets and writers. You will find information about that agency at the end of this chapter also. Another contact is The Foundation Center. Its directory lists some 26,000 foundations which can offer assistance. The center is also listed at the end of this chapter. I wish you luck.

PROMOTION

"If you don't tell 'em, you don't sell 'em!" is an old but good adage. Tell everyone, even the cop on the beat, about your special event, even while you're still in the planning stages. Who knows...s/he may have a suggestion or a resource person for you. Be sure, if you have a large staff, that they are all informed about the forthcoming event. Get them involved. Enthusiasm is contagious.

Know the media and their special interests and deadlines. Get your news release out at least two to three weeks prior to the event. I prefer three to six weeks to allow for a possible follow-up story. If you have time and money, and the special event warrants it, prepare a press kit containing a news release, photos, fact sheet, brochures, fliers, buttons, balloons, invitations, etc.

If you publish a newsletter, use it as the first place to tell your community about the big event. Your community deserves to know first. Sometimes word of mouth is the best form of publicity. People love to talk. If you are running a series of events/programs and are the one who does the introductions, take advantage of the captive audiences and do "commercials" about your special event. They all work.

If you have a central location and the space, set up displays and exhibits in conjunction with your event. No space? Then place your displays in heavily traveled walkways in town and in retail stores or banks.

Promotional fliers, brochures, posters...saturate your building and anywhere and everywhere else that you can.

For more detailed information on putting together news releases, brochures, fliers, press kits, etc., refer to Chapter 7, "Publicity and the Media."

DOING IT

The day is here! This is what it's all about. You've planned it all. So what could go wrong? Plenty. I'll bet everyone has a story to tell, but since it's my book, I get first dibs. The room was set and 125 people were sitting and waiting for another stimulating "Lunch'n Books" program. I was basically laid back after so many years of doing the series, and my speaker was only five minutes late. Parkway traffic. Still time, my heart said, but my stomach knew something was wrong. The phone rang. It was for me. "Louise, I'm sorry I couldn't get to the phone sooner, but I'm in the emergency ward of Syosset Hospital."

Thinking only of my audience and the possibility of my having to do a soft-shoe routine, I asked,

"How long will you be?" Not even a "How are you and what's wrong?"

"It's not me, it's my little girl. She fell on the nursery school playground and hurt her head. She seems to be all right."

"I'm glad she's all right. When will you be here?" I persevered.

"I'll call back soon."

In retrospect, I am embarrassed about my behavior that day, but I was desperate. I had to face an audience. Here's where knowing your community helped. I spotted a man in the audience who was newly retired, the former warden of the "Tombs" prison in Manhattan, whom I knew to be articulate, since he lectured professionally. I whispered into his ear. He grinned and nodded his head and proceeded to captivate the audience for 30 minutes with a talk on the state of the criminal justice system in our country and his own philosophy about the subject. When our speaker finally walked in, he was perplexed but pleased that the audience had such a great warm-up.

Another time, a speaker fell down her apartment stairs as she was leaving for our library. She never made it to the program and had someone call me from the hospital. I am not totally heartless; I understood. Luckily, the program for that night featured a panel discussion—and the other two speakers were able to carry the ball. One last anecdote. I will never forget the night when my two speakers were traveling together from a neighboring state and were involved in a traffic accident on the way. They phoned and said they were fine and would be on their way in a short while. Knowing it would take them another hour to reach us and also realizing they had to be in a state of shock, I said, "I think the best thing would be for you to go home. We'll reschedule the program." I faced the audience with the truth and we all went home. Thank goodness it was not a big event. Fortunately, most special events do not depend on just one or two persons.

Assume nothing.
You're the responsible one. Don't forget it. Check and recheck everything. Disasters can happen. Stay cool.

Assume nothing.
You've been efficient and have confirmed in writing all dates, etc., with everyone. Not enough. Always check with your speakers or performers a day or two before their appearance. Substitutions can still be made.

Assume nothing.
Get to the event site early. Be sure all of the equipment is in place and working. If there is food involved, be certain it's there or on its way.

Assume nothing.
When staff or volunteers arrive, hand out program schedules. Be certain that everyone who has an assignment understands what it is.

Assume nothing.
Be flexible. You may have no choice at times. If possible, meet and greet the public or have others do it. The personal touch is so important.

Assume nothing.
If it's an ongoing event, as in a month-long series of programs, treat each one as an individual event. It is.

Assume nothing.
The weather. You can't do a thing about it. So, if some of your activities or all are planned for the outdoors, have an alternate plan or an alternate date in mind...just in case.

Assume nothing.
Relax and enjoy the special event with the others, and always keep your sense of humor!

AFTER THE FACT

Tell the community how great an event it was. Do it in the local weeklies and in your newsletter. People like to share good times even if they cannot be there. Got photographs? Display them in a prominent spot in your building or other areas in the community. Thank all of those who assisted and were involved—short notes or phone calls will do. Don't forget the media, especially if they've been generous with air time or newsprint. Keep everything (well, you might part with a few items) for future reference. Some special events and programs are worth repeating, some annually and some after an interim of a few years, and some never, never again! You'll know. If you have a committee, call a meeting. Rehash the event. Keep notes and suggestions and new ideas. And then, go on to the next project!

YOU GOTTA HAVE A GIMMICK

To gimmick or not to gimmick: That may be the question. I feel it's better to gimmick sometimes than never to have gimmicked at all. Some people frown on gimmicks because they associate them with what they represented years ago: deception or trickery. Never resort to either. But looking for something offbeat or unusual to attract your audience, the community, and the media can do no harm. What it can do is promote and create a wider appeal for your event. So, think of the gimmick as an attention-getting device or feature. The commercial world has been using gimmicks for years legitimately and effectively. You're in business, too. Competition is keen everywhere, and the "big sell" is evident each day...from politicians to baby food! Don't think that just because you are presenting a special event that people will be there in numbers. What's so special about your program or event? Make it special. Sometimes something as simple as the title of your series might lure them in. Not too long ago, in doing a series of programs on Frankenstein, I called the series (made up of three events) "Frankenstein Frolics," and the theme of the promotional graphics for the fliers and newsletter was repeated sketches of Frankenstein and his bride dancing in a chorus line. It drew chuckles and favorable responses.

When Pepsi's advertising powers-to-be use someone like Michael Jackson in their television commercials and spend all those millions of dollars, they do it for its gimmick value. The celebrity is the gimmick. S/he attracts your attention, and the advertiser expects to and does sell more Pepsi.

So look for ways to hype up a simple program or an event. Something as easy as a bicycle repair workshop series can be made more enticing. Certainly the idea itself is a community service, especially if it's free. Say you've convinced a representative (an articulate one) from a bicycle shop to conduct a two-part bike workshop. The first part will deal with bike safety and include a film and discussion; the second part will take place on a Saturday morning with actual bike repairs being done. Call your resource person "Dr. Bike." Have the person wear a white medical coat (borrowed from a local hospital or doctor), and if possible, have the medical logo or a red cross stenciled on the front and back of the coat. Take some photos with the person wearing the coat, carrying a tool kit and standing next to a bicycle. Send it to the local weeklies and use it in your newsletter if you have one and in your fliers or promotional brochures. Not enough? Borrow a bicycle from the shop and hang it from the ceiling in your building or place it in a prominent space with lots of traffic. Plunk a poster on it telling about Dr. Bike's two visits and workshops. It will draw attention and get the results you want: an audience, community interest, participation, and possible media coverage.

Using the same white coat idea, we celebrated our library's "Sweet Sixteen Birthday" a few years back with many different special events. One of them was a kite fly-off at a local park. (A kite workshop had been held a month earlier.) Most of the kites were homemade and rather fragile, and the spring day was blustery. Volunteers, teen aged pages from our library staff, served as kite "medics." They rescued injured kites and took them to the first aid station for repair. In their white doctor's coats, carrying the kites on actual stretchers, these young people made quite a picture and drew lots of laughs and attention. The youngsters with the "hurt" kites took it all very seriously and walked their kites to the first aid station with the "medics." The "medics" actually did fix 85 percent of the kites! Both young and old enjoyed the whole day and appreciated this bit of gimmickry.

Sometimes there's a lull and you look for something to do just to perk things up a bit. This is the time to grab *Chase's Annual Events* book! No self-respecting program planner should be without one. One year in early August, the late summer doldrums had set in. We were looking for something small and fun for the children's room to do in mid-September. I consulted my *Chase's* and found out that the ice cream cone was invented on September 22, 80 years ago. I remembered that the children's librarians had had a craft workshop using real ice cream cones a while back and the youngsters had loved it, especially since it involved eating. Nothing too unique about this workshop, but combine it with the ice cream anniversary date and with donated gift certificates for free ice cream cones from a local ice cream shop for all the children in the workshop, and you've got a cute idea and a story for the media. Our daily newspaper sent a reporter to cover the event, and they ran a feature story about it. Much ado about nothing? Yes, you might say that, especially since that very same week we had a successful building expansion vote. That same newspaper neglected to run even a one-liner on the passage of the vote. After all, our library was just one of many libraries during this time which had a building bond vote. To the general public, there was nothing special in that news. The unique, the unusual is usually what gets the precious space. But, there is an epilogue to our library's expansion story. When we began our building expansion campaign, a new Friends group was formed and one of its leaders was a local businessperson who had openly worked against our campaign nine years before. Now, he was with us! Telling the story to the press, we played that fact up; this was the gimmick. It worked. *Newsday* ran a feature story with an interview with the man and headlined it: "Change of Heart for Library Addition."

Sometimes you can get good ideas from gimmicks other people have dreamed up, even if you have to trim them down to fit your community and/or your budget. For example, Mount Sinai Hospital in Miami Beach, Florida, did a great promotion involving the healthfulness of chicken soup. The hospital's medical director, Dr. Marvin Sackner, had received international acclaim for a study confirming the healing powers of chicken soup. So what did the hospital do to promote itself? With the help of Manischewitz, it produced 10-ounce cans of chicken soup packaged under Mount Sinai's own label—under rabbinical supervision and kosher for Passover! They also produced a delightful accompanying brochure, explaining the merits of chicken soup.

Great story, but what can I do with that idea? Forget packaging cans of chicken soup. Just think chicken soup. We have certainly all had chicken soup. Most of us have been mothered with chicken soup when we've had a bad cold. With those memories, and sparked by Mount Sinai's ingenious use of chicken soup, I plan to use just the germ of

CHICKEN SOUP: A TRADITION

Used with permission of Mount Sinai Hospital, Miami Beach, FL.

MOUNT SINAI MEDICAL CENTER: PROVING TRADITION RIGHT

Used with permission of Mount Sinai Hospital, Miami Beach, FL.

the idea in my 1987 "Here's to Your Health" series at our library in February. In conjunction with a program, probably entitled, "Staying Well by Eating Well," I plan to hold a chicken soup recipe contest. I also plan to serve chicken soup (possibly the winning recipe) to the audience during this daytime program. The prize for the winning recipe could be a bigger and better pot to make more chicken soup. To set the mood, I plan to open the program with the showing of a funny film entitled "Chicken Soup," which was made by a young Long Island filmmaker in the 1970s and shows his grandmother making her chicken soup. After reading this, I am certain you will have even more original ideas of your own.

Now your creative juices should be flowing. The following chapters should inspire you more. You can do it, and are probably well on your way. Maybe you'll pick up and borrow some ideas and incorporate them into your own creative ones. Don't be afraid to try anything. Some of the special events and programs may not be specifically in your field, but you can adapt bits and pieces, or even the whole concept, for your needs and interests. Remember again, program ideas are everywhere, not just in this book. And don't feel timid about borrowing an idea. There is no such thing as a totally original idea. Someone said that...but not first. It was originally stated in the Old Testament (Ecclesiastes, 1:9.): "The thing that hath been, is that which shall be, and that which is done is that which shall be done; there is no new thing under the Sun." Maybe there is...give it a try!

RESOURCES

General

Barber, Peggy, ed. *The Library Awareness Book.* Chicago: American Library Association, 1982.
Presents 68 great ideas.

Button, Sarah E. *You Gotta Have a Gimmick. Money* 11 (12) (December 1984): 171–74.

Chase, William D., and Chase, Helen M. *Chase's Annual Events.* Chicago: Contemporary Books, Inc.

This annual publication is an almanac and survey of the year with holidays, special events, national and ethnic days, seasons, birthdays, anniversaries, festivals, fairs, and traditional observances the world over listed.

Duran, Dorothy B., and Duran, Clement A. *New Encyclopedia of Successful Program Ideas.* New York: Association Press, 1967.
Offers thousands of program ideas and sources for speakers and films. May be dated.

Eastman, Ann Heidbreder, and Parent, Roger H. *Great Library Promotion Ideas.* Chicago: American Library Association, 1984.
Profiles the John Cotton Dana Public Relations Award winners and notables.

Edsall, Marion. *Library Promotion Handbook.* Phoenix, AZ: Oryx Press, 1980.
Contains just about anything and everything you might want to know about library promotion with examples of special events and programs.

Golden, Hal, and Hansen, Kitty. *Special Events.* Dobbs Ferry, NY: Oceana, 1960.
Gives detailed suggestions on how to put together special events, from luncheons to conventions.

Gregory, Ruth W. *Anniversaries & Holidays.* 4th ed. Chicago: American Library Association, 1983.
Provides quick identification of notable anniversaries, holy days, holidays, and special event days.

Hatch, Jane M. *The American Book of Days.* 3rd ed. New York: H.W. Wilson Co., 1979.
A revised edition of the 1948 book. It lists days of the year with facts about ways to celebrate each day and how each day has been celebrated in the past.

Leibert, Edwin R. *Handbook of Special Events for Non-Profit Organizations.* New York: Association Press, 1972.
Covers the basics of special events and public relations and cites successful examples.

Oaks, Robert. *Communication by Objective: How Non-Profit Organizations Can Build Better Internal and Public Relations.* South Plainfield, NJ: Groupwork Today, Inc., 1977.

Stevens, Art. "What's Ahead for Special Events." *Public Relations Journal* 40 (6) (June 1984): 30–32.

Periodicals

Ukman, Lesa, ed. *Special Events Report.* 213 W. Institute Place, #303, Chicago, IL 60610.
An international biweekly subscription newsletter on events, festivals, and promotions.

Grant Information

Des Marais, Philip. *How to Get Government Grants.* 2nd ed. New York: New York Public Service Materials Center, 1980.

Hillman, Howard. *The Art of Winning Government Grants.* New York: Vanguard Press, Inc., 1979.

Hillman, Howard, and Abravanel, Karen. *The Art of Winning Foundation Grants.* New York: Vanguard Press, Inc., 1975.

Kiritz, N.J. *Program Planning and Proposal Writing.* Los Angeles: The Grantsmanship Center, 1979.

Kurzig, Carol. *Foundation Fundamentals.* New York: The Foundation Center, 1980.

There exist some other good sources of general information about grants. The Foundation Center, 888 Seventh Ave., New York, NY 10106, collects and distributes information about the more than 26,000 foundations in this country that offer many kinds of support to individuals and groups. Nonprofit organizations might like to look at *The Foundation Directory.* Your local public library may be one of the many in the country that has information about the center. Oryx Press, 2214 N. Central, Phoenix, AZ 85004, produces The GRANTS Database, which lists more than 5,000 grant programs worth billions of dollars. In addition, The Grantsmanship Center, 1031 S. Grand Ave., Los Angeles, CA 90015, offers three- to five-day workshops in cities throughout the nation and publishes a magazine six times a year entitled *The Grantsmanship Center News.* Another source of information is the National Endowment for the Arts, 1100 Pennsylvania Ave., N.W., Washington, DC 20506. This independent agency of the federal government supports the arts by awarding grants to American arts and artists. Their guide, *Guide to the National Endowment for the Arts,* is available by writing to the Office of Public Affairs at the center. A final source of information is Poets & Writers, 201 W. 54th St., New York, NY 10019. Its purpose is to serve as an information clearinghouse for the literary community, to aid writers, and to sponsor organizations and schools in finding each other. The clearinghouse publishes several publications, including a newsletter and a directory.

Chapter 2
Special Events and Celebrations

✻ Baby Astor's Birthday at the Bronx Zoo
✻ The Biggest Ice Cream Sundae
✻ Jazztime
✻ Carousels, Coney Island & Cotton Candy

Special events can come in all sizes. Some require large budgets; some need only minimal funding. In this chapter you will find a range of good examples of creative special events and celebrations. Many of the other events and programs discussed in this book could easily have fit into this chapter as well; however, those that appear here best illustrate the general ideas associated with this type of function. The most common reason for a special event would be the celebration of an organization's birthday or anniversary. Yes, you could simply have a big dinner, some dull speeches, some award presentations, and a birthday cake. To make it a special event, you could turn the birthday/anniversary into a three-ring circus, literally! Just because you're so happy about the event, find a theme (could be a circus), hire some clowns, some jugglers, a brass band, and ask everyone to attend dressed as a favorite circus performer. The invitations could be printed on balloons! If you've got the funding, rent a tent and throw some sawdust on the floor. If there's a stray elephant or tiger around, invite it too, along with its trainer of course! Make your anniversary a whole month of special events. But, a word of caution: Special events take careful planning, need lots of preparation time, and could be habit-forming!

BABY ASTOR'S BIRTHDAY AT THE BRONX ZOO

For those who live in the New York City area or its suburbs, the Bronx Zoo is a fun place to be; it is loved by young and old. Like some of us, it's been around a long time. But lately, things have been perking up more than ever at the new Bronx Zoo, thanks to creative thinking on the part of the zoo administration, its public relations department, the Friends of the Zoological Society, and an outside "event maker," Karin Bacon, who came complete with ideas, a theme, and creative know-how plus professional performers and staff to help the Bronx Zoo turn its events into super special events and celebrations.

What could be more special than a baby elephant's first birthday? Astor, the baby, was the first Asian elephant to be born in the New York area in more than 9,000 years (according to zoo officials). That's big news. The anniversary deserved extensive publicity and celebrations. The news release read: "Astor the elephant is one year old and what a huge birthday party The Bronx Zoo is planning for its biggest baby! Weighing 750 pounds and standing 4 feet three inches at the shoulder, Baby Astor is big enough to need two days to celebrate, Saturday and Sunday, August 21 and 22 [1982]."

What's a birthday party without an invitation? If it's for an elephant, it has to be a *big* one. A full-page ad in the *New York Times* invited all of New York to the party at the zoo. The ad was paid

ASTOR'S BIRTHDAY:
ELEPHANT WEEKEND
BRONX ZOO
AUGUST 21ST AND 22ND, 1982

CREATED BY KARIN BACON FOR THE NEW YORK ZOOLOGICAL SOCIETY

Used by permission of Karin Bacon Special Events.

Used by permission of the *New York Post*. Copyright 1982 NGP.

for by one of the cosponsors of the event, City Investing Company & the Home Insurance Company. It featured a large photo of Baby Astor and his mother lovingly bathing and the message "Come to Astor's birthday party at the Bronx Zoo. There'll be tons of food." At the bottom of the ad, people were invited to send a $2 donation to the Bronx Zoo; in return, they would receive a free copy of the picture poster in the ad.

Another colorful brochure, "Astor's Birthday: Elephant Weekend," was produced by Bacon's office. Inside, it gave the readers some vital statistics about Astor, his birth date, what color he was at birth, etc. It also listed all the events for the weekend.

People got a chance to watch the elephants bathing at the beginning and end of each day in the Elephant Yard. And, to best see Baby Astor, all were invited to ride (for free) the Bengali Express monorail train from ll a.m.–4:30 p.m. in the Wild Asia Plaza.

What's a birthday without a birthday card? At the lawn near the Elephant House, people were asked to write a birthday message to Baby Astor. The card was 80 feet long! Astor wasn't the only one having fun that weekend. People competed in elephant events such as the elephant roaring contest, "find the elephant in the haystack," and elephant races. They got a chance to decorate an elephant by creating a ceremonial dress for it. On the following day at noon, all were entertained with an elephant show in which the animals waltzed, rolled over, and stood on their heads! This was followed by elephant dances performed by two young women from India named Sujana and Sumana.

Continuing with the elephant extravaganza, Grumpy, a 550-pound female elephant, took on the Fordham University football team in a tug-of-war, an annual event. The year before, Grumpy defeated the Fordham 5,000-pound Rams (25 men). But this year, it was their turn to win. They had been in training for a whole year for this special competition. Unfortunately, Astor was too young and lightweight to participate.

This event was followed by elephant painting in the Elephant Yard at 2 p.m., followed by a costume ceremony and a presentation of birthday cakes. A big brass band played some songs elephants might like and led the party-goers to Wild Asia to present the birthday card and Astor's birthday cake to the baby elephant. (Actually, Astor's keeper accepted the gifts.) The cake? Not your usual whipped cream or chocolate creation. It was an elephant's delight, so they say. Comprising an elephant's favorite foods, such as Italian bread, apples, and carrots, and decorated with flowers, it stood three feet high!

Summary

You know the media couldn't pass this story up. The *New York Times* did a preliminary feature story about the event and then followed it with a wonderful story and photo about the tug-of-war event with Grumpy and the Fordham Rams. The *New York Daily News* ran a story and photo about the events and featured a photo of the elephant's daily bath. The *New York Post* ran a picture story with Baby Astor and his mother, Patty, with the birthday cake.

The *New York Daily News* also ran another story in its "Midway Section" about the elephant weekend, with the emphasis on the birthday cake. In addition, the zoo held a "press" birthday party for Astor the week before so that all of the photographers could take their photos in the best conditions without the crowds. Over 45,000 people attended Astor's Birthday Weekend at the zoo and that's no elephant joke! Unfortunately, Baby Astor died from heart failure at age 17 months. But the elephant show still goes on, and Grumpy still competes with the Fordham Rams in their annual tug-of-war.

THE BIGGEST ICE CREAM SUNDAE

What kinds of special events do you plan when your town is in a recession? If you are an innovative recreation director like Jim Hilton, from St. Albans, Vermont, you plan special events that challenge the local community's imagination and perk up their spirits. How? Let us count the ways.

First of all, it seems that Jim loves a challenge himself. Beating the *Guinness Book of World Records* has been his goal many times, and twice he has succeeded! In doing so, he has put St. Albans on the map, received national media attention, and created goodwill among the people of St. Albans. He has boosted their morale and won the support and cooperation of many companies and agencies who joined Jim in bringing off celebrations and special events.

The first St. Albans *Guinness* record was set by creating a 47-foot, 10-inch-tall snowman called "Abraham" with the assistance of 800 Bellows Free Academy students and other local volunteers. Weighing 70 tons, Abraham gave St. Albans national publicity and lots of pride in a job well done. It was truly a cooperative venture. Although undertaken by Hilton, the original idea came from one of the town's aldermen and won the approval of the local chamber of commerce and the community development officer. Everyone seemed to be in on it. (The snowman was called Abraham because he was built on Abraham Lincoln's birthday adjacent to a Civil War monument in St. Alban's Taylor Park that contains a copy of Lincoln's Gettysburg address.) Not resting on his laurels after this special event, Jim went on to bigger things.

Putting It All Together

St. Albans claims to be many things: maple sugar capital of the world, hockey capital of Vermont, and home of Abraham the First, among others. And after the fun-filled special event on April 15, 1983, it can now be called the home of the world's biggest ice cream sundae! This 25,000-pound ice cream sundae contained the following ingredients:

- A planeload of pineapples flown in from Dole Pineapple in Hawaii
- A two-and-a-half-ton truckload of peaches from Alabama
- One hundred pounds of peanuts from Jimmy Carter's farm in Georgia

That was just the topping. There's more:

- 16,000 pounds of ice cream and 300 pounds of whipped cream from the St. Albans Cooperative Creamery
- 900 pounds of maple syrup from the Franklin County Maple Cooperative
- 300 pounds of strawberries and 300 pounds of cherries from the Agri-Mark, Middlebury, Vermont
- 300 pounds of liquid chocolate and a truckload of chocolate chips from Comet Confectionery, Quebec, Canada
- 900 eggs from local farmers

The event drew support in other forms as well. The National Dairy Association in Chicago provided free advertising. From nearby Burlington, IBM provided protective white coats for the 70 high school students who constructed the sundae to wear during its creation. The students even wore coverings over their shoes and sneakers, and all health standards were observed. A truckload of plastic spoons was donated to the event by the Fonda Container Company in St. Albans. Week's Dairy in Concord, New Hampshire, got into the act by having all of the ingredients for the ice cream mixture trucked to their facility, where the mix for

12 *Fireworks, Brass Bands, and Elephants*

Used by permission of the *St. Albans Messenger*.

the ice cream was concocted. Then, the mix was transported back to Ben & Jerry's ice cream factory in Burlington for processing.

Asked how he managed to get all of the companies to donate their time, money, and supplies, Hilton replied, "I've never gotten a 'no.' I have always gotten more than I asked for."

This project was sponsored by the city of St. Albans in conjunction with its 16th Annual Vermont Maple Syrup Festival. There were many other events planned for the week, but the ice cream sundae caper was to be the kick-off event. It was also the beginning of spring school vacation. So, wearing their white medical coats, cotton shoe covers, shower caps, and white gloves, the high school students constructed the actual sundae and even cleaned up the park at the end of the day with the help of elementary and junior high school students. Actually, Hilton credits the high school students with the entire project idea. Knowing he is always open to wild and crazy suggestions, they approached him in the fall of 1982 asking for ideas for a community project which would address the economy and have an impact on the people. St. Albans had one of the highest unemployment rates in the state of Vermont. This super sundae event was a real morale booster for the community, which is now "pulling itself up by the bootstraps," according to Hilton. Hilton's theme for the day was "Recession is like an ice cream sundae; you have to learn to lick it."

The Big Licking Day

Busloads of people, 20,000 in number, came from all over the country to help lick up the "Recession '83 World's Largest Ice Cream Sundae." E. F. Hutton provided buses so that several thousands of elementary school children from four counties could view and taste the super sundae, which stood 11 feet tall. It took five hours of frenzied hustle and bustle by the industrious high school students to create the sundae. Balloons lent a festive air to the park where the event was taking place. Governor Richard Snelling rode a crane lift to the top of the super sundae, poured a pitcher of maple syrup...and the feasting began! The first taste went to a local dairy farmer, Tim Maxham, who paid $375 for the honor. He made his bid at an auction conducted by Vermont Educational Television. "It was worth the money," declared a satisfied Maxham in newspaper reports.

The ice cream was served to one and all; what was left was scooped up and delivered to local nursing homes. The remaining ingredients were sent on their way to other depressed areas nearby, and to New York, Michigan, and Texas. And, yes, they did make the *Guinness Book of World Records* as the largest ice cream sundae ever created.

Promotion

I am certain that if the St. Albans volunteers had just promoted the "biggest ice cream sundae" event locally they would have had a good attendance. But, with all the national coverage they got, thousands of people came to St. Albans in April 1983 to watch an ice cream sundae be created and then to help eat it up. Thousands of people were invited including President Reagan and Prime Minister Trudeau of Canada. Fliers were distributed at the St. Albans recreation center and other popular locations in town. Local radio and television publicized the event both beforehand and after it was over. Local and regional newspapers ran feature stories with many photos. National wire services ran not only the story, but photos as well.

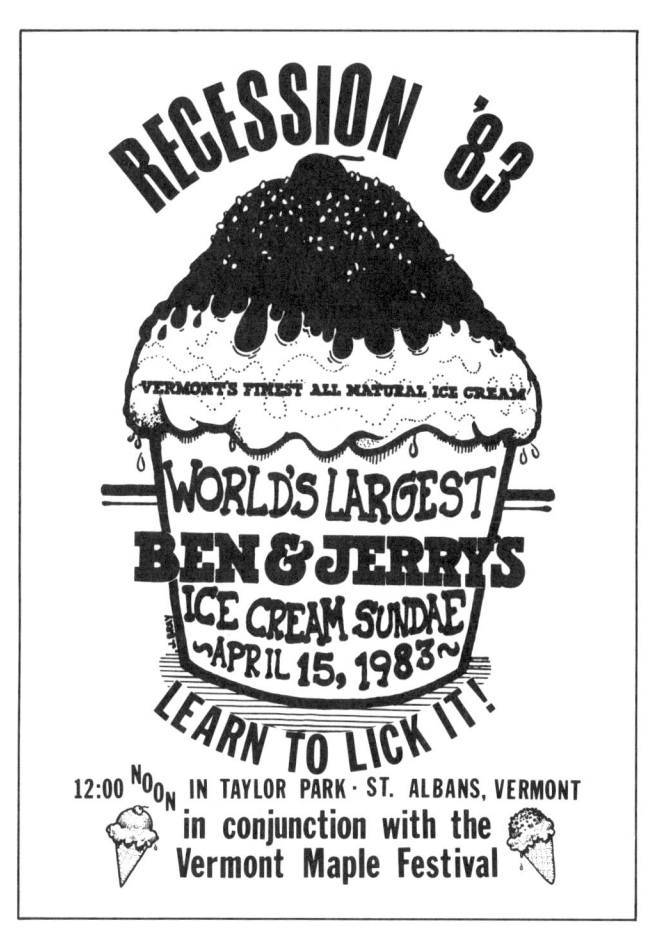

Used by permission of the St. Albans Recreation Center.

Cooperation

In 1982 the St. Albans Recreation Department had a staff of 30 people during the spring and summer. During the winter and fall, the number decreased to seven, which included both full- and part-time workers. The rest of the help came from the local high school population, the chamber of commerce, and the local citizenry. All of the participants had one thing in common: enthusiasm. It was contagious. There is a special satisfaction in being part of something that is fun, something that makes people feel good...whether it is a fund-raiser or creating a super sundae! It's the creating and the doing. You can do it on a shoestring budget, as St Albans did, with many volunteers. They proved you don't have to be a big-city operation to pull off an exciting event. I suppose you're asking, "How does a wild and crazy event like that help the mood of St. Albans residents?" Well, in town, they tell of an older woman who always called up the local radio station to complain about something. When Abraham the snowman went up, she said it would flood the city when it melted. But when the snowman was completed and the volunteers were climbing down, guess who was down below handing out hot coffee? Yes, and during the ice cream extravaganza, she volunteered to help out from the outset.

Comments

Hilton and his crew do creative programing all year, although not all of the events are blockbusters that attract national media attention. They also sponsor the usual things: macrame classes, dance classes, sporting events, and contests such as a Pet Rock Race, Stone Skipping, Frog Jumping, Ugliest Pig, etc.

Maybe setting world records is not your thing, but, then why not? If you've got a few hours, borrow the *Guinness Book of World Records* and find a challenge. Not competitive? Then do it just for the fun of it. You don't have to be the best or the first to have a successful special event. It's your enthusiasm that will entice others into joining you in creating exciting events and stimulating programs. So, don't be shy. Show your enthusiasm when you have a great idea. It will probably be the beginning of something big—maybe not the largest ice cream sundae in the world—but it will be your very own special event. Do it.

JAZZTIME

Jazz was the theme, and it sounded through the campus in song, dance, theatre, fashion shows, poetry, lectures, art shows, and even an antique car show. The scene was C.W. Post College, which is part of Long Island University and is located on the north shore of Nassau County on Long Island, New York. The celebration was the 16th annual American Theatre Festival, held April 13 to 24, 1983. Jazztime was the name of festival, and it was sponsored by the School of Fine Arts under the direction of Dr. Julian Mates, dean of the school and the founder of the American Theatre Festival. Thousands of Long Islanders would be swinging over to the college for the jazzy events taking place during April.

The focus of each year's festival is a play, which then leads to selection of a theme. The play chosen for 1983 was *Chicago,* which is based on the book by Fred Ebb and Bob Fosse. It's the story of Roxie Hart, who can literally get away with murder—all she needs is a little "razzle dazzle." Chicago was one of several cities where jazz first gained popularity, thus the choice of play. Once the play was chosen, the coordinating and planning for the rest of the festival began. *Chicago* opened on April 13 and ran through the 23rd. Admission was $5; $3 for senior citizens and students.

Casts for the shows are primarily drawn from the drama department of the school with a few Actors' Equity Association players providing needed depth. It's always a learning experience for these college students because the school has a very viable theatre department.

One of the highlights of each year's festival is the John Gassner Memorial Lecture and Luncheon. This year's speaker was the original Roxie Hart of the Broadway production of *Chicago,* dancer and choreographer Gwen Verdon. The luncheon was held at the Top of the Commons, located in the Hillwood Commons, an attractive student activities center. The menu was "Back Room Barbecued Ribs and all the Fixin's," and the admission charge was $10. After the luncheon, people adjourned to the west wing of the school's large concert theatre, where they were treated to a performance by the American Dance Machine, a professional Broadway theatre dance group which serves as a "living archive of Broadway theatre dance." Lee Theodore and her dancers presented jazzdance of the twenties. And, it was all free.

The next day (Sunday) was filled with more jazzy activities. People were encouraged to bring a picnic lunch and set up tables and blankets in the Rose Garden of the campus. Over a chicken leg and a glass of white wine, they watched a "Fashions of the Twenties" show with students modeling antique clothing provided by a local antique clothing store. This was followed by a concert by the Jazz Ensemble. If that wasn't enough, people also enjoyed an antique auto rally. After a dinner break, music lovers gathered in the college's interfaith chapel for an ecumenical service featuring Pastor John Garcia Gensel of St. Peter's Church in New York City, at which Eddie Bonnemere and his jazz trio played. (St. Peter's Church is noted for its many jazz vespers held during the year.)

Jazz continued on Tuesday, April 19, with a showing of...what else, but *The Jazz Singer,* starring Al Jolson. Film critic Gordon Hitchens introduced the program, and a selected jazz short was also shown. This too was free to the public. "Chicago Jazz of the Twenties" was the title of the next evening's lecture/demonstration by David Jasen, jazz historian and musician, in the Great Hall. Jasen plays a great ragtime piano and is the chair of the communications department. Another free offering, Edna St. Vincent Millay's "Woman of the Jazz Age," featuring an evening of drama and poetry with actress Laurie James, was held the following night, April 21, in the Great Hall. Richard Griffith played a jazz piano accompaniment.

Closing the festival was the college's Fourth Annual Collegiate Jazz Festival featuring the C.W. Post Center Jazz Ensemble, Five Towns College Lab Band, Nassau Community College Jazz Ensemble, and Hofstra University Jazz Repertory Company. International jazz trumpeter Valery Ponomarev was the featured guest artist. There was a token admission charge of $2.

And it went on. For those who loved dance and did not wish to be merely spectators, there was a master class in jazz dance with a lecture/demonstration. Professional dancer and teacher Gael Stepanek was the speaker/performer. It was held in the lecture hall in Hillwood Commons and was free. The master class was held from 4 p.m.–5 p.m., and the lecture/demonstration was held from 5 p.m.–6 p.m. "Oh, Didn't He Ramble," an exhibit of artist Ralston Crawford's New Orleans jazz photographs, was on display from March 30 to April 20. There was an opening reception on Friday, April 15, from 7 p.m.–9 p.m. Admission to the gallery was free. On Saturday evening, April 16, the festival presented a special offering to the public, a dinner and theatre package for $19.75 with a reduced price for students and seniors. A Chicago dinner consisting of prime ribs au jus was the entree, and the concluding delicacy was Windy City Strawberry Chiffon Pie. There was a cash bar and, yes, there was music during the meal provided by musician Alfred Doblin at the piano.

The Promotion

The media were first alerted to the American Theatre Festival's Jazztime series with news releases from the college's public relations department. Also, in its April issue, the School of Fine Arts newsletter, *Cakes & Ale*, did a first-page story on Jazztime. With silhouette-style illustrations by Giovanna Testani (who also did the design for the Jazztime brochure), the newsletter devoted its entire paper to historical feature stories about the individual events in the Jazztime series. Interesting to read and certainly informative, it also listed all of the events in the "Calendar of the Arts" section. The newsletter is distributed in the college and through a special mailing list, which consists of local universities, libraries, and interested individuals. It is an ongoing feature of the School of Fine Arts, student-written with guest writers.

The promotion continued with the posting of individual event fliers and/or brochures, which were produced by the department of fine arts. There was a handsome informational brochure produced for the photography exhibition in the art gallery and an attractively designed playbill for the theatre presentation of *Chicago*. Photographs of the production were taken by students of the department. The entire festival was coordinated, one might say choreographed, down to the last detail.

Used by permission of the School of Fine Arts, C.W. Post Center, Long Island University.

Used by permission of the School of Fine Arts, C.W. Post Center, Long Island University.

They even handed out classy hot pink-and-white buttons that said, "C.W. Post 1983 JAZZTIME American Theatre Festival." Probably the most attractive piece was the Jazztime promotional brochure which served as a mailer. It consisted of white, coated paper with hot pink and black ink and contained everything anyone would want to know about the festival: a brief history of the American Theatre Festival, highlights of the festival with annotations, a schedule of events, and credits to those involved. And, in bold type in hot pink (on white) were the phone numbers for general information and one for theatre reservations. Well designed and well organized...not only the graphics, but the entire Jazztime celebration.

Used by permission of the School of Fine Arts, C.W. Post Center, Long Island University.

A Brief History

According to Mates, "The purpose of the festivals is a unique attempt to demonstrate each year some aspect of this country's cultural history."

How do they choose a theme? Usually it begins with the theatrical presentation. Sometimes it originates with Mates himself or from a member of his department or a committee meeting. Everyone has input. A special festival director is chosen each year, sometimes from the faculty and sometimes from the "outside." Usually the director of the theatrical presentation is a member of the theatre department, although on occasion a professional director has been hired for a particular show.

The cost of the American Theatre Festival is budgeted into the School of Fine Arts expenditures. The admission charges help defray some of the expenses. The professionals hired for lectures, music, and dance are paid. The students involved do it as a learning experience. The department even holds a poster contest for each festival, with art students being asked to design a poster for the particular festival. All of the winning posters are framed and put on permanent display in Hillwood Commons. The art design for the brochures, buttons, and fliers is usually executed by a faculty member, student, or a freelance artist.

The American Theatre Festival follows basically the same format each year with some variations. What makes it successful is the professional manner in which it is all handled. Nothing is left to chance. It is well coordinated and well packaged...and promoted...all essentials for a successful special event or celebration. C.W. Post certainly does know how to jazz things up!

CAROUSELS, CONEY ISLAND & COTTON CANDY

So far you've read about special events dealing with a zoo, a recreation center, and a college. Now I'd like to turn to a library. Since it's about the library I work for, the East Meadow (New York) Public Library, I'd like to begin with the "how" of this particular special event. It's how a special personal interest of mine sparked a month-long celebration.

I collect lots of things. One of the things I would love to collect (but can't afford) is antique carousel animals. At one point in my career, I was public relations director of Steeplechase Park in Coney Island. The carousel animals in the park were distinctive and beautiful, and I always imagined owning one of them. This never happened because first, I didn't have the money, and second, the carousel was sold and was moved to Japan. However, because I frequent antique and flea markets, I found myself one sunny Sunday in August making the rounds of booths at a show out on the east end of Long Island. I knew I would go no farther when I reached a booth that had several old carousel animals. I was entranced. The exhibitors, a charming couple by the name of Winfield, knew they had a captive audience and told me all about their collection of carousel animals. I told them of my past carousel connection. Amused by my enthusiastic interest, they invited me to their studio to see their entire menagerie. After five minutes' worth of conversation with them that August day, I was already formulating a program idea (only one at that point). That's how it all began.

One Thing Leads to Another

By this time, the wheels were really turning in my head. After I sorted things out, I approached my library director and made my pitch. "Sounds great, but also a lot of work," was his reply. He then offered his help. Little did he know that he was to be the unofficial "director" of the midway games. More about that later on. I had read in *Newsday* that the Friends of the Nassau County Museums had purchased some antique carousel animals and hoped to set them up as a working carousel in a nearby county park. This was my connection number two! I contacted the museum director and told him of my idea. He agreed to let me have two of the "animals" on loan for one month during our celebration, "Carousels, Coney Island & Cotton Candy." Yes, by this time I had a title for the celebration.

The word was getting around. I spoke to anyone and everyone I knew who might have a carousel connection or interest. An artist who worked for the Nassau County Parks and Recreation Department made lunchtime visits to the library. From time to time, we had talked about a mutual interest, old advertising art. I caught him one day and poured out the carousel celebration story and ended with, "What have you got for me?" Well, it just so happened he had designed photo cutouts for a park promotion a few years back. The cutouts were sitting in storage. (For those who may never have seen a photo cutout, it's usually a free-standing, lifesized figure constructed of masonite. There is a cutout where the head and face should be.) "Come up and see my cutouts," was his offer. I move fast. I was there the next morning poking around the recreation department's storage area. There they were...just what I wanted. Two delightful figures, one of a man in an old-fashioned bathing suit and one of a woman in a bathing suit of the same era. The park department's photo cutouts were promised for the library's special event.

The reason for the lengthy preface to this special event is to stress again how important word-of-mouth contacts are and how important enthusiasm and interest are in planning an event. When you find people with a special interest in the project you are working on, you might find yourself overwhelmed with offers of help and suggestion. Always remember two things: one, it's your show and two, stay in charge. Every contact I made was one-on-one in person or by letter or phone.

I also want to emphasize again the importance of long-range planning for a big event. When I first met the Winfields at the antique show, it was August. "Carousels, Coney Island & Cotton Candy" was to be held the following February. Not many of us have the luxury of working on just one program or special event at a time. An apt middle name for all of us in this act might be "juggler." So, if you are committed and enthusiastic about a project, you will find yourself spending weekends (your time!) working on the planning and contact work. It can't be helped. In my case, it's always been an asset to have a husband who's understanding, patient, and willing to join in.

How It Went

While in the throes of planning the carousel event, I discovered that, because it was the Bicentennial Year, the town of Hempstead and the Nassau Library System were offering for a reduced rate several Smithsonian's Traveling Exhibits. One of the displays was the "Great American Scream Machine," an exciting photographic display of roller coasters. So, it wasn't carousels...but it was close! Since I had already planned another exhibit for our February special event, the Smithsonian exhibit went up for the month of January and continued into part of February. It was a great promo then for our forthcoming extravaganza.

The February event was promoted as a four-part celebration. By this time, everyone in the library was involved in one way or another. Opening the month's festivities was the children's room "Carousel Paint-In," held on a Wednesday afternoon. Pre-outlined carousel horses on corrugated cardboard, donated by a local resident "in the business," were waiting for youngsters when they came into the meeting room. Sitting, lying, and sprawling on the floor, the young artists painted the nearly lifesized animals (as they imagined them) with colorful poster paints. The custodians were grateful that the children were fairly competent painters and kept most of the paint on the cardboard as intended and not on the floor tiles! The painted carousel animals were hung from a high ceiling in a circle above the children's room for all to admire. No one wanted them to come down even months later. In fact, they only came down because they were needed for a new home in a school that "borrowed" them for a special project. They've never returned.

The following Friday evening, the movie *Coney Island*, with Betty Grable, was shown. The short *Popcorn Lady* was shown first. It was a night of nostalgia. The feature film was timely, even though it wasn't outstanding. But the people didn't seem to notice because they enjoyed the whole evening. (If I were to repeat the evening, I would find another feature film and hand out bags of popcorn to each moviegoer.)

Working with Poets & Writers and the New York State Council on the Arts, I planned the third program, which consisted of readings and reminiscences with author/poet Norman Rosten of Brooklyn. This program took place on a Friday evening and was called "Under the Boardwalk," which just happened to be the title of Rosten's book, which he would read from. I knew that people would not turn out in droves if I just promoted the event as "readings by Norman Rosten." There had to be a gimmick. Brooklyn, with its nostalgic Coney Island and boardwalk, was it. Knowing our community helped. East Meadow has a population of about 51,000, most of whom have migrated from one of the five boroughs of New York City. A large number are from Brooklyn. Anyway, the whole evening turned out even better than I had planned. Rosten, the writer and poet and Brooklyn-lover, connected with the audience from the beginning. The audience felt a strong rapport with him because of their Brooklyn association and listened attentively to his readings and anecdotes. And, before the evening was out, it looked and sounded like a big Brooklyn reunion.

The Really Big Show

The next Sunday was the main event! Fortunately, at this point in the library's life, it was not open for Sunday service, as it is now. The whole building was ours. To literally tear the place apart to make room for all of the events required a lot of hard work and cooperation by the staff involved (myself, a clerk/illustrator, two pages, two custodians, and the library director). Fortunately a wonderful crew of volunteers had also gotten carousel fever and joined in.

After moving things around in the children's room, the midway games were set up. "Hook the Book," "Dart the Balloon," "Pitch the Penny," "Shoot (water pistol) the Daisy," and "Have Your Fortune Told" were just some of the fun games played upstairs. Games were run by teen members of Interact, a high school Junior Rotary club. The young people were wonderful and dedicated...and had a good time too.

Also upstairs on the main floor were the photo cutouts where people could take pictures of friends or relatives for free if they had their own camera. Or they could have photographers (on hand from the Long Island Camera Club, which meets at the library) take the pictures for 35 cents each. The two volunteer photographers were exhausted at the end of the day but happy to have made a contribution.

Nearby, in the area usually occupied by the library's community information aide, a man who restored antique carousel animals held court. He was referred to us by the Winfields, my original carousel contacts. Bruno Speiser not only talked to people about his restoration work but also displayed several of the carousel figures he had restored.

People still had a chance that day, until 3 p.m., to "Guess How Many Peanuts in the Jar." The jar of peanuts had been on the circulation desk since the beginning of the month. Hundreds of people participated. The winner was announced by the day's end, and he went home with the jar of peanuts!

In the midst of all this activity was a roaming band of clowns out to make everyone laugh. They were members of Voiture 803 Nassau County 40 & 8 (American Legion). They added color and laughter to a day which, by the way, was rainy and dreary outside.

Moving downstairs, your first stop might have been the staff lounge, which had been turned into a "Cotton Candy Shoppe." Free cotton candy was available while the supply lasted. Members of Interact who manned the machine were covered, most sweetly, with pink cotton candy by the end of the day.

The "formal" presentation was held in the library's meeting room downstairs. It began at 2 p.m. with a slide show/talk, "Carousels & Carvers," with Barbara and Armand Winfield. At 3 p.m, the silent movie *Coney Island: When the Century Was Young* was shown. The walls of the meeting room displayed an art and photography show featuring the works of artists who used the carousel and Coney Island as their theme. Also on display were old-fashioned posters from Nathan's, the famous Coney Island hot dog emporium. Nathan's also provided hundreds of free hot dog recipe booklets. There wasn't one left at the end of the day.

People did not need tickets to join in the fun, but tickets were issued to everyone who entered the library. Each person received four orange tickets and one blue ticket. The orange tickets could be used to play games and to take pictures with the photo cutouts. Youngsters could use one of their orange tickets for a ride on the Voiture 803 40 & 8 locomotive bus around the block. The blue ticket entitled the holder to some cotton candy. Each person received a bright orange program which explained the day's lineup of activities. It also gave a brief history of carousels, spoke of the future of the proposed carousel to be erected in the county park, and listed reading material for carousel enthusiasts.

Over 800 people from Long Island, New York City, and New Jersey, some with babies in knapsacks on their backs, came and enjoyed "Carousels, Coney Island & Cotton Candy" on this special Sunday. All of us involved had a great time!

The Promotion

First, let's take the "why" of February for such a celebration. East Meadow is located in the northeast section of the country, and February is usually a month where you might start going downhill (and not necessarily skiing). The winter blahs set in. The weather can be anything...wet, cold, stormy, snowy. People are weary of winter, and not all can afford the warmth of Florida or the Caribbean to perk up their spirits. I have found that special events and thematic programs go over big in February.

Knowing I already had a potential audience, I began promoting the February event at library programs in December. I call such promotions "library commercials." Since I preside over the adult programs, I know I have a captive audience. After welcoming the people to the program for the night,

I give them a pitch about forthcoming events. If an event is of interest to them, people usually go home and make notes on their calendars for future events. Next, the January/February library newsletter told the whole story with a mailing to over 3,000 homes at that time. The printed word was out! The newsletter is also distributed in the library, in the Library-On-Wheels, and at one of the local banks. News releases went out to the media about the "Great American Dream Machine" exhibit and the last paragraph read, "The East Meadow Public Library is coordinating another exhibit to follow this one entitled 'Carousels,' which will be part of their month-long celebration, 'Carousels, Coney Island & Cotton Candy,' a series of programs with movies, slides, exhibits, games, clowns and cotton candy beginning on February 11."

This was followed by another news release several weeks later telling the whole February story. Next came the promotional fliers and posters. The flier (which could and did serve as a poster) was designed to resemble an old-time circus broadside and featured typefaces that typified those broadsides. "Playbill" was one of the typefaces used. The paper was a goldenrod vellum stock and the inks were black with red accents. It was produced on a mimeograph machine. With more time and money, it could have been produced by a professional printer with better results. But the color and flavor of the special event were captured. Fliers were posted everywhere in the community where allowed. Everyone was getting "carousel fever."

The library's display cases were loaded with carousel memorabilia. Authentic merry-go-round music, taped by a carousel buff, was discreetly played during the month at the circulation desk. At this point, you would have had to be living on another planet not be be aware of our forthcoming event! The print press was especially kind to us. The two large dailies sent photographers; one stayed the whole afternoon and the result was a feature photo story the next day! The other daily used one photograph. I took some photographs, which I then sent to the weeklies, and I used one for a follow-up story in our own library newsletter. My husband took color slides, which we later ran continuously in our "black box" rear-view slide projector on the main floor of the library. To see the slide show, you just had to push a button below the screen. People who had attended the special events enjoyed the reruns and people who weren't able to attend enjoyed seeing what they missed. Thank-you letters went out to all involved. The idea and the thrust of the work might have originated with me. But without the sincere enthusiasm and hard work on the part of so many, "Carousels, Coney Island & Cotton Candy" would not have been the success it was. A week later, another big special event was in the works. But, that's another story.

Summing it all up, this event was a success and did not cost much. We paid $35 for the rental of the cotton candy machine (including the ingredients to feed 500 people). Staff salaries (double-time) for six people had to be included. Two rolls of tickets cost $6 and printed promotional material cost $50. That was about it. Even the miscellaneous expenditures did not come to much more than an additional $150. The library staff heard many complimentary remarks from people long after the event and were asked, "When are you going to do it again?" Who knows? Some events are worth repeating. This one promoted goodwill, brought many people to the library (including some who had never been there before), and showed people that the public library can truly offer more than books! One last note: Like many others who have done a "good thing," I put "Carousels, Coney Island & Cotton Candy" into a scrapbook (with the slides) and won a special John Cotton Dana Library Public Relations award for it. So, you see, you can get a lot of mileage out of one event and one promotion.

Chapter 3
Cooperative Ventures

☞ How a Library Helped Preserve a Road
☞ "A Sense of Community: Diversity and Change" in Albany, New York
☞ Detroit's Cultural Institutions "Do It Together"
☞ "A Moveable Feast": Commemorating Hemingway in Key West
☞ Hooray for the Bay! Working with a Friends Group

You can't do it alone. In many of the case histories in this book, you will find the "idea" agency or person has turned to other organizations, companies, and people for cosponsorship or assistance. Here you will read about several excellent examples of groups and people working together. Awareness of resources, awareness of the local community and what its people can offer, awareness of environs, awareness of what your state can offer are all-important when undertaking a large project such as a special event or an unusual program. Sometimes that resource will be monetary, and sometimes it will be talent or time or knowledge or physical resources. If you have an arts council in your area, cultivate a relationship with its staff and let them know of your existence and what you might be able to offer them. They, in turn, most likely will include you in any arts and/or programming workshops or seminars they are planning. If you have a specialty, don't be shy; offer your services as a speaker. Establish a rapport with the chamber of commerce and Jaycee group. Keep in touch. Keep them posted on your activities. You never know when they'll need you or when you'll need them.

The following stories describe five totally different cooperative ventures. The first tells of a Long Island, New York, library and how it helped preserve a historic road in its community. In the second, the Albany Public Library's efforts to create a new awareness and the feeling of a special identity for the city's many ethnic groups are described. They were helped by a grant from the National Endowment for the Humanities through the New York State Education Department. The third story deals with a big city, Detroit, and how its cultural institutions "do it together"—create special events cooperatively. In "A Moveable Feast," a newspaper, several libraries, library Friends, and interested community leaders create a great promotional event to honor Hemingway. And the fifth story details how a dedicated Friends group works with a library to annually present a series of programs and events called "Hooray for the Bay!"

HOW A LIBRARY HELPED PRESERVE A ROAD

It was simple curiosity and an interest in doing a program about the community where she was working that started the public relations director of Half Hollows Hills Community Library (Huntington, New York) on a quest in 1976 that would happily haunt her years later. Sally Miller, a longtime Huntington resident, had driven on the Long Island Motor Parkway (also known as Vanderbilt Parkway) in her everyday travels. She had also bicycled on the parkway as a child growing up in Queens, New York. She knew there was a history behind the parkway, but until she needed ideas for a program, she hadn't bothered to seek out any information on it.

This library serves a rather well-to-do community on Long Island. Both the community and the local high school are situated right on Motor Parkway. Miller felt residents might like to know some historical information about their community. Right about that time people on Long Island and all over the country were feeling the Bicentennial spirit. Local histories were being rediscovered and celebrated. For Miller, the involvement began with reading a letter in the *New York Times* from a local resident, Haydon Rogers, who asked the newspaper for more information and history about the Motor Parkway. A correspondent of the newspaper responded on the phone with the admission that they hadn't much information at all and asked if Mr. Rogers had any. Miller called Rogers; after talking to him she decided that there must be others who had historical information about the parkway. So she decided to do a program at the library in the hope of attracting residents with information on the parkway. But first she needed a speaker who could talk expertly on the subject. At about this time a magazine called *Long Island Sound* ran an article by John Helig about the Vanderbilt Races on the parkway. The story of the races is this: William K. Vanderbilt was a wealthy man who had a number of houses throughout the country (one nearby in Centerport), and he vacationed all over the world on his yacht. One of his loves was auto racing, and he wanted America to be number one at it. So, in 1904 he organized the first race, using 30 miles of local Nassau County roads. Racers from all over the world came to participate; drivers found sponsorship from the newborn automobile industry. Vanderbilt commissioned Louis Tiffany to design a silver cup as the winner's trophy, weighing 30 pounds and able to hold 10½ gallons of champagne. The races were held annually from 1904 until 1938. Because the roads on Long Island were dangerous, many accidents occurred the first couple of years, and as a result the American Automobile Association would no longer sanction the race. So Vanderbilt called his wealthy colleagues, Henry Ford, John Jacob Astor, August Heckscher, August Belmont, and others. They committed three-and-a-half million dollars to the road improvement project, which resulted in the construction of the Long Island Motor Parkway. They hoped one day to extend the Motor Parkway farther east on Long Island to Riverhead. The races continued. Helig, a New Jersey resident, was more interested in the races than the parkway. However, in the course of researching the races, he learned much about the Vanderbilt Parkway itself. He agreed to be the library's speaker.

Miller was astounded at the turnout. "If 75 people come to the library for a program, it's because it's a hot topic. Two hundred and fifty people came that night!" It was like putting together the pieces of a puzzle. Each person who came had a little bit of information passed down from a parent or grandparent or other relative to contribute. Helig provided the biggest "piece of the puzzle." Now the picture was becoming clearer, and Miller could see she had the foundation (and the community's interest) in somehow preserving this little bit of history. A Robert Miller, who was an employee of the Queensborough Public Library (in Queens) got in touch with her and proved to be another enthusiastic resource person. He claimed he had "driven, cycled, walked, and even crawled on his hands and knees on the parkway."

After receiving all this input, Miller decided the best way to preserve this bit of history would be to try to have the stretch of the Motor Parkway that runs through Huntington Township declared a historic district. To do so she needed clout; she found it in Huntington's historian, Rufus Langhans, who had fought many a preservation battle. He set up a date for Miller to appear before the town board. Fortunately for her, town supervisor Jerome Ambro was also enthusiastic and the rest of the officials followed his lead. The board agreed that the town would pay for the historic marker and Miller would decide on the wording that would appear on the marker.

The markers were erected on the road. So then what? More had to be done! Miller had the signs covered in preparation for the dedication and did some serious researching on her own at the nearby Smithtown Public Library, which housed the Long Island Archives. The Long Island Archives contain the original plans and materials pertaining to the historic road. She photocopied pages and pages of information about the road. She found that a driver #16 (George Robertson) appeared in just about all of the Vanderbilt Cup Races held in the 1900s. She found his son, Crawford Robertson, living in Garden City on Long Island. He agreed to share with her what information he had. So Miller's resource bank was growing. She held another program and more memorabilia and information came her way. She was fast becoming a "curator" of Motor Parkway artifacts—photographs, rally ribbons, license plates, and even a game called the "Vanderbilt Game." Her research told her that there was even a play called *The Vanderbilt Cup* that had been performed on Broadway and starred Elsie Janis and Barney Oldfield. From the library at the Lincoln Center of Performing Arts, she found the music that had been "lost."

In preparation for dedication day, news releases went out. They invited all those with antique cars to come to the library on Sunday, June 10, 1976, and show off their style in the library's parking lot during the dedication. She called on the U.S. Marines, who promised to participate with a "call to colors." Music was necessary to make the event a festive occasion, so she contacted the Half Hollow Hills High School band; they provided turn-of-the century music. Just in case the crowds were large, she informed police department officials, who said they would be on hand to control traffic. High school officials agreed to allow the library to use their parking lot, which was right across the street from the library.

The day was beautiful. The news release had stated that those arriving in an antique car and/or old-fashioned dress would be allowed to park in the library's parking lot; 65 people arrived in cars and "old clothes." Spectators went from car to car, querying owners about the year and make. The gimmick of the afternoon was the 1930 Long Island Bee Line Bus, which had been perfectly restored. Its job was to travel the historic road with the many dignitaries, including local legislators, state and federal elected officials, and special guests, filling the seats. The day was most successful, but that was only the beginning of the Motor Parkway saga.

Used by permission of Sally Miller.

Re-creating the Vanderbilt Cup Races

How do you top the preservation of a historic road? Take it one step further and actually re-create the Vanderbilt Races! A re-creation of the famous auto races was planned with the library as the starting spot. Since the actual first race was held on October 8, 1904 (a Saturday), it was hoped this date would have been available for the re-created race. Unfortunately, the high school parking lot would be unavailable for the event because a football game was scheduled. So, the race (really, a rally) was moved to an early September Sunday afternoon. The antique car owners who had attended the historic preservation dedication would be there. Again there would be music to entertain those waiting for things to begin. There were about 60 cars entered from Nassau and Suffolk counties and Queens. Each car was a 1925 vintage or earlier.

A purist, Miller began the race by using a megaphone to count off the time in French! Auto races had never been held in America before the first Vanderbilt Race years ago, and she wanted to be as authentic as possible. Ribbons were given to all who participated, and those who "won" received special ribbons. Both spectators and participants had a good time, and all said, "Let's do this again!" And they did, under the library's sponsorship, for five more rallies!

Comments

To "pull off" something as big as these events takes a great deal of planning and lots of hard work. The bulk of the work fell to Sally Miller. Without her enthusiasm and perseverance, the event would not have happened. On the other hand, she involved just about everyone: community members, parkway buffs, politicians, antique car owners, and anyone else who voiced an interest in the parkway and the Vanderbilt Cup Races. By involving the community, particularly the new residents of the area, in the history of a famous road on which they drove, she succeeded. The road became a historic district and was suitably marked. It was a first for the community.

To this day, many years after she retired from the library and began her own public relations firm, Miller is used as a Motor Parkway/Vanderbilt Race resource person by the community. When people inquire about the historic district, people say, "Send 'em to Sally!" The library is now the home for Motor Parkway and Vanderbilt Race memorabilia such as maps, archives, deeds, news stories, and photographs, plus the prize-winning scrapbook of the event created by Miller.

While she was still at the library, Miller convinced a local theatrical group to present *The Vanderbilt Cup* play at the library. Another after-the-fact story: A group of students from the Human Resources Center in Albertson, Long Island, who came to the library and "rode" on the famous road in their wheelchairs, wrote, produced, and presented (with the help of their teacher, William H. Frohlich) a slide show titled "Vanderbilt's 30-Year Wonder: History of the Motor Parkway, 1908–1938." They invited Sally Miller to their premiere showing.

Also during its operational years, the Motor Parkway had toll booths, and the toll-takers lived on the road with their families. Miller found several toll-takers still alive in their 70s and 80s and brought them to the dedication. And, for the first time, the toll-takers and their families were able to meet and talk to one another. They had never done this in all the years of working on the road. There were many such human interest stories connected with this event.

One coup she did not pull off was getting the real Vanderbilt Cup, which is in the Smithsonian Institution. But, did she try! She was informed if she wanted to borrow the cup for display purposes, she would have to not only hire an armored truck for its transportation to and from Washington, DC, but would also have to hire armed guards while it was on display at the library! That was the *only* thing too rich for her blood!

"A SENSE OF COMMUNITY: DIVERSITY AND CHANGE" IN ALBANY, NEW YORK

Albany, the capital of New York State, contains a strong ethnic mix including people of Irish, Dutch, Italian, and Jewish descent. The Albany Public Library wanted to participate in the National Endowment for the Humanities project "A Sense of Community: Diversity and Change." But before officially applying for the grant, it wanted to obtain input and involvement in the project on the part of as many neighborhood people as possible. So three community forums were held: one at the main library in downtown Albany, one in a neighborhood branch library, and the last in a local school. A neighborhood with a strong local history and active neighborhood associations was chosen for the first forum. Although the first meeting drew only 21 people, those present were vocal and participated in the forum, providing the library staff with lots of good ideas. A steering committee first met in 1979 for the project, which was to take place in 1982.

The second forum was held in the Pine Hills community. About 11 people showed up. Most of the people in this area were relative newcomers to Albany; the contrast was great between this meeting and the first, which was mostly attended by "old-timers." The library staff and the project's steering committee conducted the meeting in an open-ended "you tell us what you would like" format. After a brief presentation by the library staff, members of the audience made suggestions and comments. One of the majority sentiments that came through was an interest in Albany's history. The Pine Hills group felt that a series of informed debates or panel discussions on the idea of community (e.g., what is a community?) would be interesting. Unlike residents from the first forum, who lived in the city of Albany proper and in older neighborhoods, these people lived in a relatively new community and did not have the same sense of Albany's past.

The third forum took place in a Delaware Avenue school. Delaware Avenue was cited in the initial forum as an example of an intact community where many people had lived all their lives with most of their relatives and friends. So, this forum was totally different from the Pine Hills forum. Whereas the people in Pine Hills were looking for identity, these people had strong community ties and feelings. Much of this meeting was filled with reminiscing and talking about the "old neighborhood." There was talk of the Prohibition days in Albany. The group discussed the various churches and ethnic groups and how the streets in the area were named. One suggestion made was for people to study the cultures, contributions, and settlement patterns of the various immigrant groups and then to make oral or written presentations using music as an accompaniment.

"All in all, I think we enjoyed the community forum process, and I think the participants enjoyed it too," commented librarian coproject director Cheryl Gregory-Pindell. "We did have some people who came to at least two community forums, and the steering committee members tried to make all of them."

The Series of Programs

Reference librarians Michael Catoggio and Gregory-Pindell, who were named coproject directors, planned a diverse schedule of programs as a direct result of the open community forums. They also obtained input and assistance from the steering committee. The series included exhibits, slide and sound productions, films, music, lectures, tours, and discussion programs. "The roaring twenties, when brewing was a major industry, music and politics were hot, and prohibition gave the city its share of gangsters, is the focus of programs in October," read the promo in the library's newsletter, *The Half Moon*. The series included:

- "Swingtime," music of the 20s & 30s played and sung by Doc Scanlon's Rhythm Boys and the New Moon Swing Band - Friday, October 9 at 7:30 p.m.
- Saturday afternoon seminar, noon–5, Oct. 24. Lectures included: "An Overview of Albany in the 1920s" by William Rowley, professor of journalism at the State University of New York–Albany and one-time assistant city editor of the *Knickerbocker News*; "Political Transformation: From Barnes to O'Connell" by Albany Human Resources Director Jack McEneny; "Prohibition" by William Kennedy, author of the novels *Ironweed* and *Billy Phelan's Greatest Game*; "Brewing in Albany" with Fred Childs, Humanities Professor, Albany College of Pharmacy.
- Tour of the Newman Brewery (Visitors sampled some of the beer following the talks. Bus transportation to and from the brewery was provided by the library.)
- Classic Gangster Films (*Little Caesar*, *Public Enemy*, *The Roaring Twenties*, *Underworld*) were shown at the main library—two showings for each film in October.
- Depression Era Films (*Scarface*, *Bonnie and Clyde*, and *Grapes of Wrath*) were shown in November with two showings of each film. Jack Hotchkiss, Bernie Allen, and Bill Lowenberg shared their recollections of Albany in "Hard Times: Albany in the 1930s" November 18. (Videotaped for telecasting)
- "Albany's Changing Skyline" with Paul Goldberger, architecture critic, *The New York Times*, January 27. (Videotaped for telecasting)

Also as a result of the project, two exhibits were developed by the library and displayed at the main branch. "History of Brewing in Albany" contained photographs, silk screens, and memorabilia from 15 major breweries, now part of local history. "Albany's Theaters at the Turn of the Century" displayed photographs, posters, and playbills from when Albany was an integral part of the Northeast theater circuit between Boston and New York City. Four slide shows were produced, two from the exhibits and one of the "Corner of State and Pearl," which traced the events on this central intersection from the pre–Civil War period to after the Vietnam War, with period photographs, short poems, and a thoroughly researched script. The last slide show, "Delaware Neighborhood" was a compilation of a valuable old glass print photo collection with new photographs and taped interviews of residents.

Local history scholars conducted 41 videotaped interviews of Albany residents who remembered Albany at the turn of the century. These interviews were produced in the main library's own television studio. The tapes were transcribed, indexed, and added to the library's Pruyn Library of Local History for future public use.

Comments

From all reports, this project was an immense success and one of a lasting nature. The project directors and the steering committee should feel a sense of accomplishment. Although the main project idea and coordination were executed by the library staff, there was much community involvement. To begin with, the library was able to tap a community-based planning committee.

They also made use of local celebrities and personalities. One of the tools used to get people to come to the initial community forums was a personal letter from author William Kennedy (who later won the Pulitzer Prize for his novel *Ironweed*). It was their best "advertising tool." According to Gregory-Pindell, "People called the library and responded to it [the letter] in a very personal way and most of the people who did show up at the forums mentioned that they had gotten a letter from Bill Kennedy inviting them. And some people even called and said they couldn't make the forums but they'd be very happy to do whatever they could and this was all in response to that personal letter."

Three other locals—Bernie Allen, Bill Lowenberg, and Jack Hotchkiss—who talked about Albany in the 1930s, also were a big hit. In her project report, Gregory-Pindell said, "Bernie Allen stole the show with his touching personal memories, sneaking into theaters, skipping school, dayliner trips to N.Y.C., and other light anecdotes of the period." Again, it's a matter of knowing what and who will appeal to your community.

Of course, a nationally prominent figure also draws a big crowd. The Paul Goldberger lecture drew the largest attendance, nearly 300 people.

More important than obtaining the grant money for this project was the library and its planning committee's success in reawakening a spirit and pride in Albany both as a city and as a community. Quality planning and creative thinking were evident. Not only the regular library users but also those who had never set foot in the library before were attracted. It certainly was a cooperative project!

The Promotion

One thousand project fliers were printed by the library and sent to target groups. The letter from William Kennedy was sent to 65 leaders of neighborhood associations and the city's history and arts organizations. Notices were included in calendars for Albany League of Arts (600), *What's Happening at APL* (library monthly activity newsletter, 1,000), *Friends of the Library Newsletter* (830), and *Empire*

State Plaza News calendar notice. Posters were hung on community bulletin boards. Press releases went out to local newspapers and radio stations. Publicity for "A Sense of Community: Diversity and Change" inundated Albany. The interest was there all along, but if the promotion had not been as thorough and as good, the response would not have been so great. Always, in your planning, include all aspects of promotion. Albany Public Library obviously did and succeeded in creating an interesting community series.

DETROIT'S CULTURAL INSTITUTIONS "DO IT TOGETHER"

The geographic proximity of different groups vying for the attention of the same public can be destructive for all. This is the story of three separate institutions which, instead of competing with each other, chose to pool their ideas and resources, and came up with a creative program jointly. Each had its own programs based on a common theme. The result: everyone benefited, particularly the public.

The Cultural Center of Detroit, Michigan, which is made up of the Detroit Public Library, the Detroit Institute of Arts, and the Detroit Historical Museum, heralded its 12th Annual Open House, "American Fanfare," on a Wednesday evening in mid-September. These three institutions, although housed separately, are clustered and have chosen to "do it together" for many years. The Open House goes on, rain or shine, between 6 p.m. and 10 p.m. Even the street on which the buildings are located is closed. The purpose of this night's series of events was to introduce the fall season at these three city institutions, and, most important, to promote goodwill, cultivate new friends, and influence supporting friends.

At the Detroit Historical Museum

For "Parade And Panoply," the historical museum's presentation, the museum practically reconstructed a Civil War encampment on its front lawn with uniformed soldiers staging artillery demonstrations from 6 p.m. to 10 p.m. The "soldiers" were members of Battery B and Loomis Battery of the 1st Michigan Light Artillery and the 17th Michigan Volunteer Infantry. The patriotic spirit of the Revolutionary War was relived with the music to which the armies of 18th-century Europe and America marched. The First Michigan Colonial Fife and Drum Corps performed this lively concert from 7 p.m. to 7:30 p.m. and again from 8 p.m. to 8:30 p.m.

People felt they were strolling through the past as they listened to "old-time" music performed by the group State of Grace in the section of the museum which housed 19th-century streets of Old Detroit. Costumed interpreters were available all evening long to share information about the old buildings, and costumed storytellers brought to life the days of the French settlers and their Indian friends in the Moran Cabin, from 6 p.m. to 7 p.m. and from 8 p.m. to 9 p.m. Two museum exhibits celebrated the auto industry: "General Motors 75th Anniversary" was on display in Dodge Hall on the main floor, and "Cars of Old Detroit," a sampling of such early makes as the 1898 King Car and the 1915 Scripps-Booth Cyclecar, was on display on the ground floor. "Crafts and Trinkets," another part of the celebration, featured heritage craft demonstrations on the main and ground floors of the building from 6 p.m. to 10 p.m. Also on display were rare and colorful artifacts acquired over the past 54 years in the display entitled "Curator's Choice."

At the Detroit Public Library

The "joyous tantaras" of the Renaissance Brass Quintet were first heard from on the library balcony; afterward, the public adjourned to the Biography Room to hear the band play in concert. A multimedia trip "down memory lane" came next, with attendees joining in the singing of songs of America's yesteryear, and films, slides, and live singers re-creating the sights and sounds of over a century of American history in the Friends' auditorium; shows were at 6:45, 7:45, and 8:45 p.m. The show was repeated nightly during that week and was cosponsored by the Friends of the Library and a local clothing store. It was free, but reserved tickets were necessary.

Jazz played an important role in Detroit's history; top performers and crowds would gather in the city's many dance halls, ballrooms, theatres, and clubs. On this night, people got the chance to vicariously relive some of Detroit's musical heritage by viewing the photographic exhibition "Detroit: City of Jazz, 1930–80," in the library's exhibit hall.

More nostalgia was offered in an exhibit of baseball materials from the Ernie Harwell Collection, which is a permanent part of the library. Harwell, a well-known sportscaster recently admitted to the Baseball Hall of Fame, donated his lifetime collection of books and memorabilia to the library. For this occasion, many of the materials were displayed in the first floor exhibit cases.

At the Detroit Institute of Arts

Songs of the late 19th century were presented by pianist Bernard Katz and vocalist Faith Foster in the Kresge Court from 6 p.m. to 9 p.m. Light refreshments were served in the Court for a small charge. There was even some entertainment here for the children. A puppet show, "American Puppet Review," by the Fred Cowan Puppets, was presented in the institute's theatre at 6, 6:45, 7:30, and 8:15 p.m.

Comments

By planning special events accented with plenty of pizazz, three side-by-side city institutions showed their community what a good time they could have at a library, a historical museum, and an art institute, all on the same night. Staff, Friends, a local store, local talent, and many community organizations were involved in this Open House celebration. The gimmick for the Detroit Cultural Center was that the buildings were located right next door to each other. The same idea could work in other locales with cooperating agencies. It just might be better and more practical to spread the Open House idea over a two-day time period (preferably a Saturday and Sunday) so that people would have the chance to hit more activities. In any event, such promotional possibilities can work for your group as well as they did for Detroit.

"A MOVEABLE FEAST": COMMEMORATING HEMINGWAY IN KEY WEST

When notable people have lived and worked in your community, it is certainly a cause for celebration. Key West, Florida, has been and still is the home for many writers and poets. In 1984, some Key Westers decided they had some good reasons for honoring one of their most famous residents, Ernest Hemingway. They wanted to commemorate both his 85th birthday and also the 30th anniversary of his receipt of the Nobel Prize. So the Council for Florida Libraries, along with the Hemingway Society, decided to present a four-day Hemingway seminar in Key West called "A Moveable Feast." Cosponsors were the *Miami Herald*, the Monroe County Library, and Friends of the Monroe County Library and the Broward County Library.

Many well-known writers as well as friends and scholars of Hemingway appeared as speakers, including *Paris Review* founder/editor George Plimpton; Hemingway's son Patrick; and Hemingway's publisher, Charles Scribner, Jr. Three hundred people—writers, teachers, librarians, housewives, stewardesses, salespeople, and soldiers—each paid $100 for the privilege of being there. Key West proved an accommodating host by providing balmy weather for the mid-January affair.

As the initial speaker at the seminar, George Plimpton described his 1950s visit with the 59-year-old Hemingway in Cuba. Patrick Hemingway, the second of three sons, came from his home in Montana to participate in a session of reminiscences, "Remembering Hemingway." Other speakers in this series included publisher Scribner and other people who knew Hemingway. Other panel topics included "The Hemingway Style: The Man and the Writer"; "Hemingway: The American Myth, the Created Image, Hollywood and Popular Culture"; "Hemingway's Women In His Life and Work"; and "Hemingway In Cuba." Novelists Philip Caputo, Timothy O'Brien, and Robert Stone spoke on the panel "Hemingway and War: His Literary Inheritors."

KEY WEST BOOK & AUTHOR LUNCHEON

January 14, 1984

A&B Lobster House

Used by permission of Libraries Division, Florida Center for the Book, Broward County, Florida.

These were the main events. But there were others. People attended a reception at Sloppy Joe's Bar, had supper at the Pier House, and viewed a fireworks display with George Plimpton. They went to a cocktail party and tour of the Hemingway house and saw a slide show and exhibit from the Hemingway Collection of the Kennedy Library. They watched films and dramatic presentations, attended another cocktail party at the East Martello Art and Historical Museum and a coffee reception at the Key West Library, and went on a "Hemingway in Key West Walking Tour," led by author David Kaufelt.

People magazine covered the event. They followed and photographed a group of Hemingway look-alikes (complete with white beards) sipping a few in Sloppy Joe's Bar, where it's said Hemingway spent much of his time. Then they all joined the residents of Key West in their nightly ritual of watching the sun set at Mallory Dock.

Scott Donaldson of William and Mary College spoke of Hemingway's fascination with older women. Feminist Bernice Kert, author of *The Hemingway Women,* said of the writer, "the better they [women] treated him, sadly enough, the worse he treated them. Though he dominated the world of literature, I don't think Hemingway was so different from most men." Fiction writers Ambrose Clancy (*Blind Pilot*), David Martin (*The Crying Tattoo*), and Tim O'Brien (*Going after Cacciato*) spoke of what Hemingway meant to them and their work.

There were other highlights: While touring Hemingway's house in Key West, those who liked cats had a chance to touch and pet some of the many that still inhabit the house, descendants of Hemingway's original cats. Besides the usual tourist items, visitors bought books about Florida and Key West writers such as *In Residence: Key West Writers and Their Houses* by Lynn Kaufelt, who with her husband, David, served as the local coordinator of the seminar. The *Miami Herald* printed copies of the "Ernest Hemingway and Key West Friends" poster as a souvenir of the Key West Literary Tour and Seminar. WPA artist Erick Smith had created the caricature-type painting in 1933 when Hemingway was living in Key West. For many years it hung in Sloppy Joe's Bar on Duval Street. The original now hangs in the Key West Historical Museum; Sloppy Joe's has a copy on the wall.

Back on the mainland, the Broward County Library presented its "literary feast" for those who might not be able to attend the seminar farther south. The Broward festival took over where Key West left off; its "feast," from January 14 through March 19, consisted of films based on Hemingway novels, a panel discussion, a photo exhibit, and cable television interviews with some of the Key West seminar participants. A Hemingway bibliography was printed on the back of the "literary feast" promotional brochure.

Topics offered were similar to those at Key West. The speakers were academics from Florida colleges and universities; the films shown were *To Have and Have Not, A Farewell to Arms,* and *The Sun Also Rises.* Some were repeated at various branches of the library. Jean Trebbi, Broward County's library program coordinator, interviewed Bernice Kert, Scott Donaldson, and others on the television cable show *Library Edition.* Discussions included: "Hemingway's Paris," "White Wall of Spain," and "Hemingway and the Movies."

Summary

It all has to begin some way, usually with one or two enthusiastic people. To make it truly successful, it takes the cooperation and assistance of a great many others. Paul Smith, past president of the Hemingway Society, helped coordinate the program along with Bill Robertson, book editor of the *Miami Herald* (both also served as moderators); Jean Trebbi, program coordinator of the Broward County Library, was a planning committee member and the grants writer for the seminar; and Lynn and David Kaufelt were local arrangements people in Key West.

The seminar was funded in part by the Florida Endowment for the Humanities with support from the National Endowment for the Arts and the Key West Tourist Development Council. Special donors included Sloppy Joe's Bar, Pier House Inn, Marriott's Casa Marina Resort, the Hemingway House, the Tennessee Williams Fine Arts Center, the Art and Historical Society, and the East Martello Museum.

Comments

Since Ernest Hemingway is still an international literary figure, a celebration of his works and life could be held in just about any community. Commemorate his birthday, his first book, his first movie, his death...anything. Borrow some of the topics that the Florida group covered or some of the ideas from the hometown Foundation. Create your own ideas...have reviews of several of his books during the month of July with people bringing box lunches to the event, possibly in a park setting, near a college or university. You will find many professors who would love to give a talk on Hemingway the writer or Hemingway the man. Research and devise a Hemingway trivia quiz for all to play in conjunction with your programing. The prize could be a simple one such as a Hemingway book or, if possible, a Hemingway film night at the winner's home with invited guests. You would provide film, projectionist, and projector! The winner provides the popcorn. But, don't stop with a study of Hemingway and his works. Go on to other activities! Have a Hemingway look-a-like contest or a Hemingway 1920s dance which could serve as a fund-raiser with everyone dressing in the fashion of that era. Once you start rolling with ideas, there's no end...except a happy one!

HOORAY FOR THE BAY! WORKING WITH A FRIENDS GROUP

This could be described as a cooperative venture. It's a good example of a Friends group and a library working together on creative programming. The Friends of the Virginia Beach Library have been presenting "Hooray for the Bay!" celebrations at their library branches for the past several years. What could be more natural than commemorating Chesapeake Bay, which is right in their front yard? The waters and the weather here can be rather

HOORAY FOR THE BAY!

Sunday, October 9 3:00 P.M.	**THE VIRGINIA PILOTS ASSOCIATION — OCEANFRONT AREA LIBRARY.** Drs. Jane and George Webb of Christopher Newport College who made such a hit last year with their program on Virginia Beach at the turn of the Century, return with a behind-the-scenes look at the Virginia Pilots, the group responsible for guiding all commercial ships into Hampton Roads. The lecture and slide presentation, co-sponsored by the Virginia Beach Maritime Historical Museum, will be followed by a reception. Funds for this lecture were provided by the Virginia Foundation for the Humanities. Registration in advance is required. Call 428-4113 for reservations.
Wednesday, Oct. 12 7:30 p.m.	**CRAB PICKING — BAYSIDE AREA LIBRARY.** Library Assistant Laura Ashworth will teach school-age children the ins and outs of picking a crab. Children participating in the workshop must bring a permission slip from home in order to eat the product of their labors. Registration in advance is required. Call 428-4113 for reservations.
Saturday, October 15 9:30 a.m.	**GO BAREFOOT IN SALTWATER WITH MAC RAWLS — OCEANFRONT AREA LIBRARY.** Mac Rawls, Director of the Virginia Museum of Marine Sciences, will again lead a marine collection trip at Rudee Inlet. The trip will leave from the Oceanfront Area Library and is limited to 20 persons, 12 years of age and older. Group enrollments are prohibited. Specimens collected will be observed and returned to the water or temporarily housed in a saltwater aquarium at the Oceanfront Area Library throughout the Chesapeake Bay celebration. Registration in advance is required. Call 428-4113 for reservations.
Sunday, October 16 3:00 p.m.	**CHESAPEAKE, A PORTRAIT OF THE BAY COUNTRY — KEMPSVILLE AREA LIBRARY.** Awardwinning photographer Margaret J. White of Maryland will present this slide-lecture. She is the associate photographer who with photographer-author James A. Warner produced the magnificent book of color photographs, **Chesapeake, a Portrait of the Bay Country.** Prints from the book will be on sale for $20 and $50 apiece. A reception will follow. Advance registration is required. Call 428 4113 for reservations.
Thursday, October 20 7:30 P.M.	**VIRGINIA'S ROLE IN MANAGING THE CHESAPEAKE BAY — OCEANFRONT AREA LIBRARY.** Sheila M. Prindiville of Richmond, Administrator of Virginia's Council on the Environment, will speak on the part the state will play in the Bay's future. Call 428-4113 for reservations.
Sunday, October 23 3:00 p.m.	**AUTHOR AND CHOWDER AFFAIR — OCEANFRONT AREA LIBRARY.** Larry S. Chowning, author of **Barcat Skipper: Tales of a Tangier Island Waterman**, will be featured at the traditional lecture and clam chowder feast. This new book, just out, is based on the reminiscences of Elmer Crockett, an 80-year-old Tangier native whose tales tell the story of this independent island community. Books will be on sale. Tickets to the Author and Chowder Affair are available for $1.00 at all area libraries.
Sunday, November 6 Noon	**FISHERMAN'S ISLAND FIELD TRIP FOR BIRDERS, SHELL COLLECTORS AND NATURE ENTHUSIASTS.** Dan Dinkler, Outdoor Recreation Planner with Back Bay National Wildlife Refuge, will lead a two-to-four-mile walk on Fisherman's Island. The trip will begin at noon at the Chesapeake Bay Bridge-Tunnel, South Toll Gate Plaza parking lot where participants will arrange car pools. Participants are responsible for a one-way tunnel toll. This is a special opportunity to visit this refuge which is normally closed to all public entry. Come prepared. There are no shelter, restroom or refreshment facilities on the island. Advance reservations must be made by calling 428-4113.
Saturday, October 15 - Sunday, October 23	**CHESAPEAKE BAY — OCEANFRONT AREA LIBRARY.** This new exhibit and continuous slide show is being made available by Virginia's Council on the Environment. It stresses the importance of the Bay's resources to Virginia, the State's current efforts to solve the Bay's problems and to manage the Bay. The Council will have informative brochures on the Bay available for the public.

Used by permission of the Virginia Beach Public Library.

warm and inviting; the program titles were inviting as well: "Go Barefoot in Saltwater with Mac Rawls," "Virginia Beach at the Century's Turn," "The Ghost of Cape Horn," "An Oceanographer's View of Chesapeake Bay," "Seafood Cookery Demonstration," "Fisherman's Island Field Trip for Birders, Shell Collectors and Nature Enthusiasts."

On the first Saturday of this celebration, Mac Rawls, director of the Virginia Beach Museum of Marine Sciences, took a group of 20 people (ages 12 and up) on a marine collection trip to Rudee Inlet. Specimens collected were put on display in the saltwater aquarium at the Oceanfront branch library.

At the library on Sunday evening, people were treated to a slide/talk show, "The Beach at the Century's Turn: A Place Defines the People," with Drs. Jane and George Webb of Christopher Newport College. Their presentation described the physical nature of the beach and how it set a certain spirit and expectation for early residents, farmers, summer visitors, and life-saving personnel. Refreshments were served; funding for the program came from the Virginia Foundation for the Humanities.

Both dyed-in-the-wool mariners and Sunday sailors would have loved the next offering on Monday night at the Oceanfront library branch with boat builder and waterman Billy Moore. He had built a Chesapeake Bay deadrise boat, which is designed to endure the rigors of oystering and crabbing in the bay. A film which documents the building of the boat and its actual use in the bay was shown with comments by Moore.

The film *Ghost of Cape Horn* was shown at three branch libraries during the week on separate nights. "Immerse yourself in the thrill, majesty and sometimes terror of the great age of sail" was the promotional flier's phrase touting this program.

To get another view, perhaps unknown to most laypeople, a slide/talk show, "An Oceanographer's View of Chesapeake Bay," was presented at the Windsor Woods Library on Tuesday night. Dr. Carvel Hall Blair, professor of oceanography at Old Dominion University, was featured. On that Friday morning, Fay Foster of Bud Roe's Fresh Seafood Restaurant presented a "Seafood Cookery" program at the Kempsville Branch Library. She described how to prepare shrimp, crabmeat meatballs, Hatteras-style clam chowder, and other seafood delicacies.

Would you believe a chowder reception for an author? Why not, if you're living right on a bay and your speaker's book is *The Living Chesapeake*. Seems natural and delicious. The "Author and Chowder" speaker was Dr. J. R. Schubel, director of the Marine Research Center of the State University of New York and former associate with the Johns Hopkins University Chesapeake Bay Institute. The chowder reception followed his talk.

Those seeking more information about the history and ecology of the bay found it in a talk by Dr. E. T. Buchanan, dean of student services, Tidewater Community College (Virginia Beach campus). Buchanan, who is the past leader of the Lynnhaven Chapter of the Chesapeake Bay Foundation, described the development of the bay estuary and its complex ecological system.

Concluding the series was a field trip to Fisherman's Island with Dan Dinkler, outdoor recreation planner with the Back Bay National Wildlife Refuge. It attracted many bird watchers, shell collectors, and nature enthusiasts from the community. Many of the programs were made possible by a grant from the Citizens for the Chesapeake Bay. The library promoted the activities with news releases and promotional fliers.

Summary

The world around you can be a great theme. Think about this as a potential program idea, especially if you live and work near a famous body of water. Live in the part of the country where the nearest body of water is your bathtub? Fantastic! You really have more of a challenge. Take the sea or water as your theme and flow with it...have slide show/talks with naturalists, show films about the sea (perhaps a documentary), feature a film like *On Golden Pond* with Katherine Hepburn, exhibit model-scale boats and ships created by local residents, hold a travel night with films or slides and talks on exotic cruises. If you work for/with a library, why not hold a used book sale on the main floor with all the books dumped into a borrowed rowboat? There are many more great ideas you will dream up. Of course, your event doesn't have to be about water or the seas. It's just a suggestion. Look around you. Each natural environment offers its own creative program ideas.

There is no better way to produce an event than to work cooperatively with someone else. There are so many others out there: other institutions, communities, Friends (or friends), private industry. This way you not only share ideas, space, and funding, but the rewards of a successful event.

Chapter 4
Thematic Programing

- It's a Mystery!
- Let's Fly!
- Year of the Trains
- Strictly for Laughs
- Selected Short Subjects

Thematic programing, designing and scheduling a series bound together by a common thread, can produce gray hairs as well as crowns on the planner's head. The legwork and attention to detail to make each and every step dovetail can be staggering. Each program should build on those preceding it, but should also stand alone as an individual presentation. Because the series is related in both theme and time, the pressures can mount accordingly. But at the other end of the rainbow, it is these same factors which allow in-depth examination of your theme, to also increase your audience as well as their appreciation and applause! It's worth the work. Short staffed? Don't try to do it alone. Think cooperative venture and contact other staff members, Friends, and other community organizations and work on a theme together.

The possibilities of unlimited creativity are yours when you undertake thematic programing. The case histories you will be reading about here center on such themes as mystery, flight, trains, food, humor, health, hair, family, baseball, and love. Actually, most programing can be considered thematic; many such activities are presented in other chapters of this book.

IT'S A MYSTERY!

Murder and mayhem at a museum? Why not? As long as it's all in fun. As part of a series of events, films, and lectures on mystery, visitors to the Strong Museum in Rochester, New York, were invited to join in the fun one October weekend in 1984 to test their powers of observation and deduction, to follow clues, to solve riddles, and to see if they could solve the "murder" in the museum.

Mystery weekends are offered at hotels, resorts, and on trains and ships, so why not at a local museum or at any location? After all, mystery books are being read more than ever. Marie Hewett, director of education at the Strong Museum, and her associates devised a clever weekend for mystery buffs. They offered not only a mystery to solve but also films, old-time radio programs, exhibits, and lectures on the history of the detective story. The attractive promotional brochure (grayish tan paper with black and maroon ink) announced the various programs and exhibits available at the museum. Sleuths were given a three-page information sheet which described the "Murder in the Museum." Clues were scattered all over the museum. Amateur Sherlocks and Inspector Poirots were then handed "Tracking Down the Clues" sheets (riddles leading the sleuth to clues scattered about the museum). When a sleuth had figured out who the murderer was, s/he would take the sheet to the "solution checker" in the main lobby and claim a certificate.

The museum's film and lectures series covered the American mystery story from its earliest days to 1939. For those interested in learning the origins of

IT'S A MYSTERY!

AMERICANS AND THE MYSTERY STORY TO 1939

October 27 & 28, 1984

The Strong Museum
One Manhattan Square
Rochester, New York

Used by permission of the Strong Museum, Rochester, NY.

the mystery story, English professor George Grella of the University of Rochester elaborated on "From the Rue Morgue to the Mean Streets: Detective Fiction in America." Sherlock Holmes buffs were treated to "Sherlock Holmes in America," by longtime Sherlockian Donald Pollock, a University of Rochester anthropologist. He spoke about the American fascination with Sherlock Holmes from the 1890s through the 1930s as it was manifested in stories, parodies, comic strips, radio programs, plays, and movies. Concluding that day's lecture series was Jon Lazar from the Rochester Public Library, who spoke of "Sherlock Holmes on Stage and Screen." All of these activities took place on Saturday beginning at 10 a.m.

Sunday was mystery movie day at the museum. At 1:30 p.m., visitors saw *The Hound of the Baskervilles* with Basil Rathbone and Nigel Bruce. And for those still game, the museum showed *The Maltese Falcon*.

On both Saturday and Sunday, children and adults listened to *The Shadow*, the old-time radio show which so delighted and terrified listeners in the 1930s. The mystery man "in the shadows" began and ended each broadcast with a nasal, frightening laugh. In between, he taught criminals that "in the end, crime must fail." It was nostalgia time for those who remembered the broadcasts from their childhood, and for the younger set, it was pure fun. There were more treats: six episodes from 1938 with Orson Welles and two 1939 shows with Bill Johnstone as Lamont Cranston. More listening pleasure was added with the airing of four Sherlock Holmes broadcasts from the same period. *And*, people listened to the programs via a 1930s Philco radio! How about that for authenticity?

Besides the big murder game, there were two games for both adults and children. "Sherlock's Lost Pipe" was played on a computer. "The Collections Caper," a Hardy Boys/Nancy Drew game, tested the mettle of 20th-century detectives on both Saturday and Sunday until 2 p.m. "Murder in the Museum" was repeated on Sunday also. Everyone in the family was included in the museum's mystery weekend. Exhibits included mystery books from the museum's own collection and "Holmesiana," two local collections of books, posters, paper ephemera, and other materials based on Holmes.

Timing was great for a mystery weekend—the weekend right before Halloween! Local experts responded with pleasure, and the weekend was a great success. The "Murder in the Museum" game was copyrighted by the museum and plans are afoot to repeat the entire programing series. Variations on this mystery weekend can be adapted by any organization looking for something creative and fun to do. It does take some creative thinking, careful planning, and promotion. Think about it. Then, for more inspiration, read this next mystery program.

Have Mystery, Will Travel

A couple I know—she, a classical pianist and he, an English teacher, editor, and author—together are deep into mystery and "horror." They have fun while providing even more fun for their audiences. Joyce and Arthur Liebman live on Long Island, and for the past five years or more they have been entertaining audiences with slide/talk shows complete with background piano music provided nickelodeon-style by Joyce. Arthur and Joyce are costumed as Sherlock and friend. They come with their own "set," a fringed shawl for the piano, candle, wine and wine glasses, and magnifying glass. They also "do" Dracula, Frankenstein, and Agatha Christie in costume with the proper musical accompaniment.

I read about their Sherlock Holmes Halloween show in a weekly newspaper. It sounded like a potential program idea. I love birthday celebrations and have learned the value that a birthday celebration can add to a program. After some quick research, I found out that Sherlock Holmes would have been 128 years old the following January 6. So, I thought, why not hold a birthday party for him at our library on his birthday? The Liebmans loved the idea. We qualified for a matching grant from the Nassau County Office of Cultural Development, and our plans and promotion began.

"Sherlock Holmes Lives!" declared the headline on our gray/tan brochure with purple ink. Everyone was invited to a "Sherlock Holmes Birthday Party. No tickets needed...bring a friend or a ghoul!" The news releases had gone out weeks earlier to all the media. Little did we know the monster we were creating.

This is as much a promotion story as a creative program idea. Our library is located in East Meadow, 35 miles from New York City. Most of the community's residents lived "in the city" or in one of the other boroughs before they migrated to the space and sea of Long Island. Long Island's public television station does little remote coverage because of budgetary problems. And, to make the "big time," getting air time on New York City's television stations, is practically impossible. Remember, I said practically. Miracles do happen. Long Island's only daily newspaper, *Newsday*, ran our special event, ("Sherlock's Birthday Happening") as the top spot in its "Tonight" entertainment section that day. The phones were busy in my office all day long. Half of the calls were from people wanting to know directions to the library, and the rest were from Channel 4-WNBC staff, including Jim Van Sickle, the reporter who covered the Holmes program. They had picked up on our special event from *Newsday*, not from my news release.

Back at the library the night of the program, it was like the invasion of the bodies! People jammed our doors as early as 7 p.m. for an 8:30 p.m. presentation; they came from as far away as Connecticut and New Jersey on a weekday night. Jim Van Sickle arrived at 7 p.m. with his television crew. (If you've ever had television coverage for one of your events, you know the way the crew takes over.) The Liebmans, who are the most delightful couple to work with, were pleased, at ease, and most willing to please all. I finally had to inform the television crew that the show had to go on; an audience was waiting for the real show of the evening, even though they enjoyed being part of the television taping for the 11 o'clock news. So, I got my stage back, and the show went on. It was a huge success, and the birthday cake was the icing on the whole evening's happenings. Our meeting room overrunneth...all chairs were filled and the rest sat or stood on the floor. I prayed that the fire department would not walk through for an inspection. We would have failed.

It was an entertaining, educational, and hectic evening. Even Arthur Liebman, who began the evening wearing his full Sherlockian attire of deerstalker hat, Inverness cape and coat, spats, and a calabash pipe, was down to his pants and dress shirt by the evening's end, although Joyce was still resplendent in her long black dress and white Victorian hat.

As far as the TV coverage was concerned, we ended up receiving four to six minutes of air time on the 11 o'clock news! Luckily, there were no murders, no fires, no late-breaking stories. Precommercial promos kept announcing our Holmes birthday celebration during the TV news. Several people in the community even taped the television segment for us to view later. I thought it would be a successful evening, but it went beyond my wildest expectations. I have stressed the promotion of this event more than the event itself because the press coverage results became the major event for all concerned.

As a result of this "big time" coverage, the Liebmans received requests to "do Sherlock" from many points on the compass, including a Queen Elizabeth 2 cruise to London. Arthur ended up taking a sabbatical from teaching so that they could take on all the bookings for their mystery shows. They are still going strong.

Back to the library's celebration. It was a month of mystery at the library with the showing of *Phantom of the Opera* and *The Hound of the Baskervilles* on the two following Friday nights after Sherlock's birthday gig. A "Just about Everything You Ever Wanted to Read about Sherlock Holmes" reading list was compiled by Arthur Liebman and published by the library. Many people played the "Sherlock Holmes Quiz" devised by Liebman; the winner received a gift book about Sherlock Holmes. The library's exhibit cases displayed Sherlockian memorabilia collected by the

Used by permission of Arthur Liebman.

Liebmans. The demand by people who had seen the television coverage was so great that we repeated the Sherlock Holmes program on a Wednesday afternoon later on that month. It was the only free time the Liebmans had open.

Later on that year, the Liebmans did their thing again with a "Frankenstein Frolics" night at our library, followed by a showing of the movie *The Bride of Frankenstein* on another evening. Recently the Liebmans came again, this time to celebrate Agatha Christie. The library printed an "Agatha Christie Quiz and Crossword" developed by Arthur. Mystery buffs loved and played the games.

Of all of the events, the Sherlock Holmes program proved to be the most popular, with the Agatha Christie program running a close second. The Liebmans are a pleasure to work with because they are creative not only in their presentations but in their promotional thinking. They have learned that they are their own best promoters. So they prepare "homemade" fliers ready-to-go, complete with press information. This kind of attitude is always most welcome to a program planner.

Comments

Just about anyone can do a mystery month. Pick a theme. You might even want to go with the most popular, such as Sherlock Holmes, Agatha Christie, Dracula, or Frankenstein. Check the film catalogs in your public library and consult with the film librarian. There are so many fine mystery, horror, and detective movies that it'll be a snap. Plan a "Murder at the Y" or a "Murder at the Library" or a "Murder at the Rec Center." Your committee could be mystery buffs, academics, and amateurs. Use the mystery quizzes in this book or better still, make up your own. It takes time and research, but it can be a lot of fun. Always remember the *fun* of things. The prizes? Mystery books or mystery games. For the booby prize winner: a magnifying glass for better sleuthing the next time around. The "It's a Mystery" series should be a natural program series. With permission from Arthur Liebman, I have included two of his popular quizzes, Sherlock Holmes and Agatha Christie, ready for your use.

Sherlock Holmes Quiz

1. Holmes and Watson lived at _____ Baker St. in London
    a. 378B
    b. 123
    c. 437A
    d. 221B
2. Holmes's favorite musical instrument was _____
    a. piano
    b. cello
    c. violin
    d. flute
3. The famous Sherlock Holmes hat was called _____
    a. Lord Acton Cap
    b. deerstalker
    c. bowler
    d. Hill-and-Dale
4. Sherlock Holmes's landlady was _____
    a. Mrs. Brown
    b. Mrs. Turner
    c. Mrs. Carter
    d. Mrs. Hudson
5. Professor Moriarty had once been an outstanding _____
    a. historian
    b. mathematician
    c. biologist
    d. painter
6. Prof. Moriarty visited Holmes's rooms in _____
    a. "The Dying Detective"
    b. "A Case of Identity"
    c. "The Final Problem"
    d. "The Red Circle"
7. Holmes's older brother was _____
    a. Edmond
    b. Sackmorton
    c. Mycroft
    d. Hosmer
8. The first movie in which Basil Rathbone played Holmes was _____
    a. *The Adventures of Sherlock Holmes*
    b. *Sherlock Holmes and the Secret Weapon*
    c. *Sherlock Holmes Faces Death*
    d. *The Hound of the Baskervilles*
9. When Dr. Watson was in the British Army, he served in _____
    a. Australia
    b. South Africa
    c. The Sudan
    d. Afghanistan
10. Who played Dr. Watson opposite Basil Rathbone's Holmes?
    a. Edmund Gwenn
    b. Alan Napier
    c. Lionel Atwill
    d. Nigel Bruce
11. When the first Sherlock Holmes stories were published, _____ was on the throne of England
    a. Queen Elizabeth
    b. King Edward
    c. King George
    d. Queen Victoria
12. Which of the following played Holmes in a silent movie?
    a. Douglas Fairbanks
    b. Lon Chaney
    c. John Barrymore
    d. Frederic March
13. One of Holmes's most famous lines was "The _____ afoot"
    a. plot's
    b. game is
    c. job's
    d. kill's
14. The group of young boys who often helped Holmes with his cases was called _____
    a. London Gang
    b. Roving Boys
    c. Junior Detectives
    d. Baker St. Irregulars
15. What was the name of "the woman" in Holmes's life?
    a. Rose White
    b. Irene Adler
    c. Helen Stoner
    d. Virginia Fairfax
16. Who was the bungling inspector from Scotland Yard?
    a. Stapleton
    b. Milverton
    c. Lestrade
    d. Stoner

Used by permission of Arthur Liebman.

34 *Fireworks, Brass Bands, and Elephants*

17. Dr. Watson fell in love in _____
    a. "The Boscombe Valley Tragedy"
    b. *The Valley of Fear*
    c. *The Sign of the Four*
    d. "The Missing Three Quarter"
18. Which Holmes story took place out on the mysterious moors?
    a. "The Yellow Face"
    b. "The Beryl Coronet"
    c. "The Copper Beeches"
    d. *The Hound of the Baskervilles*
19. Sir Arthur Conan Doyle, creator of Holmes, studied to be a _____
    a. painter
    b. professor
    c. lawyer
    d. doctor
20. Complete the following title: "The _____ League"
    a. Mysterious
    b. Empire
    c. Red Headed
    d. Barefooted
21. Holmes encountered Jack the Ripper in the movie _____
    a. *Terror by Night*
    b. *The House of Fear*
    c. *A Study in Terror*
    d. *The Woman in Green*
22. Which story took place at Christmas time?
    a. "The Illustrious Client"
    b. "The Red Circle"
    c. "The Blue Carbuncle"
    d. "The Golden Pince-nez"
23. Holmes and Watson searched for a fabulous treasure in _____
    a. *The Sign of the Four*
    b. *A Study in Scarlet*
    c. "Silver Blaze"
    d. "The Second Stain"
24. Watson and Holmes looked for a missing pearl in "The Six _____ "
    a. Necklaces
    b. Pendulums
    c. Napoleons
    d. Garidebs
25. While Holmes was an undergraduate at the University, he solved the case of "Gloria _____ "
    a. Scott
    b. White
    c. Brown
    d. Russell
26. Holmes and Watson searched for a missing London businessman in "The Man with the Twisted _____ "
    a. Leg
    b. Arm
    c. Lip
    d. Mind
27. Holmes's snuff box was given to him by _____
    a. The Duke of Cornwall
    b. Queen Victoria
    c. Benjamin Disraeli
    d. The King of Bohemia
28. Which of the following was not a title of a Holmes movie?
    a. *Pursuit to Algiers*
    b. *Terror by Night*
    c. *Death at Dawn*
    d. *Dressed to Kill*
29. In which story did Holmes decipher a code?
    a. "The Bruce-Partington Plans"
    b. "The Three Students"
    c. "The Devil's Foot"
    d. "The Dancing Men"
30. According to most experts, Holmes was born in _____
    a. May
    b. August
    c. November
    d. January
31. Holmes kept his cigars in a/an _____
    a. special humidor
    b. coal scuttle
    c. old violin case
    d. special pouch given him by the Queen
32. One of Watson's great unwritten cases was "The Giant Rat of _____ "
    a. Sumatra
    b. Borneo
    c. Brazil
    d. Tibet
33. Holmes and Moriarty struggled at the Falls at _____
    a. Norfolk
    b. Reichenbach
    c. Geneva
    d. Salzburg
34. The first story in which Holmes's older brother appeared was _____
    a. "The Solitary Cyclist"
    b. "The Greek Interpreter"
    c. "The Veiled Lodger"
    d. "Thor Bridge"
35. A king visited Holmes in _____
    a. "His Last Bow"
    b. "The Norwood Builder"
    c. "The Cardboard Box"
    d. "A Scandal in Bohemia"
36. _____ was the great English illustrator who illustrated the original Holmes stories
    a. Sidney Paget
    b. Payson Russell
    c. Algernon Abernathy
    d. Trelawney Basehart
37. Holmes and Watson searched for a stolen horse in "Silver _____ "
    a. Blaze

b. Streak
c. Mine
d. Light
38. The first Sherlock Holmes novel appeared in _____
    a. 1895
    b. 1887
    c. 1875
    d. 1880
39. Holmes retired to a little cottage in _____
    a. Cornwall
    b. Sussex
    c. Paris
    d. Dartmoor
40. A snake played a venomous role in _____
    a. "The Yellow Face"
    b. "The Illustrious Client"
    c. "The Noble Bachelor"
    d. "The Speckled Band"
41. Which line was not said by Holmes? "_____"
    a. I am lost without my Boswell.
    b. You know my method.
    c. Crime is common. Logic is rare.
    d. Elementary, my dear Watson.
42. Which of these actors has not played the part of Sherlock Holmes?
    a. John Neville
    b. Robert Stephens
    c. Robert Duvall
    d. Arthur Wonter
43. Which actor once played the role of Mycroft Holmes?
    a. Ralph Richardson
    b. Robert Morley
    c. Robert Donat
    d. Michael Redgrave
44. Holmes captured a German spy in _____
    a. "A Case of Identity"
    b. "The Adventure of the Mazarin Stones"
    c. "The Devil's Foot"
    d. "His Last Bow"
45. The coal mines of America were important in _____
    a. "Black Peter"
    b. *The Valley of Fear*
    c. "The Second Stain"
    d. "The Retired Colourman"
46. In the movie *The Pearl of Death*, Holmes defeated a horrible villain known as the _____
    a. Zombie
    b. Caveman
    c. Creeper
    d. Crusher
47. The American illustrator who immortalized the image of Holmes in the U.S. was _____
    a. Norman Rockwell
    b. Charles Dana Gibson
    c. Frederick Dorr Steele
    d. Payson Smith
48. During his retirement, Holmes devoted his time to _____
    a. raising roses
    b. studying tropical fish
    c. raising a special kind of wheat
    d. keeping bees
49. The role of Prof. Moriarty was played by _____ in *The Adventures of Sherlock Holmes* (1939)
    a. Lionel Atwill
    b. Lionel Stander
    c. Ian Hunter
    d. George Zucco
50. Holmes disguised himself as a book dealer in _____
    a. "The Priory School"
    b. "The Empty House"
    c. "The Dancing Men"
    d. "The Five Orange Pips"

Answers to Sherlock Holmes Quiz

1=D 2=C 3=B 4=D 5=B 6=C 7=C 8=D 9=D 10=D 11=D 12=C 13=B 14=D 15=B 16=C 17=C 18=D 19=D 20=C 21=C 22=C 23=A 24=C 25=A 26=C 27=D 28=C 29=D 30=D 31=B 32=A 33=B 34=B 35=D 36=A 37=A 38=B 39=B 40=D 41=D 42=C 43=B 44=D 45=B 46=C 47=C 48=D 49=D 50=B

Agatha Christie Quiz ¿?

1. Agatha Christie's great detective, Hercule Poirot, was a retired member of the _____ police force
    a. French
    b. Dutch
    c. Swiss
    d. Belgian
2. Hercule Poirot first lived in England _____
    a. during World War II
    b. in 1926
    c. during World War I
    d. in 1933
3. During most of his professional career, Poirot resided at _____ London
    a. Fairview Apartments
    b. Whitehaven Mansions
    c. Victoria Mews
    d. Wimpole Manor
4. Poirot was very proud of his _____
    a. very shiny teeth
    b. dark eyebrows
    c. strong heart
    d. wonderful mustache
5. Poirot often said that he solved his cases by using his _____
    a. continental mind
    b. little gray cells

Used by permission of Arthur Liebman.

c. detective's instincts
d. infallible intuition
6. The name of Poirot's faithful valet was _____
    a. Emile
    b. Pierre
    c. Georges
    d. Gaston
7. Poirot's secretary and receptionist was _____
    a. Mrs. Gump
    b. Miss Cavendish
    c. Miss Lemon
    d. Mrs. Blue
8. A not-so-bright member of Scotland Yard who appeared in a number of Agatha Christie novels was Inspector _____
    a. Tick
    b. Hound
    c. Shaw
    d. Japp
9. The great detective Hercule Poirot died at the end of _____
    a. *Elephants Can Remember*
    b. *Postern of Fate*
    c. *Sleeping Murder*
    d. *Curtain*
10. The first Hercule Poirot novel was _____
    a. *Murder on the Links*
    b. *Easy to Kill*
    c. *The Seven Dials Mystery*
    d. *The Mysterious Affair at Styles*
11. Most of the early Poirot novels were told by Poirot's friend and confidant _____
    a. Captain Summerhill
    b. Colonel Gilchrist
    c. Captain Simpson
    d. Captain Hastings
12. Miss Jane Marple first appeared in the Agatha Christie novel _____
    a. *Crooked House*
    b. *The Listerdale Mystery*
    c. *Murder at the Vicarage*
    d. *The Regatta Mystery*
13. Miss Jane Marple lived in the tiny village of _____
    a. Kenworthy
    b. St. Mary Mead
    c. St. Luke
    d. Timothy on Thames
14. _____ played the role of Miss Marple in four films
    a. Edna May Oliver
    b. Martita Hunt
    c. Gladys Cooper
    d. Margaret Rutherford
15. Miss Marple was a member of the distinguished _____ club
    a. Sunday
    b. Tuesday
    c. Friday
    d. Faraday
16. Miss Marple's nephew who appeared in a number of novels was the famous novelist _____
    a. Newton Keith
    b. Dorian Shaw
    c. Raymond West
    d. Trelawney Wells
17. The last novel in the Jane Marple series was _____
    a. *The Pale Horse*
    b. *By the Pricking of My Thumbs*
    c. *Sleeping Murder*
    d. *Crooked House*
18. A writer of detective stories who often appeared in Agatha Christie novels was _____
    a. Phaedra French
    b. Emma White
    c. Mathilda Crane
    d. Ariadne Oliver
19. The Agatha Christie novel which first made her name world famous was _____
    a. *The Man in the Brown Suit*
    b. *Ten Little Indians*
    c. *Passenger to Frankfurt*
    d. *The Murder of Roger Ackroyd*
20. In the film *The Alphabet Murders*, Poirot was played by _____
    a. Henry Fonda
    b. Lawrence Olivier
    c. Tony Randall
    d. Gregory Peck
21. _____ played Poirot in Agatha Christie's play *Alibi*
    a. Lawrence Olivier
    b. Emlyn Williams
    c. Charles Laughton
    d. Eric Portman
22. A husband-and-wife team of detectives who appeared in a number of Agatha Christie novels was _____
    a. Nick and Nora Charles
    b. Mr. and Mrs. North
    c. Tommy and Tuppence Berresford
    d. Freda and Freddy White
23. _____ took place in ancient Egypt more than 3,000 years ago
    a. *Death Comes at the End*
    b. *Easy to Kill*
    c. *Endless Night*
    d. *The Hound of Death*
24. Which of these movie stars did not appear in *Witness for the Prosecution*?
    a. Tyrone Power
    b. Marlene Dietrich
    c. David Niven
    d. Charles Laughton
25. The movie *Love from a Stranger* was based on a short story by Agatha Christie called

    a. "Philomel Cottage"
    b. "The Arcadian Deer"
    c. "Accident"
    d. "Double Sin"
26. Christie's play _____ was the longest running play in the history of the modern English theatre
    a. *Alibi*
    b. *Dial M for Murder*
    c. *The Mouse Trap*
    d. *An Inspector Calls*
27. _____ played the part of Poirot in *Murder on the Orient Express*
    a. David Niven
    b. Michael Caine
    c. Sean Connery
    d. Albert Finney
28. All the suspects in *Murder on the Orient Express* were at one time connected with a young girl named _____
    a. Susan Wallace
    b. Hester Shaw
    c. Daisy Armstrong
    d. Myrna White
29. _____ was the name of a sleuth created by Agatha Christie
    a. Paul Pruit
    b. John Jantor
    c. Coleman Cole
    d. Parker Pyne
30. A group of guests were invited to an island by a mysterious, unknown host in _____
    a. *Endless Night*
    b. *They Came to Bagdad*
    c. *Partners in Crime*
    d. *Ten Little Indians*
31. Agatha Christie's mother was English. Her father was _____
    a. French
    b. American
    c. Canadian
    d. Australian
32. For more than 40 years Agatha Christie was happily married to the noted archeologist _____
    a. Sir Max Mallowan
    b. Sir Harold Porter
    c. Sir Gerald Abernathy
    d. Sir Temple Johnson
33. Agatha Christie wrote a number of romantic novels under the pen name _____
    a. Gladys Traherne
    b. Mary Westmacott
    c. Cynthia Sheldon Shaw
    d. Susan St. Regis
34. In 1926 Agatha Christie, suffering from amnesia, disappeared for _____
    a. two months
    b. 11 days
    c. three days
    d. four months
35. Agatha Christie's novels have been translated into more than _____ languages
    a. 40
    b. 60
    c. 80
    d. 100

Answers to Agatha Christie Quiz

1=D 2=C 3=B 4=D 5=B 6=C 7=C 8=D 9=D 10=D 11=D 12=C 13=B 14=D 15=B 16=C 17=C 18=D 19=D 20=C 21=C 22=C 23=A 24=C 25=A 26=C 27=D 28=C 29=D 30=D 31=B 32=A 33=B 34=B 35=D

LET'S FLY!

Space and air flight are more exciting today than ever before. The Smithsonian's National Air & Space Museum, in Washington, DC, records the highest attendance of all of their museums. Programing that celebrates flight is a natural. There are so many ways to commemorate flight...let's explore a few!

Paper Airplanes

Admit it. You fashioned a paper airplane in school with a piece of composition paper and set it sailing aloft when the teacher wasn't looking. If it's been that long since you've created a paper plane, maybe it's time you took flight with a piece of paper again. Thousands of people design, make, and fly paper planes. Remember the 1st International Paper Airplane Competition in 1967? *Scientific American* magazine announced the contest in December 1966, with judging to take place in 1967. However, the planners never dreamed that so many would enter the contest. They had to move the judging from the hallways of *Scientific American* to the New York Hall of Science. All told, 11,851 entries arrived from 5,144 people representing 28 countries. Of those, 5,000 entries were from children. It was overwhelming; even the international press covered the event. The First International Paper Airplane Competition awarded the Leonardo, a trophy of a hand holding a paper plane (now the logo of the Second Great International Paper Airplane Contest) to winners in each of four categories: duration, time aloft, distance flown, aerobatics, and origami. There was such interest and enthusiasm about the contest that a book, *The Great International Paper Airplane Book*, was published in 1967 as a direct result.

Eighteen years later, the Second Great International Paper Airplane Contest was announced by the three sponsors: *Science 85* magazine, the Seattle Museum of Flight, and the National Air & Space Museum. The judging took place in late May 1985

/ Fireworks, Brass Bands, and Elephants

MUSEUM OF FLIGHT NEWS

January/February 1985   *For Future Generations*   Volume 7 Number 1

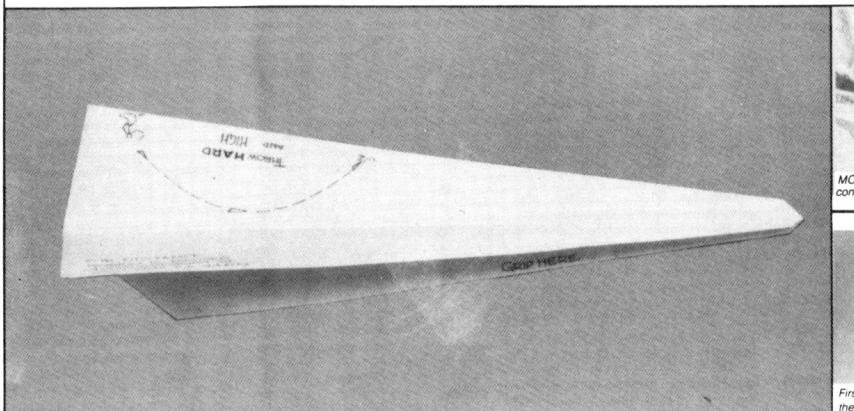

MOFs Howard Lovering at press conference in D.C.

First airplane entry to arrive at the museum.

IT'S ONLY A PAPER PLANE...

But it flew 58 feet, two inches, winning in the nonprofessional category of *Scientific American's* paper airplane contest in 1967. A lot has changed since then. Real planes have traded heavy, metal parts for pieces made of layered and fibrous composite materials. And, we assume, the paper plane buffs of the world have been tinkering too, folding along different lines and perhaps learning a few tricks from the nonpaper engineers. So *Science 85* magazine, Seattle's Museum of Flight and the Smithsonian Institution's National Air and Space Museum announce The Second Great International Paper Airplane Contest of the Century.

THE EVENTS:
Time Aloft
Distance
Aerobatics
Aesthetic Design (all these planes must fly at least 15 feet or three seconds)

THE CATEGORIES:
• Professional—teachers and graduate students in aeronautics and related fields as well as engineers, designers, and others employed in the aerospace industry
• Nonprofessionals—everyone else
• Junior—entrants under 14 years old, eligible for time and distance events only (parent-child teams must enter under the professional or nonprofessional categories)

THE JUDGES
A high-flying panel will test your design in the wide open spaces of a Boeing aircraft hangar in Seattle
—Michael Collins, former director of the National Air and Space Museum and Apollo astronaut
—Dennis Flanagan, editor emeritus of *Scientific American*
—Ilan Kroo, NASA aerodynamic designer
—Yasuaki Ninomiya, designer of WHITEWINGS toy airplanes
—Sheila Widnall, MIT aerodynamics engineer

THE AWARDS:
THE BERNOULLI MEDALLION for paper flight goes to first-, second-, and third-place winners in each event. First-place winners will be flown, all expenses paid, to Seattle to receive their awards and fly their planes during a special ceremony at the Seattle Kingdome in June. Some of the winning designs will be published in the September issue of *Science 85*.

THE RULES:
All entries must be made only of paper. Glue and cellophane tape may be used only for bonding purposes, not to add weight. Paper lamination and paper reinforcement *is* allowed.
Your entry is your airplane, properly folded, with your name, address, phone number, and any special throwing instructions written clearly on the plane. Also write which event you would like to enter (only one event per plane) and whether you are in the Professional, Nonprofessional, or Junior group. Planes missing any of the required information will be disqualified.
Entries should be sent to: International Paper Airplane Contest, Museum of Flight, 9404 E. Marginal Way South, Seattle, Washington 98108.
Entries must be received by May 1, 1985. All entries become the property of *Science 85*, the Museum of Flight and the National Air and Space Museum. By submitting their designs, entrants agree to allow *Science 85*, the Museum of Flight and the National Air and Space Museum to publish and use them in subsequent promotional material. Employes and relatives of employes of *Science 85*, the Museum of Flight, the National Air and Space Museum, and AG Industries/WHITEWINGS are not eligible.
The Second Great International Paper Airplane Contest is sponsored in cooperation with AG Industries/WHITEWINGS.

MUSEUM OF FLIGHT
SCIENCE85
NATIONAL AIR AND SPACE MUSEUM

THE SECOND GREAT INTERNATIONAL PAPER AIRPLANE CONTEST

Annual Membership Meeting
5:00 pm, Wednesday
March 20, 1985

A report on annual operations, fund-raising, and announcement of elected trustees and members of executive committees.

MUSEUM OF FLIGHT FOUNDATION
9404 E. Marginal Way S.
Seattle, WA 98108

Dated Material—
Postmaster Please Expedite

NON-PROFIT ORG.
U.S. POSTAGE
PAID
PERMIT NO. 3196
SEATTLE, WASH.

ABOUT OUR CO-SPONSORS

SCIENCE 85
SCIENCE 85 was founded in 1979 by the American Association for the Advancement of Science (AAAS) to help "bridge the gap between science and the citizen" by providing science and technology information in a readable, relevant, and stimulating style. Written for an educated lay audience, SCIENCE 85 is an authoritative source of information and has been consistently recognized as the highest quality publication in the science field—and in the magazine industry. For two years in a row the National Magazine Award for General Excellence was given to SCIENCE 85.

AG INDUSTRIES
Over the years AG Industries has become one of the leaders in the field of toys and hobbies. After successfully introducing many new items into Japan and maintaining a high market share, AG came to Seattle in 1982 to develop a U.S. market for their quality products, which include WHITEWINGS paper airplanes—27 gliders in 8 styles for all ages at all performance levels. AG also produces the Heron 12 Radio-Controlled Sailboat, the Winner of the Hobby Industry Creative Excellence Award.

NATIONAL AIR AND SPACE MUSEUM
The Smithsonian's National Air and Space Museum opened in 1976 and offers its visitors an array of flying machines and spacecraft. NASM is the most popular museum in the world and is internationally accepted as having one of the greatest displays of air and space exhibits.

The Museum of Flight is proud to be associated with these fine co-sponsors.

Used by permission of the Museum of Flight, Seattle, WA.

at the Seattle Museum of Flight. AG Industries, manufacturers of Whitewings paper airplanes, later joined the sponsorship. Judging considerations were: time aloft, distance, aerobatics, and aesthetic design. The categories were professional (teachers and graduate students in aeronautics and related fields), nonprofessionals (just about everyone else), and junior (children under 14). Parent-child teams had to enter under the professional or nonprofessional categories. The entries had to be made of paper only. Glue and cellophane tape were allowed for bonding purposes but not to add weight. Paper lamination and paper reinforcement were also allowed. Bernoulli Medallion awards were presented to first-, second-, and third-place winners in each event. First-place winners were flown, all expenses paid, to Seattle to receive their prizes and flew their planes during a special ceremony at the Seattle Kingdome in June. Some of the winning designs were exhibited at the National Air & Space Museum in Washington and featured in a story in the September issue of *Science 85*.

According to Ali Fujino Miller, director of special events for the Museum of Flight in Seattle, regional contests and tie-ins sprung up all over the world, generating local enthusiasm for the international contest. Local museums, such as the Cranbrook Institute in Bloomfield Hills, Michigan; corporations like the Seibu Company in Japan; and engineering schools, including the University of California at Berkeley, were some of the organizations that took the opportunity to involve their communities.

The Museum of Flight first announced the competition in its newsletter, *Museum of Flight News* (January/February 1985), devoting the opening page to the news. The museum held paper airplane workshops monthly from February through April along with other related programs. In May, when the judging for the contest was held, the museum featured a special exhibit, "Early Flight," a collection of photos from the Wright Brothers. It was a traveling exhibit of rare photos of the Wright Brothers accomplishments. The display came from the National Air & Space Museum and was made possible by a grant from a local company, Hamilton Standard. On Saturday, May 25, the day after the judging of the international contest, the museum held a Whitewings Paper Airplane Day with a hands-on workshop led by Dr. Y. Ninomiya, designer of Whitewing paper airplanes and gliders. Continuing with its programing, the Museum of Flight presented a "Flying Apparatus Day" on September 14 from noon to 4 p.m., with live demonstrations and workshops on the "how" and "why" of flying objects—Frisbees, Toobies, aerobies, boomerangs, kites, and more. Weifang Kitemakers of China presented kite workshops at the museum in September for school groups and then for the general public on Saturday, September 28, at 10 a.m. and 1:30 p.m.

There are innumerable ways to celebrate flight. The Hudson River Museum in Yonkers, New York, decided that April would be a fine time to commemorate its "Lighter Than Air Day," a free community celebration of the aerial arts and sciences. Staff presented a whole potpourri of events: a paper airplane contest, kite workshops (and flight contests), balloon rides, a rocket demonstration, parachute games, origami workshops, a giant board game called "Race to the Moon," poetry writing, and dancing. The guest of honor was Sabina, a giant hot-air balloon named for the wife of balloon enthusiast Malcolm Forbes, Jr. All of this took place on a Saturday afternoon from noon until 5 p.m.

One more flight experience...this time a personal one. The public library I do public relations and programing for is down the road from the Cradle of Aviation Museum. It's a relatively new museum with a couple of curators and lots of volunteers, most of whom are members of the Early Fliers' organization, a national group made up of fliers from aviations early days. I had recently seen the film *To Fly* at the National Air & Space Museum in Washington and was smitten with the film and the idea to do a program on flight. The program turned into a month-long celebration called "Come Fly With Us!" February is my favorite month to do in-depth thematic programing; because of the winter weather, everyone is ready to do something different. From the Cradle of Aviation Museum, I borrowed photographs of Long Island aviation history with emphasis on Charles Lindbergh and his flight from nearby Roosevelt Field in 1927. Model airplanes on loan from local airplane buffs hung from the library ceiling, and others were placed in display cases to localize the exhibit as much as possible, I included a display of photographic panels about Elinor Smith, a former Long Island resident who had been chosen the best woman pilot in 1930. She was not available during that month but did make a speaking appearance at our library in May when her book, *Aviatrix*, was published. Here's how the February celebration went.

- *The Spirit of St. Louis*, starring James Stewart, started the series and commemorated the Lone Eagle's 79th birthday. February 4 at 8 p.m.
- "Come Fly With Us!" super Sunday opened with the film *To Fly*, which takes the viewer breathlessly aloft suspended in a balloon during colonial times and in progressively more sophisticated aircraft as it goes through each flight era and finally into space. February 8 from 1 p.m. through 5 p.m.
- "Restoring the Spirit," a talk/slide show presented by William Kaiser, curator of the Aviation Museum, detailed the restoration of Lindbergh's plane, Jenny, which hangs in the museum.
- "The Ninety-Nines," a talk/slide show narrated by actress/flier Susan Oliver. (The Ninety-Nines is an international organization of women pilots.)

- The film "Technology of the 90's" was hosted by John Pereira, engineer from Grumman Aerospace Corporation.

The following Wednesday, the children's room staff presented a paper airplane workshop and contest. On Friday, youngsters viewed three short films on flight: *Dawn Flight*, *Sky Dive*, and *Master Kiteman*. The last program for the month was the silent movie *Wings*, starring Gary Cooper and Clara Bow with musician Harry Weiss playing the live piano accompaniment. The audience loved it, especially the younger members of the audience who had never seen a silent film. (By the way, did you know that *Wings* was the first film to win an Academy Award? The year was 1929. Add that to your trivia list!)

During the month, people were encouraged to bring their cameras and willing family members to the library's main floor to pose in photo cutouts of Charles Lindbergh and Elinor Smith. Everyone could be a flier for a day!

Comments

When the series was still in its planning stages, I did my usual amount of sleuthing to try and track down community people who were interested in airplanes, were former pilots, or had any connections with flight organizations. I began my detective work with the library staff, and sure enough, the husband of one of the staff members was an Early Flier. Early Fliers members spread the word quickly. Not only that, most of them came to every program and were truly disappointed when the month's activities ended. The Cradle of Aviation staff were most cooperative and eager to generate interest in their museum. Although the programing appealed to a special audience, it did still draw the "regular" library program attendee. It was "standing room only" at the events.

The promotion began officially with an announcement in the library's newsletter, which was mailed to a special mailing list of over 4,000 people. A bright goldenrod vellum paper flier (with red and black ink) appeared next with all the events listed, followed by news releases to the media. It all seemed to work. The Sunday edition of the *New York Times* (Long Island section) declared that "February is Aviation Month at the East Meadow Public Library!" They took the words right out of my mouth. It was an exciting time and worth all the work. Lots of new friends were made for the library. Many of the Early Fliers now make regular visits to the library. After the last program that month, a couple of them turned to me to offer thanks and some free flying lessons! Sensibly for me, I declined. The memories of that high-flying time at the library still linger. Who knows, in a couple more years, a repeat program may be done.

In discussing promotional ideas related to flying, I would be remiss not to mention kites. Next to, or possibly before, paper airplanes, kite flying is universal. Kite flyoffs or festivals are held annually all over the world. The Venice Pier's recent 11th Annual Kite Festival attracted 12,000 participants. Early spring is usually a good time to a hold a kite flyoff. Begin with a kite workshop—make it a parent-child one. Your volunteer instructor could be an aerospace engineer or just a local kite enthusiast. Try these four categories for your contest: most novel design, best box kite, best decorated kite, and best flying kite. Hold a special category for store-bought kites. The entry blank could serve as a free raffle ticket for a handsome commercial kite.

A Note on Boomerangs

It all began 14 years ago when Ben Rhue, a world traveler, discovered boomerangs in Australia. He was hooked. He has since passed on his boomerang "fever" to thousands of others. The whole world seems to be boomeranging!

While working at the Smithsonian Institution in Washington, DC, Rhue initiated the first boomerang workshop, which was open to youngsters ages eight and up. The youngsters learned to make a simple style of boomerang, then went out onto the mall to test them. The workshops evolved into a tournament planned as part of the Smithsonian's Resident Associate's program. From this, the Annual Boomerang Festival began and continued until 1984; since the Smithsonian's Resident Associate's program is primarily an educational one, the event was then turned over to the U.S. Boomerang Association, which now holds festivals all over the country. Things have literally boomeranged for Ben Rhue and his boomerang colleagues. The group is called upon to boomerang at such places as Yale University, the University of Massachusetts, the University of Buffalo, and the University of Washington, and in such cities as Seattle, Syracuse, and New York.

The boomerang originated in the stone age and is generally associated with the Australian aborigines. One of the nicest things, according to Rhue, is that you can throw boomerangs indoors as well as outdoors, in large areas like gyms or arenas. This may be something to keep in mind when contemplating your own competition. Begin with a boomerang workshop, or purchase some inexpensive lightweight ones. Have demonstrations on how to throw a boomerang...and then hold your competition, indoors or outdoors. Tie in the activity with an entire month of aeronautical events, or simply enjoy the boomerang event itself. Flight can be fun and informative, whether you are high in the skies or down on earth enjoying flight vicariously. So fly!

Resources for Flight Programs

Bahadur, Dinesh. *Come Fight a Kite*. New York: Harvey House Publishing, 1978.

Barnaby, Capt. Ralph. *How to Make and Fly Paper Airplanes*. Bristol, FL: Four Winds Press, 1968.

Cassidy, John. *The Boomerang Book*. Palo Alto, CA: Klutz Press, 1985.

Downer, Marion. *Kites: How to Make and Fly Them*. New York: Lothrop, Lee & Shephard, 1959.

Hall, Stephen S. *Boom in 'Rangs Launches Old Toy Into New Orbit*. Smithsonian 15 (3) (June 1984): 118–25.

Kaufmann, John. *Fly It*. Garden City, NY: Doubleday, 1980.

Kettlekamp, Larry. *Kites*. New York: Morrow, 1959.

Mander, Jerry. *The Great International Paper Airplane Book*. New York: Simon & Schuster, 1967.

Marks, Burton, and Marks, Rita. *Kites for Kids*. New York: Lothrop, Lee & Shephard, 1980.

Rhue, Benjamin, and Darnell, Eric. *Boomerang, Making, Throwing & Catching It*. New York: Workman Publishing, 1985.

Wagenvoord, James. *Flying Kites*. New York: Macmillan, 1968.

Wiley, Jack. *The Kite Building and Kite Flying Handbook with 42 Kite Plans*. Blue Ridge Summit, PA: Tab Books, 1984.

Yolen, Jane. *World on a String: The Story of Kites*. Cleveland, OH: The World Publishing Co., 1969.

YEAR OF THE TRAINS

I wish I had been there. Next to carousels, I love trains best. The creative personnel at the Spokane Public Library declared 1984 the "Year of the Trains" with the mayor of Spokane making it so in a formal proclamation. Although the idea originated at the library, those involved knew they needed help, and not just financial help; more than anything else, the library wanted to involve the people and organizations of Spokane, Washington, in this celebration.

It was the library's centennial year, so the commemoration had to be a big one. They had to find a theme. The director of the library and staff tossed around many ideas, but the one that came up consistently was trains, since railroads had played an important role in the development of Spokane.

Planning began about a year before the date it was all to begin. They knew a grant was needed to accomplish their goal. Input and support was given to the library by the following community organizations: Eastern Washington University–Spokane Center, Spokane County Library District, Friends of the Spokane Public Library, Spokane Public Schools, Inland Empire Railway Historical Society, Union Pacific Old Timers, Eastern Washington Historical Society, Hillyard Community Concerns, Retired Senior Volunteers Program, Project Joy (City Parks and Recreation), Spokane City-County Historic Preservation Office, and the Burlington Northern Veterans Association. With their advice and support, the library applied for a grant from the Washington State Commission for the Humanities. A $13,247 grant was approved in January of 1984 and the "Year of the Trains" was rolling on the rails!

A paid project director, Ron Manheimer, was appointed, and it was full steam ahead. After Mayor James E. Chase's proclamation, the news releases and promotional materials began to hit the community. The scheduled events were varied and many. In its monthly publication, *Previews*, the library told its patrons:

> There is a deep and continuing fascination with trains and lore of the rails for young and old alike....Railroads established Spokane as the center of the Inland Pacific Northwest and helped shape the social, political, cultural and economic history of the region. It is to this theme of railroad history—past, present and future—that Spokane Public Library has coupled itself in 1984.

The Events

Opening the train series were four Sunday afternoon programs held at the Higher Education Center in downtown Spokane. All were free and began at 2 p.m. "Songs & Lore of the Iron Rail" officially set the rails humming with Utah Phillips, who shared songs and stories of unions, hoboes, heroes, and villains of the rails. Phillips is "Spokane's own nationally renowned folksinger and Grand Duke of the Hobos." This opening program took place on the last Sunday in February.

A narrated slide/talk show, "Western Railroads & the National Parks" with Alfred Runte, University of Washington historian and national park ranger/naturalist, was the initial program for March.

"Once There Was a Streetcar" took people on Spokane's trolleys via a narrated slide show with Charles Mutschler, one of the region's most knowledgeable railroad buffs. This was another March event. For its final Sunday program, the library turned to Carlos Schwantes, a historian from Walla Walla College, who presented, "Railroad Violence: 19th Century Perceptions of the Railroads in the Inland Empire."

A free film series on the theme of trains was presented at the Spokane County Library District's North Argonne Branch on Tuesday nights. The movies included *Emperor of the North*, *Sleeping*

Car to Trieste, Bound for Glory, Union Pacific, The Train, The Great Locomotive Chase, 3:10 to Yuma and a silent double feature, *The General* and the 1903 *The Great Train Robbery,* with Buster Keaton. The film series was repeated at another library branch on Wednesday nights.

Working with the Union Pacific Railroad, the Spokane Public Library declared Saturday, July 14, as the "Day of the Train." According to library spokesperson Lisa Wolfe, "It was the highlight of the Summer!" An open house was held at Union Pacific headquarters in Spokane. Keith Durant, Union Pacific trainmaster, was the official host. People were invited to come down and climb aboard the trains, including a diesel locomotive and bulkhead flat car. Union Pacific employees were on hand to demonstrate the computerization of modern railroads and answer questions about the "ole days of railroading." There were movies, book displays, and a poster exhibit, "One Hundred Years of Trains." A trivia game, "Railroad Slang" was distributed to over 400 people. Popcorn made it more of a party and was supplied by the Spokane Public Library's staff association. The library's Bookmobile represented the library in the Union Pacific yards that day. The staff answered questions for 106 people and issued 10 new library cards. More than 1,500 people came out on a sunny Saturday to be "railroaded." A pun is intended!

Even National Library Week at the library centered on the "Year of the Trains." Patrons were greeted by staff members wearing railroad hats and treated to cake provided by the library's staff association. There were four exhibits of model railroads and an exhibit of railroad prints. They continued with their special railroad book displays and introduced more train reading lists.

Hobo Party

Using railroading as a theme with related programs and activities, the library hoped to encourage children to read through the summer. "Whistle-stops on the Reading Express" was the heading on the attractive summer reading game brochure for youngsters that year. On the back of the brochure, the "Spokane Public & Spokane County Library Railroad" issued "free passage" to (child's name) on a series of "whistle-stops" which included sing-alongs, creative dramatics, a Hobo Party, movies, and a special day excursion invitation to the "train day" at the Union Pacific yards.

Vivian Fetty, children's coordinator, held a Hobo Party at each branch library at the end of the reading game. Youngsters were invited to attend in costume, wearing something hobos might wear. A delightful promotional brochure tempted children to "help the hobo find the Mulligan Stew!" In a fun graphic maze, children could find their way to the pot of Mulligan Stew. The brochure also contained

Used by permission of the Spokane Public Library.

a hobo quiz with such questions as "What do you call a hobo who picks apples?," and "What do you call a hobo's bedroll?," and "What do you call a hobo with cooking utensils?."

The young readers found some interesting information and facts about hobos such as "Hobos wandered from town to town looking for food, shelter and work. To help each other, they developed a secret message system: symbols chalked on a fencepost, mailbox or other inconspicuous place."

The hobo symbols were graphically placed on railroad tracks in the same brochure. Children even sang, "Hallelujah, I'm a Bum!" at the Hobo Party. The words to the song were supplied on the back of the same brochure. By the way, here are the answers to the three hobo questions: Appleknockers, Bindle, and Chronicker. And, just in case you're pining for a recipe for Mulligan Stew, here it is!

Mulligan Stew

Hoppins (any and all vegetables that can be bought, begged, borrowed or stolen)

Meat (acquired the same way)

Gumps (chicken or other fowl)

The whole savory mess is cooked outdoors.

You can't take something out unless you put something in!

By the way, more than 6,000 children in the county library district played the Reading Express Summer Reading Game. The theme appealed to both boys and girls.

The Promotion

All the graphics produced for the "Year of the Trains" were attractive, simple, and certainly appealing. Consistency of theme was evident throughout the promotion in all of the materials produced. It was planned. Credit should be given to then library public information officer Nancy Greer, graphic artist Gerry Krueger, library director Betty Bender, and all others involved in the project.

Annual Report

If you've got a good gimmick such as the "Year of the Trains," why not flaunt it! The library was 100 years old and it was annual report time again. It was easier this year because the library had a theme—railroad history and its impact on the Inland Empire, an area including Spokane and eastern Washington and northern Idaho. Utilizing the attractive library logo and interesting typeface headlines, the annual report began 100 years earlier. "In the 1880's people of Spokane turned out in large numbers for a 'necktie social.' No, not a lynching, but an evening's entertainment where men purchased a necktie at the door and shared supper with the lady wearing a matching apron and the proceeds of the evening went to support a library. . . ."

That's how the library began in Spokane. In the report, the current library director then spoke about the "Year of the Trains" celebration in 1984 and how the community and library were both involved. An old-fashioned "choo-choo train" was sketched on the cover of the annual report. Well done.

Brochures, Booklists, Etc.

There were many, all good-looking, using basic white stock paper with red and black inks. The annual report was a pale alabaster grey with black and red ink and the reading game brochure was yellow with black and red ink. The handsome "Year of the Trains" promotional piece which listed all of the events for Spring and Summer 1984 was black and grey on white stock. The reading list for adults was tastefully done in black ink on white stock and the "All Aboard" reading list for young people was on white stock with red ink. The pièce de résistance in graphics for this promotion was the lovely glossy poster which announced the train celebration.

The poster (500 produced) was displayed in Spokane libraries, schools, community centers, businesses, and institutions. They even sent some to nearby cities in Washington and Idaho and top national, state, and local railroad organizations and publications. Some of the posters were mounted on stands with holders which held schedules and booklists. Total cost for printing, supplies, mailing, etc., was $603.76.

To get the word out first the library produced a special "utility flier." The City Utilities Department included this flier with the monthly bills sent out in February at no cost to the project. Results were excellent. It swelled the library's special railroad mailing list to 600, and also brought response from other community organizations and businesses who promised support. So, the cost of $362.91 for the preparation of 65,000 fliers was well worth it.

Used by permission of the Spokane Public Library.

Used by permission of the Spokane Public Library.

Ten separate news releases were produced in conjunction with this promotion. Seventy-five of each were sent to radio and TV stations, daily and weekly newspapers and specialized publications such as the *Senior Times*, and to the National Model Railroad Association and nearby schools, libraries, and university publications. The results were gratifying. Initial press coverage was very extensive and included a four-page spread in the Sunday issue of the *Spokesman-Review*, a Spokane newspaper, in late February. Then radio and TV coverage picked up. "Day of the Trains" was aired by three local TV stations; one radio station invited Keith Durant for a telephone-call-in interview.

Ten thousand, five hundred program brochures were created at a cost of $479.49 and distributed to people on mailing lists and placed in poster display pockets in libraries, schools, and businesses. The "Day of the Train" flier (4,500) cost $39.09 and was distributed the same way. The game "Railroad Slang" which was given to 400 people at the "Day of the Train" event cost the most, at $1,015. The game was created by graphic artist Gerry Krueger along with community consultants Charles Mutschler (historian), Utah Phillips ("King of the Hobos"), and Keith Durant, Union Pacific trainmaster. Help was needed to fund the printing of the game; it came from the Union Pacific Railroad, Burlington Northern Railroad, Spokane Railway Credit Union, and Trade Graphics Typesetting. The game was featured on a local radio show. It is now copyrighted.

The Railroad Booklists (4,000) cost $223.35 and were available at the libraries, at the special events, and film programs.

The film series, which was shown in both city and county libraries, attracted audiences of 70 to 150 people and cost $963.68 in rental fees. Speakers' fees came to $1,250. Over 1,500 people attended the lecture series. The opening songfest with Utah Phillips drew 400 enthusiasts and was heavily covered in the media. By the way, signing for the deaf was provided at four lectures and several of the lectures in the series were repeated at neighborhood community centers.

The Children's Summer Reading Game, Reading Express, had 14 different programs which cost $502.08, provided by the Friends of Spokane Public Library. A total of $280.62 was spent for printed materials (bookmark, "Reading Express" brochures, and "Hobo Party" brochures) for the summer reading game.

Comments

Spokane Public Library and its community got its money's worth! But more important, the library reached out and touched many untapped portions of the community—people and organizations. They certainly serve as a great example of working together. Another example of a good idea, carefully planned, skillfully executed...and one that can be borrowed.

STRICTLY FOR LAUGHS

Much has been written by medical scientists and psychologists about the relationship between humor and good health. It's been said that a laugh a day can keep the doctor away. In any case, it can't hurt, and you and your community might have a lot of fun. So keep everyone in good health by trying some creative programming using humor as the theme. Create your own National Laugh Month or National Joke Month and plan a series of special events and programs during a time of the year when the weather itself can make you feel down in the dumps. For quite a few years at our library, we have declared February "Here's to Your Health!" month with a variety of health-related programs focusing on nutrition and special diets ("When Your Feet Hurt, You Hurt All Over," "Fears and Phobias," "Holistic Medicine Centering on Managing Pain and Self-Health by Guided Imagery"). All programs have featured reputable professionals and have drawn large audiences. People today are health-minded and aware of the options open to them when they need health care. The aforementioned were just some of the programs offered one February. I have long been gathering material on how laughter and humor affect our health and intend to do a series soon. Here are some more ideas and suggestions.

First, make your declaration. You're going to hold a National Laugh Month. Brainstorm with your staff. Read some books about humor and laughter. Need to convince people of the positive effects of laughter? Tell them you read that research suggests laughter produces some of the same beneficial effects as exercise does. It raises the heart and breathing rate as well as skin temperature in peripheral areas of the body and increases activity, tone, and metabolism of the muscles involved in laughing. In other words, laughs are good for what ails you; according to some medical scientists, laughter even serves as preventive medicine. Once you've convinced people, follow through on some of these ideas (or your own).

- Have a local psychologist talk about humor and how it affects us. Ask him/her to give the audience a humor test during the program and go over the results with them. The test could simply consist of some sample jokes with a place on the test paper for each member of the audience to rate the joke. Each joke could be rated 1 (not funny) to 5 (very funny) as in the Humor Self-Test offered by a team of California psychologists in 1983 (see Blakeslee listing in the "Resources" list at the end of this section). One of their jokes was: "A man falling from a cliff clutches at a protruding root. Hanging in midair, he casts his eyes to heaven and cries, 'Is anyone out there?' A voice from the clouds responds: 'Yes, my son. Let go and I will bear thee up.' After a pregnant pause the man calls out, 'Anyone else?'"

- Hold a film series for the whole family and call the showings "Laugh-Ins." Feature oldies but goodies with Buster Keaton, Harold Lloyd, Laurel and Hardy, and Charlie Chaplin. Have a lunchtime series for senior citizens and serve coffee and tea for the brown-baggers. Have an evening series just for adults and teens and show some of the more contemporary or classic funny movies. Have more fun by selling popcorn or boxes of caramel corn. Bring back old memories. Bend the rules a bit. I liked the funny films series offered by the Campbell County Public Library in Gillette, Wyoming, on Thursday nights in 1984. The series was called "Madcap Comedies" and featured a drawing of the laugh masters Laurel and Hardy and Charlie Chaplin with a can of film as the graphic design. The annotated film brochure was purposely printed upside down just for laughs. The films served up were "2 parts Danny Kaye, 4 parts Marx Brothers, 1 dash Jerry Lewis, 1 pinch Peter Sellers, 3 Stooges and for class, add a drop of Cary Grant." The brochure continued: "Combine the ingredients seasoning with a touch of Laurel & Hardy then add a bit of Abbott and Costello. Blend well, garnish with Lucy and Bob. Top the entire thing off with Charlie Chaplin." Some of the films shown were: *The Delicate Delinquent, Me and the Colonel, The Three Stooges in Orbit, Abbott and Costello in Hollywood, His Girl Friday*, and *Sons of the Desert*.

- Have a Clown-Full Sunday Special for the Family! Hire a clown or tap some volunteers in your community. Ask them to put on a show first and then involve the audience, young and old. After all, you're never too old to be a clown. Hold a clown workshop where the audience can learn clown tricks and how to apply clown make-up, etc. Have a Friends group available with instant cameras to take pictures of the new clowns. Got a button-making machine? Great. Take a close-up clown picture of each new clown and make it into a button and charge a dollar or two. Could be a fund-raiser.

- Have a "Make a Fool of Yourself" afternoon or night. Hire a local comic and ask that person to do his/her routine. Then ask that person to serve as emcee while the audience is asked to "make a fool of yourself" right in front of everyone! Sometimes the best laughs are ones we have on ourselves. Invite people to stand up and tell a few jokes. Have categories, e.g., the best jokes, the worst jokes, the longest jokes, the shortest jokes, etc. The prize? A joke book, what else? Don't stop there. Buy a bunch of kazoos and invite adults as well as youngsters to come up and play, solo or as a group. I'd like to see anyone play the kazoo in front of an audience and keep a straight face. The best kazooers get to keep their kazoos, and the master kazoo player might be given a copy of the book *The Art of Playing the Kazoo*. I would recommend that in your preprogram promotion material you ask people to register in advance for the joke segment to ensure that you have some participants. Want a silly ending to your afternoon or evening? Hand everyone a stick of cotton candy as they are leaving, whether they want it or not. Leave 'em laughing...how can anyone keep a straight face with cotton candy all over his/her face? While you're at it, why not hold a "Juggling for Klutzes" day? It couldn't hurt and should bring out a few giggles. Hire a professional or experienced amateur juggler to show and tell. Then let the audience do their act. The best juggler gets a pat on the back, while the worst juggler gets a book on how to juggle!

- In conjunction with all of this frivolity, hold a cartoon art exhibit. There are many ways to do this. First of all, you could display the works of a reputable cartoonist, or you could invite local amateur cartoonists to submit their works for your art show which you might entitle "The Laugh's on Us." You might even have a "Name the Cartoon Caption" contest. Place some funny cartoons on a bulletin board or have them printed on fliers and ask people to submit the funniest captions. The prizes could range from a year's subscription to *The New Yorker* magazine to a comic book or a how-to book on drawing cartoons.
- Somewhere along with one of the other programs suggested, or as a program by itself, hold an afternoon of music and songs with an entertainer who will not only entertain with fun songs but will also involve the audience in sing-alongs. You know how good you feel after you've stood around a piano and sung songs, off-key or not. (There are more laughs promised if you sing off-key!)

These are just a few simple suggestions. Now that you're into the idea of humor and programs you will certainly create many of your own.

Resources for Humor Programs

Books and Periodicals

Blakeslee, Sandra. "Tests Show You Are What You Laugh At," *The New York Times*, August 30, 1983, p. C1.

Cousins, Norman. *Anatomy of an Illness*. New York: Norton Publishing, 1979.

Goodman, Joel, ed. *Laughing Matters*. Saratoga Springs, NY: Sagamore Institute.
A quarterly magazine.

Moody, Raymond A., Jr., M.D. *Laugh After Laugh: The Healing Power of Humor*. Jacksonville, FL: Headwaters Press, 1978.

Stewart, Barbara. *How to Kazoo*. New York: Workman Publishing, 1983.

Conferences and Programs

Gesundheit Institute, Patch Adams, M.D., director, 404 N. Nelson St., Arlington, VA 22203.
Medicine: A Musical Comedy (developed by the Institute) is a traveling multimedia show with preventive medicine and holistic living information.

Humor Project, Joel Goodman, director, 110 Spring St., Saratoga Springs, NY 12866.
Programs, seminars, and graduate courses are offered to explore the constructive use of humor personally and professionally.

Institute for the Advancement of Human Behavior, Box 7226, Stanford, CA 94395-0164.
Conducts conferences on the healing power of laughter and play. Also offers conference-related materials such as records, cassettes, books, and periodicals by mail.

SELECTED SHORT SUBJECTS

There are many directions you can take when planning thematic programs, and there is no way that they can all be covered in this one book. I have just brushed the surface with the many possibilities. Here, I would like to talk about a few selected short subjects which can be used in thematic programing.

Food

Look on the shelves in your local bookstore and public library and you will find hundreds of cookbooks. People are into cooking, some for better health and some just for the fun of it. And most are in it for the eating, too. So, food demonstrations, recipes, and films on food are excellent programing ideas. You can approach this subject from many directions. For example, in just about every community, there are cooking classes, interesting restaurants, and gourmet chefs; certainly audiences would be willing to be guinea pigs for tasting new recipes at cooking demonstrations. So, give it a try.

"A Taste of America"

The Brooklyn (New York) Public Library is not too far from Brooklyn's main downtown area, a district with many restaurants, some old and some new. Brooklyn has a mixed population, representing a wide variety of ethnic backgrounds. All of these ingredients, plus some interesting programing

Brooklyn Public Library Bulletin

FALL 1984

AMERICAN COOKERY

Joel Wolfe, owner of the well-known Lisanne's restaurant, in his kitchen.

"A Taste of America: A Celebration of Regional and Ethnic Diversity" is an exciting round of events planned for the holiday season. All will take place at the Central Library, Grand Army Plaza; everything's free.

Brooklyn restauranteurs speak on three Monday evenings in December, from 6:30 to 7:45. Each will discuss American cookery as it pertains to the restaurant; each will give out one holiday recipe to the audience. Hear Joel Wolfe, owner and chief of Lisanne, on December 3; Mr. & Mrs. Dewey, owners of Gage and Tollner's, on December 10; and John Quimby and Stacy Cretekos, owners of the New Prospect Cafe, on December 17.

On Tuesday, December 4, 11 and 18, the Central Library's 2 pm film series will be devoted to food and cookery. And a "Career Opportunities in Cookery" seminar will be presented by a guest lecturer and the Library's Education and Job Information Center. Details were not available at press time, but will be listed in the December Calendar of Events.

Finally, there will be a major exhibit of cookbooks, some new and some out-of-print, at the Central Library from November 26 through January 31. The books on display, many of which will also be available for borrowing, will reflect the current interest in America's gastronomic diversity, including Southern Creole and Cajun, Tex-Mex, California, Black, Puerto Rican, Jewish and native American cookery. If you can't wait, check out the extensive cookbook collection in the Science & Industry Division, Central Library, 2nd floor.

NEWS NEWS

★ ★ ★ ★

Years of fiscal cutbacks curtailed the Library's ability to buy books and forced the shortening of hours. Now, thanks to the Omnibus Library Legislation signed by Governor Cuomo on July 10, there's a chance to catch up. Increased state aid this year will help to replenish our depleted book stock and to support Sunday hours at five more branches.

The following libraries are now open on Sunday from 1-5: Borough Park, Brooklyn Heights, Canarsie, Central Library, Greenpoint, Kings Highway, Midwood, New Utrecht.

Many thanks to all of the Brooklyn members of the New York State Legislature for their support of the bill.

★ ★ ★ ★

Books-By-The-Pound, the Library's biggest and best fund raiser, brought in $7,777 in only six hours. Thanks to all of the dedicated volunteers who worked at cash registers and carried out the 20,000 or so hardcover books which were sold at 50¢ a pound. The slogan of the sale: Buy Our Old Books and Help Us Buy New Ones. Next sale will be held in the spring.

★ ★ ★ ★

The Education & Job Information Center, located in the Central Library, Grand Army Plaza, has just been awarded a one-year grant by the State Department of Education for the re-establishment of a program to help women entering or re-entering the job market. Watch for announcements of special programs. The center offers guidance and special collections of materials for people who want schooling (from adult education classes to high school equivalency degrees) and jobs (want ads, information about job training programs and books about resumes, interviews, etc.).

★ ★ ★ ★

Sylvia Mechanic, head of the Business Library, received the Disclosure Achievement Award for "excellence in information and library management." The award is given yearly by Disclosure, Inc., official representative of the Security & Exchange Commission for printing documents.

★ ★ ★ ★

Cyril Acham, one of the Literacy Program volunteers, was chosen as the Outstanding RSVP of Brooklyn for 1984. RSVP, an organization that works with volunteers throughout the city, presented Mr. Acham with a special citation at the annual recognition event on October 25.

"NEW" LIBRARIES

A new look — part of a new concept in library service — will be coming to four more branch libraries. The Leonard, Carroll Gardens, Flatlands and Rugby branches will be closed for several weeks in coming months.

When they reopen, they will have new shelving and furniture and, most important, a new arrangement of books. Popular categories such as "Health" and "Cooking and Entertaining" will be used to promote browsing and borrowing.

"This kind of organization has been extremely successful at the Cortelyou library," according to Larry Brandwein, Deputy Director of the Library. "We were so pleased with it there that we scheduled six other branches for the same treatment. McKinley Park and Sheepshead Bay were recently completed."

Closing of the four branches will be announced in advance.

TRUSTEES' AWARD

Dr. Esther Lopato, member of the Brooklyn Public Library's Board of Trustees, received the Velma K. Moore Award at the 91st convention of the New York Library Association on October 24. The award is the highest state honor given by public library trustees.

Dr. Lopato, who has served as a Library trustee since 1973, was vice-president of the Library for three terms and then the first woman president for three terms.

FOR STUDENTS

The Term Paper Clinic is again in progress at the Central Library's Youth Services Division (first floor, near the children's area). You can get one-to-one help with a term paper already in progress on Wednesdays from 3:30-4:30 and 6:30-7:30. Help is free — just ask the librarian at the desk.

Used by permission of the Brooklyn Public Library.

ideas, produced the month-long series "A Taste of America: A Celebration of Regional and Ethnic Cooking" at the Brooklyn Public Library.

In order to make the primary programs accessible to working people, the library offered the cook talks on three Monday evenings from 6:30 p.m. to 7:45 p.m. Joel Wolfe, owner and chef of Lisanne, a French restaurant, spoke on December 3. Ed and Gertrude Dewey, owners of Gage and Tollner (a Brooklyn landmark restaurant), were the speakers at the December 10 program. John Quimby and Stacy Cretekos, owners of the New Prospect Cafe, spoke on December 17. Holiday recipes were given out at each talk.

Understanding that people also respond favorably to food in films, the library presented three Tuesday afternoon film programs, featuring *Garlic Is as Good as Ten Mothers*, *Always for Pleasure*, and five shorts: *Chicken Soup*, *Le Plat du Jour*, *Sunday Dinner*, *Part of Your Loving*, and *Zea*. But the food programing didn't stop there. Equipped with the information that many men and women enjoy taking cooking lessons and that many have since entered the field of cooking on a professional level, the library staff decided to offer a restaurant career night on Wednesday, December 5, from 6:30 p.m. to 7:45 p.m. with talks by representatives from the New York Food and Hotel Management Schools and the Brooklyn Public Library's education and job information center.

Another idea that the library came up with revolved around cookbooks. You've heard people say, "Cookbooks are so tempting today that I feel I gain weight just by browsing through them." Chancing that, the library put its best cookbooks on display for a two-month period. The exhibit, reflecting the current interest in America's "gastronomic diversity," included Southern Creole and Cajun, Tex-Mex, Californian, Black, Puerto Rican, Jewish, and Native American cookery. Library visitors were reminded that there were many more cookbooks in the library's extensive collection in the science and industry division on the second floor of the Central Library.

Because all kids like to eat and some kids even like to cook, the library presented seven "Programs to Make Your Mouth Water" during December. Some were held in the morning, while others were held after school. Here's a list of the children's activities:

- Story/Craft. "Design Your Own Candy Bar and Name It." Ages 6 to 9. December 3, 4:15 p.m.
- Story/Craft. "Fish Fry." Ages 8 to 10. December 6, 4:15 p.m.
- Story/Craft. "Gingerbread Paper Playmates." Ages 2½ to 3½. December 14, 10:30 a.m. to noon.
- Filmstrips. "Let's Eat." Ages 4 to 8. December 14, 4 p.m. to 5:30 p.m.
- Preschool Films. "What's Cooking." Ages 3 to 6. December 26, 10:30 a.m.
- Films. "Food and More Food." Ages 6 to 12. December 26, 4:15 p.m.
- Story/Craft. "Candy Cane Bookmarks." Ages 4 to 5. December 28, 10:30 a.m. to noon.

The results of all of the food activities, according to a library spokesperson, "were overwhelming." The public relations department promoted the series first in the Fall issue of its newsletter, *Brooklyn Public Library Bulletin*. A photo of chef/speaker Joel Wolfe drew attention to the food series. News releases were sent out three weeks in advance; two weeks prior to the first program, public service announcements were sent to the radio and television media. The library's art department produced two simple promotional brochures for the adult and children's series. Posters were placed in prominent spots in the Central Library and branches.

The library staff knew their community. They had a "hot" topic for a theme. They promoted well. They had a successful series. A series similar to this or a whole new approach would go well in just about any part of the country. You will find even more food ideas in Chapter 6, "Games, Contests, Festivals, and Fairs." But, here's one more proven idea.

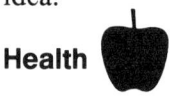

Health

According to a survey released by the American Board of Family Practice, Americans are assuming more responsibility for decisions regarding their life, health, and even death. The study, a nationwide telephone survey of 1,007 men and women over the age of 18 and of 303 family doctors, was conducted between December 20, 1984, and January 31, 1985. The study revealed that people want to keep up-to-date on health issues and want to be involved in their own health care. Personal experience at my library, where I have conducted many health series over the years, demonstrates that health-related programs draw large audiences and tremendous responses. Here are some tested ideas that you might consider.

Nutrition

Anything to do with this subject will be a hit. Nutrition is in. Many books and articles have been written on the subject. Get a nutritionist, a doctor who's into nutrition, and other experts as speakers. Have a cooking/tasting demonstration of healthy foods and mimeograph or offset the recipes for handouts. Working with children? Hold a craft workshop in which the youngsters create a healthy creature, using apples, raisins, celery, carrots, etc. The children can then eat their healthy creations. You might check with one of your health or social service agencies to see if they have available coloring books or sheets dealing with nutrition. These could be used as give-aways at the end of the craft program. The options are many.

Exercise

This is another "hot" topic. Get experts not only to lecture but also to give a hands-on program. Everyone could bring a mat and wear comfortable clothes and shoes. Who knows? From this may spring a series of regularly scheduled exercise classes!

Diets

Anything to do with losing weight will also sell. Get varied opinions. Bring in a doctor or a nutritionist to review and discuss a current popular diet book. Have a behavior modification psychologist speak about dieting. Hold a panel discussion with all three speakers. Even though people are dieting, they still like to eat, so hold a cooking demonstration/tasting program of low-calorie foods. Print and give away the recipes featured that day.

The Mind

People are just as interested in mental health as they are in physical health. Subjects to try include insomnia, dreams, and hypnosis. "How to Control Stress In Our Lives" is another good subject. Or how about "Psychic Powers of the Mind" with a parapsychologist? "Fears and Phobias" is another interesting subject.

Holistic Medicine

There are many holistic health centers springing up around the country, and many good books and speakers on this topic. Do some research and then offer some programing.

Health Fairs

Hold a health fair and invite health agencies to participate. Offer free blood pressure screening, free hearing tests, etc. Gather plenty of free informative literature from county, state, or local health agencies (even commercial food and drug companies) for distribution at the fair. Book a bus and take people on a tour of the county medical center or other health facility if this seems appropriate.

Other Topics

Cancer is a sensitive subject but can be handled properly with professional speakers. Alzheimer's disease is another. Backaches are universal. The heart, the feet, hearing loss, diabetes, and arthritis would also be good subjects.

The Family

Some people feel that the family is being threatened by changes in our lifestyles today. Explore this theme in a program, or even a series. Once you get started you will find many family lifestyles other than the traditional. I did a series at our library one month with such topics as "Fathers and Daughters," "Alternative Family Life Style," and "Aging Parents" as the top titles.

The father in this "Fathers and Daughters" program was a local psychology professor; the daughter was his real 20-year-old daughter. These two talked about their relationship in front of the audience. The mother, divorced from the professor, and her new husband, and the professor's woman companion were all in the audience. A few of them participated in the discussion part of the program. It was an interesting evening and drew a considerable response.

"Alternative Family Life Styles" drew the largest audience. The panel/speakers consisted of a husband and wife who live apart five days a week and get together on the weekends (either at their home in the suburbs or at her apartment in the city where she works); a divorced mother who left the home with her husband and child behind; and a practicing psychologist who reacted to the lifestyles, commented, and drew the audience into a discussion.

"Aging Parents" was probably the most controversial subject in our series. The audience consisted almost entirely of middle-aged people who have aging parents. It was a lunchtime program presided over by a well-known family therapist. At times, his views differed strongly from some of those in the audience. Some wanted definitive answers to their personal problems. Of course there were none forthcoming, but he did give suggestions, referrals, and sympathy.

Much more can be done with the family as the topic. Look, observe, listen, read what concerns people in your community about family life. That should be your lead.

Women

Since the late 60s, much has been written and spoken on the subject of women, their equality, their freedom, their rights. It's still a good topic. Only this time you might want to approach it on a different level. Do a series of film programs with women as the chief protagonists.

The Clark County (Nevada) Library District held an excellent film discussion series, "Working Women: Reflections and Stereotypes." They were joined in the endeavor by the University of Nevada and the Las Vegas Women's Center "to examine and illustrate diverse images or concepts of the 'working woman' in our society and to examine the ways in which modern cinema either reflects or reacts against the problems, difficulties and rewards associated with these various roles...."

The film programs included introductory lectures by professors Lynn Osborne and Chris Hudgins, who also led discussions after each screening. The films shown were *Klute* with Jane Fonda; *Norma Rae* with Sally Field; *I'm Dancing as Fast as I Can* with Jill Clayburgh; *The Pumpkin Eater* with Anne Bancroft; and *The Stepford Wives* with Paula Prentiss and Katherine Ross. You may wish to use this film list or create your own.

Don't forget film/book/discussions on women in literature, women in history, women in art, and Black women. And, to avoid being labeled a sexist, I would recommend a series of film discussion evenings with men as the theme and how they are depicted in films and books. That should provide you with some lively encounters with your audience. A few years back, the Michigan City and Westchester Public Libraries in Indiana presented a series, "Men's Lives: Male Roles in Society and Film." Funded by the Indiana Committee for the Humanities, the series offered 10 films with speakers (some of whom were women). The films were: *The Last Picture Show; The Paper Chase; Dirty Harry; Marty; Blume in Love; Boys in the Band; Five Easy Pieces; Play It Again; Sam; Save the Tiger;* and *Harry and Tonto.*

Hair

What, you ask, can you do with hair except grow it, cut it, or curl it? The New York State Museum in Albany took the subject of hair and gave it a special twist in one of its "Family Fun-Addicts" special events series on Saturday afternoons in 1981. "Hair at the Museum" featured a vintage 20th-century Manhattan barber shop to set the scene. Volunteer hair stylists from a beauty school gave demonstrations and 120 free haircuts! Barber shop quartets entertained and the fun-packed W.C. Fields movie *The Barber Shop* was shown. All of this took place between the hours of 1 p.m. and 4:30 p.m. Approximately 3,200 people of all ages enjoyed "Hair at the Museum." A traveling "Hair" exhibit which originated at New York's Cooper-Hewitt Museum in 1980, and consisted of a historical survey of styles, fashion, and symbolism in hair design shown in prints, drawings, sculpture, and artifacts from many periods and cultures, was on display at the same time. The Saturday special events at the State Museum were cosponsored by the Mobil Foundation Inc.; events were promoted with news releases to the local media and brochures sent to people on special mailing lists and contacts with local schools.

Baseball

Baseball events can be fun and informative and another way to draw out a special interest audience. There are many things you can do; some might even turn into fund-raisers.

The New York State Museum had a series of events and exhibits entitled "Bases Are Loaded at the Museum" in 1983. Baseball lovers converged on the museum to view displays of uniforms, lockers, bats, etc., of former baseball stars. Visitors were encouraged to use a batting practice machine, enjoy a demonstration of bat-making, and obtain the autographs of local baseball players. Movies with a baseball theme were also included in the series.

Retired professional baseball players have to live somewhere. Who knows? One may be living in your town or nearby. Ask around. He may be willing to share some baseball anecdotes at a program or donate some baseball memorabilia for a permanent or temporary display. Ernie Harwell, a major league baseball broadcaster in Detroit, was recently installed in the Baseball Hall of Fame. He is a Friend of the Detroit Public Library and has many fans in the city and the state. The Friends hold an annual "Evening with Ernie Harwell at the Old Ball Game" each September. Harwell, who has been broadcasting Tiger games since 1960, has gained additional fame as a songwriter, inventor, and compiler of the world's largest private archive of written materials on the history of baseball (which he donated to the Burton Historical Collection of the Detroit Public Library). He's been an inspiration to kids and baseball fans of all ages.

Since 1977, Ernie Harwell has been the special guest at this annual baseball night, greeting people and raffling off Tiger items to the youngsters and taking a lucky family on a tour of the broadcast booth. Here's how the annual baseball night went in September 1983:

- 5:45 p.m. to 6:45 p.m. Hot dogs, potato chips, beer, and pop were served in the Cass Concourse at the main library.
- 6:30 p.m. A raffle of "Tiger Trivia" by Ernie Harwell, including autographed baseballs and bats for kids aged 12 and under, was held. Also held was a drawing for a lucky family to be Ernie's guests in the broadcast booth prior to the game.
- 7 p.m. Chartered buses take participants to Tiger Stadium.
- 7:35 p.m. Play ball, game begins.

For a $12 ticket, attendees get food, refreshments, round-trip bus fare, and a reserved seat behind home plate; 50 cents of this goes to the Harwell Collection Endowment Fund. Sounds like a real home run night for the Friends, the library, and baseball fans!

Another idea revolves around baseball and collections. Collecting baseball cards has long been a favorite hobby for young and old. Why not have a Saturday morning baseball card exchange? Make it a program with a local collector as the speaker and moderator of the exchange. Hype the event with a display and program posters in prominent locations around town.

Plan a fund-raiser with your local community/company team against another group. It's all for fun and funds. Or, you could simply "open" the baseball season by creating and printing a neat reading list, "Play Ball!" as the Lincoln Public Library of Springfield, Illinois, did. Combine that with a display of baseball books and memorabilia and some baseball movies, and you've got a fun series.

Love

Love, the many-splendored thing, has been the theme for many an event or program. Give it a try. Valentine's Day seems to be the favorite time to celebrate love. But you can do it anytime. Nassau Community College in Garden City, New York, declared an "academic love-in" at its school on Valentine's Day in 1985 from 9 a.m. to 2:30 p.m. Participants certainly got a lot of love in during that short time! "What Is This Thing Called Love?" featured a series of lectures, discussions, and performances entitled "Love Scenes" performed by students from the dance and theatre department. There was also a sampling of love songs and love poetry, and talks dealing with "Love, Pure and Impure, on Film," "Images of the Embrace in Art," and "Love on a Grand Scale: Tristan and Isolde." Admission was free.

Our library used love as the theme for its 16th birthday in 1971. Psychedelic colors and love-ins were "in" then. So using hot Day-Glo colors (which are now "in" again in the mid-80s), we invited one and all to our "Library Love-In Sweet Sixteen Party" on our birthday, April 18. The hot pink and dazzling orange wowed them. Our annual report/newsletter also used love as its theme. Library director Tom Dutelle, together with other staff members, invented a "Game of Love" for all to play. One community member was a bit concerned when he read about our love-in and "Game of Love," so he came to the Sunday party to protest. But after an hour's observation, he left saying, "Oh, you're just having fun."

One of the highlights was the roving love reporter. Cassette recorders and mikes in hand, teenaged pages approached party-goers and asked them, "What does love mean to you?" and "What do you love most about your library?" You can imagine some of the amusing answers prompted by the first question, and we took some good quotes from the second for our annual budget vote promotion. It was all for fun...and love!

Chapter 5
Special Events Fund-Raising

$ Tips for a Successful Fund-Raiser
$ A Night of 100 Dinners: Variations on a Theme
$ "Hot-Stuff" Fun
$ Short Subjects
$ Short Short Subjects

Short of robbing a bank, I can't really think of an easy way to raise extra funds for an organization. Planning a successful fund-raiser is a lot of work. But the results can be rewarding and fun. First and foremost, you must have a purpose for the event, and everyone, those working on the project with you and the general public, must know right up front what it is you're trying to achieve. You've done all the usual things—dinner/dances, card parties, flower sales, bake sales, casino nights, luncheons, etc., and now you're looking for something fresh and different. That's great. But sometimes, you can take the old and tired and, with a little twist or gimmick, turn it into a fresh new idea. It takes some creative thinking and brainstorming with others. Remember, if it's a successful fund-raiser, you have not only raised funds for your cause but you have also promoted goodwill and established a better public relations image with the general public and your volunteers. And, yes, you can still have fun doing it. Here are a few practical thoughts and tips which will be followed by examples of some exciting and refreshing special events that were fund-raisers. Many of the other programs and special events in this book could also be turned into fund-raisers. So, remember, always look at all the possibilities an idea can offer.

TIPS FOR A SUCCESSFUL FUND-RAISER

Planning

If this is your first time, start small. Be certain to have enough committee members. Plan well in advance, six months or more, depending on the event. How much money do you want to raise? Who is the event for? Will you need seed money or donations?

Where is this event to be held? How many people can be accommodated? Think about parking problems. Do you need a license or permit?

Keep weather conditions in mind. Do you have a rain date or an alternate plan? Check on other details. Do you need security or insurance? Is food being served or sold? Are there conflicts on the local community calendar of events? Your local chamber of commerce can tell you.

Tickets and Invitations

Be sure to send invitations to the VIPs and past donors in your community first; their invitations should be mailed at least six weeks in advance, followed by invitations to all your members or community, whether it is in an invitation form or in a newsletter or fliers and posters. It is usually better to have some advance ticket sales, especially if you need a count for food. You can buy simple tickets in a stationery store or have some printed; the printer might even donate the tickets, if you include his/her name as a donor. When selling tickets, appeal to the general public as well as your organization's membership. When it comes to a special event, you must reach out to all and not depend on a small group for success.

Donations

Always look to those who helped you out in the past. They know you. They'll help. Then look to souvenir programs from other organizations' fund-raisers for new donors. Go door-to-door, asking local merchants for either advertising support or for merchandise to be raffled off at the event. Be sure to offer either a letter or a receipt of contribution, and don't forget the all-important thank-you letter to all donors!

Promotion

You can never do enough of it, so do it all. Word-of-mouth is probably one of the best ways to spread the word. Prepare a professional news release and get it out to the local media—newspapers, radio, regional magazines, and television—well in advance; I would say six weeks with the first story followed by another story with more details two weeks prior to the event. If it's really a big event, prepare a press kit (see sample in Chapter 7, "Publicity and the Media") and even hold a press conference if your event features a celebrity or a gimmick. "One picture is worth a thousand words," so if you have a good black-and-white glossy print (preferably 8 x 10 inches) that illustrates your story, send it to the editors as well. (It's best to send each editor a different photo.) Sometimes it pays to spend some money. Hire a photographer to take your pictures if you can't get a volunteer from a local camera club. You might even get yourself or another representative on a radio or TV talk show ...anything to hype the event!

Be sure to tell it all in your news release. Don't forget the Five W's: who, what, where, when, why. List a phone number for more information about the event and a location where tickets are sold. Don't make it a mystery or a puzzle! You will find examples of good news releases throughout this book. Study them. We all make mistakes, and no matter how well you plan, the unexpected will happen. But the show will go on as long as you remain cool and are prepared. Be flexible. Ask others who have run fund-raisers about their experiences. You can learn a lot. And why not keep a diary of all the things that went wrong and those that went right so you can have a laugh and not repeat the same mistakes next time around? Have a recap meeting with your committee. Have all their suggestions and thoughts written down and kept for future reference.

Wrapping It Up

Thank everyone...those who donated services or merchandise or talents, those who were on committees, and those who came. Most, if not all, should get letters of thanks. If you have a newsletter, do a thank-you story listing all contributors. Remember...you'll need their continued support. After all, there'll be more fund-raisers coming up.

A NIGHT OF 100 DINNERS: VARIATIONS ON A THEME

It began with an idea from one of the trustees of the New York Public Library Board who was then given the "go ahead" sign from the chair of the board. Chair Andrew Heiskell admitted later: "When Barbara first told me her idea I said 'Go ahead' but I thought she was off the wall! I can't believe this extraordinary success!" Event chair Barbara Fleischman chose a cochair, Sonny Sloan, and they were off to convince others of the feasibility of "A Night of 100 Dinners." They had to persuade the rest of the trustees of the library board, organize a 16-member committee of volunteers, and form a committee of three advisers with direct links to the New York City metropolitan culinary world. They didn't have to worry about expenses though, because the dinners would take place in private homes, corporate headquarters, or private clubs, and the hosts would assume all the costs. The idea was for each host to be as creative as possible in selecting a literary, artistic, historic, or culinary theme for his/her dinner. The only library expense would be the salary of one employee for six months and production of an invitation, and postage. All other work would be handled by volunteer members. The cost of the souvenir booklet was underwritten by a local gourmet-type supermarket.

New York's Night of 95 Dinners

"1000 Feast at 95 Fetes To Help Library" was the headline in the *New York Times* feature story in the Wednesday "Living Section" the day after the event. (For one reason or another five of the original 100 dinners had to be canceled. But there were still 1,000 guests present, and more than $200,000 was raised for the New York Public Library.)

The whole idea was to hold multiple dinners on the same night. Of course the New York Public Library, with its connections, came up with extra-added attractions which made a greater story and a special, special event. People like James Beard, Craig Claiborne, Marcella Hazan, and other notables were chefs and hosts that night. Some of the homes had such celebrity guests as Eli Wallach, Anne Jackson, Henry and Nancy Kissinger, John Chancellor, and of course, Brooke Astor, the person the New York Public Library could not live without, probably New York City's most enthusiastic philanthropist.

People paid (donated) $150 each for dinner. Some of the parties were formal, with black-tie attire, and some were more casual. Dinners were held in private homes, apartments, private clubs, restaurants, hotels, an auction house (Christie's), and even a specialty store (Henri Bendel).

The *New York Times* quoted the city's mayor, Ed Koch, as saying "I don't think this could happen with the same dimensions in any city other than New York and never with the same verve." Koch, by the way, was the special guest at a black-tie kosher "Dinner in an English Library" at the home of Ellen and Arthur Liman, well-known New Yorkers.

A $10,000 bottle of wine was flown over (it had its own seat on the plane!) from France and was served that night. It was a gift from Baron Philippe de Rothschild and was chaperoned in

54 *Fireworks, Brass Bands, and Elephants*

flight by a Madison Avenue wine merchant. An "imported" cook from North Carolina made she-crab soup and persimmon tarts for one party. Former library board chair Richard Salomon and his wife Edna entertained 50 guests at the Carlyle Hotel with a 1920s theme; a speakeasy door was installed to lend atmosphere! Menus varied... everything from sumptuous feasts to ethnic foods to casual buffets. Some of the parties featured magicians, actors, or musicians. Dinners were held in New York City, Connecticut, Westchester, Long Island, and Brooklyn. Entertainer Peter Schickele was the star at Barbara and Donald Eliott's "P.D.Q Bach" dinner in Brooklyn. Other innovative dinners were: "A Russian Country Dinner" with Alan and Hannah Pakula; "A Kitchen Buffet" with James Beard; "A Feast" with Kay and Warner LeRoy; "Homage à Rousseau" with Ariane and Michel Batterberry; and "Heartburn" with director Mike Nichols and his wife, Annabel, all well-known New Yorkers. These were just a few of the themes.

Results

Needless to say, a good time was had by all. Fifty percent of the donors had never previously contributed to the New York Public Library. "Guests" came from New York City, Long Island, Westchester, Connecticut, and Philadelphia. The dinners were covered by 15 newspapers and wire services. *Vogue* and *House Beautiful* featured color stories of several table settings, and other magazines and trade publications spread the story further afield. Not only did the New York Public Library net a tidy profit, it made a host of new friends. Here are three of the menus.

Craig Claiborne
New York Times Food Editor and Author
Theme: A Summit Meeting (6 guests; black tie—in East Hampton, Long Island)

MENU

American caviar with iced vodka

Striped bass with champagne sauce (Batard Montrachet, 1981)

Stuffed squab Derby (Chateau Margaux, 1964)

Braised endive

Assorted cheeses and mélange of salad greens vinaigrette

Chocolate mousse (Perrier-Jouet's Fleur de Champagne)

Coffee with cognac

Christopher Idone
Director of Glorious Food II and Author
(Guest chef for dinner being hosted by Mr. and Mrs. Howard Sloan)
Theme: Nineteenth-Century (Special guest: John Chancellor; 20 guests)

MENU

Creole oysters

New England boiled dinner with 4 meats and 6 vegetables

Horseradish cream sauce and a piquant sauce

Johnny cakes

Bread pudding soufflé with whiskey sauce

Mr. and Mrs. Michael Batterberry
Authors and Founding Editors of Food and Wine *magazine*
Theme: Homage à Rousseau (Special guest: Paula Robison, playing Eric Satie; 20 guests; Bohemian black tie)

MENU

Wine tasting of 1906 Chateau Margaux

Buffet Exotique—foods of many cultures

Patisserie Marie Laurencin

The dinner will re-create the famous "Banquet Rousseau" given in Picasso's Montmartre studio in 1908 in honor of Rousseau and attended by Gertrude Stein, Apollinaire, and others. The garden room will resemble the jungle depicted in Rousseau's paintings, the food will be equally exotic.

Laramie's Night of 100+ Dinners

The Albany County Public Library, based in Laramie, Wyoming, is certainly not in the same league as the New York Public Library. Laramie's population is only 25,000. The library has a staff of 30, of which only 3 are professionals, but it too has an active Friends group. Without them, the library certainly could not have held its successful fund-raiser, "The Night of 100 Dinners," Wyoming style. According to public services librarian Susan Simpson, adult programming is not too successful at the library, but children's activities sponsored by the Friends do well. Many clubs and community organizations hold fund-raisers for the library. For example, during the same month that the "Night of 100 Dinners" was held, the local Women's Club coordinated a community-wide flea market, with a breakfast and lunch, raffles, and a sale featuring books, plants, and crafts. About 20 organizations participated, and over $6,000 was raised for the library. "The Night of 100 Dinners," which appealed to the more affluent members of the community, raised $3,000, bringing to a total of $9,000 the amount raised from two special events in one month!

The library worked actively with the Friends group, especially in the promotional aspects of the endeavor. Usually in smaller towns, the local newspapers, even the dailies, are more community-minded and give more space to community functions, especially if the event is unique. "Laramie Cooks Prepare for Library Benefit" was the local newspaper's headline. Not only did the article tell the story but it also included menus plus photos of chefs/hosts at work in their kitchens.

Tickets were $25 each and $45 for a couple (tax-deductible). There were 116 dinners served with 18 homes participating. Exciting menu themes such as "Middle Eastern Nights I," "Fondue Festival," "Eclectic Edibles," "Southern Laramie Cooking," "The Beanery Special," "Creole Flambeaux," "Country Inn Cuisine," "A Vegetarian Venture," and "You Cannoli Live Once" were offered. Many did group bookings. One group called themselves the "Laramie Happy Cookers."

After the fact, the Friends and library staff convened for a rehash meeting and put the results down on paper for future "Night of 100 Dinners" events. Some of the suggestions that came up were these:

- provide souvenir menus
- provide souvenir recipes
- collate a cookbook and sell it as a fund-raiser
- provide menus (so people can take them home and study them)

Other information gleaned from the session included the following:

- the publicity received was good
- many thought the dinners should not be all on the same night, while some said they should have them on a weekend to retain the "oneness" of the event
- some said having the dinners all on the same night gave a bigger impact
- some suggested a brunch idea to accommodate those who cannot afford the dinners
- have meals on a sliding price sale, ranging from a $20 picnic to a more elaborate dressed-up $100 affair
- have the event in February or March when there is less going on (this group held their event in September)

When asked whether they would consider "The Night of 100 Dinners" as an annual event, cook/hosts replied:

"We'd be happy to have this an annual event."
"Maybe every other year."
"I look forward to next year."

"Not for me. Next year I may just contribute the $135."

Some comments from the guests were:

"We loved the evening very much. Part of the pleasure was the unknown aspects such as the menu."
"I thought the manner in which it was done was great."
"We had a wonderful time. Enjoyed seeing old friends and making new ones."
"Will go again. It was a beautiful idea."

The dinners made $3,000 from the attendees and from nonattendees. Some people couldn't attend and donated the money, while others gave additional monies for the cause. Here are some sample menus from the Laramie "Night of 100 Dinners."

Middle Eastern Nights I
Jeff Alford, Host/Chef
(8 guests)

MENU

Angourasalata me Yiaourti

Hummus Tahini

Pita

Dukkah

Mushroom Pilaf

Arni Yahni me Melitzana

Greek Salad

Baklava

Retsina

Coffee

Fondue Festival
Judy and Bob Lavigne, Chef/Hosts
(8 guests)

MENU

Fondue Gruyere

French bread

Garden greens

Dipped prawns

Cheesey meatballs

Batter-dipped vegetable platter with assorted gourmet sauces

Banana split fondue

Australian wines

> *Southern Laramie Cooking*
> *Walter and June Edens, Chef/Hosts*
> *(10 guests)*
>
> ### MENU
>
> Crudités
>
> Chutney glazed ham
>
> Potatoes au gratin
>
> Biscuits
>
> Wine
>
> Pecan pie
>
> Rum cake
>
> Coffee

> *You Cannoli Live Once*
> *Sandy and Charlie Ksir, Chef/Hosts*
> *(8 guests; Dianne Cawood-Cvell, singer)*
>
> ### MENU
>
> Fettuccini Alfredo
>
> Scampi
>
> Salad
>
> Wine
>
> Cannoli

Summary

As you can see, each of these "Night of 100 Dinners" was different, and if you do it in your community, you will probably take a totally different approach. There are many variations on any theme...that's what makes special events and creative programming so much fun! This is a novel idea, but it has its drawbacks, so it's best to face them in the beginning. Since this is a totally volunteer event with the host/hostess supplying the place and food, you may have difficulty getting volunteers. If you do experience difficulties, attempt only what you can handle. Don't be too ambitious. Neither you nor I have the clout of the New York Public Library. Is this type of event worth repeating? Do it once, and then talk about it. New York Public Library repeated their "dinners" successfully. I also served as a hostess for the Friends of the East Meadow Public Library "Night of Many Dinners," and I, for one, would be very reluctant to do a repeat performance. But was it worth doing? Yes!

Note: If you think this particular special event idea originated with the New York Public Library crowd, you're wrong. The Tucson Museum of Art sponsors dinners for eight to 20 in members' homes. For $50 a ticket, guests choose from up to 23 different theme dinners, all held on one evening. A good idea is a good idea, even when it's a borrowed one!

"HOT-STUFF" FUN

Whether you're into chili or not, it seems to be a very popular food throughout this country, and fundraisers find it a fun way to make money and friends! There are many, many chili cook-offs held annually for some cause or another. The folks in the Clark County Library District of Nevada decided to join them and try their hand at a chili cook-off.

The first cook-off was held in 1983; it has since become an annual event. First, let's take a look at the Clark County library district. It's in Las Vegas, and it serves all of the residents in both the rural and urban unincorporated areas. Right away, a gimmick, all that glitter and glamour everyone associates with Las Vegas. Then, there's the influence of the "Old West," lots of color and atmosphere. Of course, the main purpose of the fundraiser was to raise money, but the library also wanted to reach out to nonlibrary users by showing them that libraries are really "hot stuff!"

The "Now You're Cookin Hot Stuff" Las Vegas district chili cook-off was a one-day special event cosponsored by the library district and a local food store. In order to attract chili enthusiasts, both locally and regionally, a membership application was submitted to the International Chili Society requesting permission to conduct the cook-off. The society's approval is required for it to be official. Forty teams of four persons each paid an entry fee of $25 to compete and win prizes for the "perfect bowl of red." Each team built their own booth and decorated it in keeping with their team name: "Hill Billy Chili," "Wyatt Burp Chili," "Dinghy's Hot Stuff," and "Federales" were just some of the names. The public paid $5 to watch the competition from the initial slicing and dicing of tomatoes and peppers through the three hours of cooking. The admission fee also bought them a large "Now You're Cookin Hot Stuff" button plus live entertainment. There was a "Miss Chili Pepper" beauty contest, music by western and bluegrass bands, and drawings throughout the day for $5,000 in prizes donated by local merchants. In addition, concessions sold "hot stuff" T-shirts, mugs, hats, aprons, and small collector buttons, as well as food (chili, hot dogs, hamburgers, soft drinks, and alcoholic beverages).

The more than 2,000 attendees proved that this fun-filled fund-raiser was a success. The major goal was to raise monies to advocate the passage of a statewide $10 million construction bond which was to go on the ballot the following November. But from the library's point of view, it was intended also to increase the library's visibility with a different segment of the population. The library netted $6,228 for its awareness campaign. There was a high level of community participation not only from the committees but also from merchants, businessmen and women, and those who just served as volunteers. The library's visibility was also increased with the chili cook-off attendees, who left their names and addresses with the library staff. These new names swelled the library district's prospect list for their annual direct mail fund-raiser, "Bucks for Books." And, let's not forget the more than $5,000 that was donated to the cause in the way of prizes and merchandise. The two grand door prizes were tickets for "anytime, anywhere" on a major airline carrier, and a Hawaiian holiday for two for six days and five nights. There were many other door prizes (furniture, small appliances, dinners for two, etc.) given out during the day as well. A very positive response was received from the local print and electronic media. There was a live broadcast from the cook-off site during the event, and local radio personalities served as emcees during the day. Yes, even the politicos made appearances. It was a real community show of spirit!

The Event

The cook-off was held on a Sunday in late September from noon to 7 p.m. The contestants began their chili cooking while people watched. Door-prize drawings and country and western bluegrass music by the Warburton Family Bluegrass Band and Don Holiman's Country Fever entertained from noon to 3 p.m. From 3 p.m. to 4 p.m. the Miss Chili Pepper contest was held. (Entrants paid $10.) Between 4 p.m. and 5 p.m., everyone had a chance to enter or just enjoy the country and western music-dance contest. Five o'clock was the hour all of the chili enthusiasts were waiting for...the cook-off awards would be announced! This was also the time for the announcement of the big door-prize winners. The "Wyatt Burp" team came home first with a prize of $500; second prize money went to the "Desert Prospectors;" and the "Silver Dollar Saloon" group took third prize. The party went on until 7 p.m. that evening with more country and western music and door-prize drawings.

The Organization

It takes time, lots of effort on the part of many, long-range planning, and proper funding to get a good special event fund-raiser off the ground. In this instance the idea came first. Bob Wiseman, a well-known chili competitor and local businessperson, was the cook-off chair. He was instrumental in coordinating a committee that had expertise in many areas: contests, community relations, public relations. Las Vegas, with all of its gambling chips and neon signs, is still a place where people live, raise families, go to church, and have a community feeling. Sure, some of the hotels and lounges were sponsors, but so were local insurance companies, laundries, health clubs, hospital auxiliaries, radio stations, food companies, and retail stores. Not much different from any other locale.

After the ad hoc group had received the International Chili Society's permission to conduct the cook-off, a committee was formed comprising local businesspeople, library trustees, Friends, and library staff. The library's staff artist created the graphics. A western-style invitation using the cook-off's characters, "The Good, the Bad and the Ugly," along with the slogan "Now You're Cookin' Hot Stuff," was sent to local groups and businesses as well as International Chili Society members throughout the Southwest. The idea, the committees, the sponsors, and donors were now all one. Now came the actual promotion.

The Promotion

Even though the idea was good, without promotion it would not have been the success that it was. A great graphics piece featuring "The Good, the Bad and the Ugly" was incorporated into just about everything. An identity was established for the promotion. The slogan "Now You're Cookin' Hot Stuff" was part of the graphics. The colors were striking, bright green and black ink on white, coated stock paper. It was everywhere.

"Somethin's Always Cookin' at the Library!" was the headline on the attractive September/October library district newsletter. The chili cook-off was the lead story ending with, "Y'all come now, Ya hear!" In case you got bored at the chili cook-off that Sunday afternoon and wanted something more cerebral, the events section of the newsletter announced an art opening/reception in the main library at 3 p.m. After all, everyone's not into chili!

The news releases were sent out to all the media and the story got quite a play, before and after the fact. Photos of committee members, such as library director Charles Hunsberger, appeared in local newspapers. The *Las Vegas Review-Journal* ran a marvelous picture story a week or so after the event with action photos that really told the fund-raiser story. The *Las Vegas Sun* did the same, with great crowd shots plus a picture of Miss Chili Pepper herself.

Colorful printed programs of the day's events were available, listing the time and schedule of all the events. The programs credited the sponsors, donors, committees, judges, and contestants. The next library district newsletter told the story of the event's success and thanked all involved.

But even after all of this, there was no time to rest. It was time to plan next year's cook-off! The planners decided the general public should have a greater opportunity to sample the chili. Since the International Chili Society's rules prohibit the public from observing the judging or in any way participating in the winner selection process, some

SOMETHIN'S ALWAYS COOKIN' AT THE LIBRARY!

District Chili Cook-off Sept. 25

SEPTEMBER/OCTOBER 1983

CLARK COUNTY LIBRARY DISTRICT

Used by permission of Clark County Library District.

proposed giving a People's Choice award after the panel of expert judges had made their choices. Not a bad idea. Of course, there's another option. You could just hold a chili cook-off without abiding by the rules of the International Chili Society; however, it wouldn't be "official."

Financial Report

Money can't buy the goodwill and new friends that this fund-raiser generated for the Clark County library district. But they did make a tidy sum.

> Revenue received from gate and contestant fees, T-shirts, hats, mugs, apron sales, Miss Chili Pepper entry fees, concession percentages......$12,469.20
>
> Revenue paid out for International Chili Society dues, merchandise for resale, equipment rental......$6,240.91
>
> Net profit for Clark County Library District Library Awareness Fund $6,228.29

Chili Cook-Off, Eastern-Style

Although the geopolitical center for chili is the western or southwestern United States, converts in the eastern United States, Europe, Canada, and Australia are ardent lovers of chili and have chili cook-offs too! Who would have thought a botanical garden in New York City would sponsor a chili cook-off? Why not? You don't have to be Texas-born to be a super chili enthusiast and cook. It was 90 degrees under a clear blue sky when 27 teams of chili cookers competed amongst the flowers in the Queens Botanical Gardens in the New York State Chili Cook-Off, sanctioned by the International Chili Society. They were vying for a spot in the World Chili Finals, which are held annually in California.

The Easterners had interesting names for their teams too: "Hot Steamin' Yankees," "Dave's Supersonic Tonic," "Death Row Gang," "Moonshine Chili Cooks." Cooking was not the only thing being judged. Costumes were varied and were judged separately. The "chief" of the "Death Row Gang" was dressed in a black pinstriped suit, a cowboy hat, and pointed boots. Texas drawls dominated the arena, where the sun and heat were cooking the cookers. Many tried to beat the heat with umbrellas overhead and by chugging beer.

Roland Wade, executive director of the Queens Botanical Gardens, was the official organizer of this annual chili cook-off. News releases went out from his offices. A beer company was a cosponsor. Local food editors served as judges and even New York City mayor Ed Koch made an appearance, traveling from booth to booth in a bright yellow apron, cowboy hat, and red bandana, tasting the chili. So, as you can see, a chili cook-off can be done just for the fun of it or as a fund-raiser.

International Chili Society (ICS)

The ICS is based in Newport Beach, California, and its director is Jim West. The principal purpose of the society, according to its fact sheet, is "to develop and improve the preparation and appreciation of true chili and to determine each year the World Champion Chili cook through officially sanctioned regulated competitive cookoffs."

The year 1984 marked the 17th annual "quest for the best bowl of chili in the world." One hundred state and regional winners from all over the world competed for the grand prize of $25,000 and a trophy. In 1983, the ICS sanctioned 200 events, and an estimated $750,000 was raised with over one million people attending. For more detailed information on the society, contact Jim West, International Chili Society, P.O. Box 2966, Newport Beach, CA 92663. One source of chili recipes to check is *The International Chili Society Official Chili Cookbook* by Martina and William Neely, New York: St. Martin's Press, 1981. It's a compilation of just about all the chili recipes you might ever want to have. By the way, "official" chili is made *without* beans!

In case your mouth has been watering for a bowl of the "hot stuff," here's the 1984 winning recipe:

1984 WORLD CHAMPION CHILI RECIPE FROM THE KITCHEN OF DUSTY HUDSPETH, Irving, Texas

---

BOTTOM OF THE BARREL GANG RAM TOUGH CHILI

4 lbs. beef chili grind
2 8 oz. cans Hunt's tomato sauce
2 onions, finely chopped
2 tsp. garlic powder
½ cup Gebhardt's chili powder
2 tsp. oregano
3 tsp. salt
4 tsp. ground cumin
2 tsp. Tabasco sauce
½ tsp. cayenne pepper
1 can Old Milwaukee Beer
2 tbsp. Wesson oil

Sear meat in covered 2-quart pan with Wesson oil. Add tomato sauce, onion, and garlic powder. Cover and simmer for 30 minutes, stirring occasionally. Add remaining ingredients and stir. Simmer for one hour. Add water if necessary. Serve with side dishes of pinto beans, chopped onions, and grated cheddar cheese for garnishes. Enjoy! Serves 6–8.

A cold glass of beer or a large glass of water is suggested...after that, you're on your own!

SHORT SUBJECTS

There are many levels and varieties of fund-raising; in this section you will find several successful and varied examples. The fund-raisers run the gamut from a baseball competition in New Jersey, to an autumn winefest in St. Louis, a cruise party in Yonkers, a lawn mower race in Indiana, a Jello Jump in Ohio, to a dog's tale in Washington, DC.

The Soaps vs. the Libraries

Take a willing group of soap opera stars from the New York City area and add two libraries willing to do the organizing, mix it with the cooperation of two Friends' groups and various other community organizations, and you end up with a successful special event/fund-raiser. Hold on, it's not all that simple and without problems, but it can work and did for the East Brunswick and Milltown, New Jersey, public libraries.

This fund-raising idea, first conceived by the East Brunswick Library, was to be a baseball game between the cast and crew of the popular television soap opera "The Guiding Light" and local community "celebrities" (school and library officials). According to Sharon Karamzin, East Brunswick Library public information officer, the library had the soap opera connections but did not have the baseball field for the fund-raiser. By asking around, they found that Milltown not only had a ball field but also the use of the VFW hall across the street to use during and after the game for the players. So, the two libraries worked together to orchestrate one great baseball game between the Library All Stars and the "Guiding Light" stars.

The library team was outfitted with team shirts featuring the national library symbol. (The shirts were to be used again in future games.) Planning began two months in advance for ticket sales, transportation, refreshments, publicity, and the many details that demand attention. In most cases when you're dealing with special events, you would start planning and promoting more than a couple of months in advance, but when you are dealing with celebrities such as a soap opera troupe, you must be flexible. Their shooting dates are unpredictable. But then, those are the chances you take.

Sunday, the day of the game, was clear but hot. Nearly 500 excited fans paid admission ($3 adults, $2 children) to see the game and have the chance to win autographed baseballs and scripts in a raffle, as well as cash. The final score was Library All Stars 9, Guiding Light 5. Both teams and fans agreed it was a great game and probably one of the few baseball games with more women than men in the stands! East Brunswick's own Channel 8 cable television cameras caught this memorable event on videocassette for all to enjoy later. After the game, all adjourned to the VFW hall, where the Friends' groups hosted a buffet for players and workers. A great time with plenty of laughs. The "take" was $1,000, which was divided between the 2 libraries.

You too can plan and bring off a celebrity baseball game even though you may live in a town short on movie stars, models, and soap opera stars. How about local politicians versus the local TV and radio station staffs? Or schoolteachers versus students' parents? It's the same game; only the names have changed. And it's just as much fun.

Expenditures

Most of the time, to get something, you must spend a little. Sometimes you must advertise to reach your audience. That's what was done in this case. The libraries advertised in several New Jersey weeklies. Cost: $68.67. Transportation for the soap opera stars was needed. Bus cost: $375. Beer and soda came to $220. Food and T-shirt lettering cost $148. It seems there were some Library logo T-shirts left over from a prior event, so an enterprising Sharon Karamzin just had the names of the two library teams printed on a batch of them. The food for the after-the-game party consisted of deli platters (purchased) and salads (donated by the Friends). The gross was $1,800; each library netted $500 after expenses.

You might say, "All that work and effort and you only end up with $500 each?" True, but some fund-raisers are worth doing just for the fun of it and just to enhance your image with the public. In this case, the larger library provided services such as printing tickets, organizing and contacting the soap opera stars, promoting the event, and handling the cable TV taping. The smaller library did its part by providing the baseball field and the free use of the VFW hall and assisting in the food preparation and other jobs. Involvement of people and community is the major "profit" of a fund-raiser. By the way, some of the most active on the sidelines were the young teens from both library communities.

The East Brunswick Library's Friends seem to have an active fund-raising schedule; many of their fund-raisers are annual events. The biggest money-maker is a used book sale held in a shopping mall, which brings in $15,000 each year. Every successful book sale or special event should have a few gimmicks. For example, East Brunswick Library Friends have compiled a special book sale mailing list; visitors are asked to self-address a postcard for the next year's sale. Good idea. Each school-age child takes home a book sale promotional flier. Another good idea. But there's more. Those who remember to bring that postcard to the sale win a paperback book. The postcards are used a second time in a drawing for a free "Trivial Pursuit" game. As an extra-added attraction and to keep the youngsters happy and occupied, the library puppeteers put on shows several times during the day.

A "quality" Chinese auction is run annually, and it not only draws from the local community but also snares Chinese auction "junkies." It takes a lot of hard work on the part of the library and volunteers to put the event together and acquire quality prizes, e.g., Atlantic City show tickets, restaurant dinners, in addition to the usual merchandise. The auction usually attracts 500 people and has made $5,000 in one night! Not bad. The event is held at a local high school large enough to accommodate everyone.

Not every event is successful, but it is hoped that at least lessons can be learned from the failures. The East Brunswick Library purchased a Kurzweil machine for the blind but needed funds to cover training and servicing. Word went out to the Lions Club. In response, the Lions' president organized a basketball game between the New York Giants football team and a local team. The library realized a profit of $3,500. Great. But a repeat of the event the following year flopped. The first time, 700 people attended, but the next year drew only 350. So, what went wrong? Perhaps the Lions Club should have waited a year before repeating the event. Maybe there wasn't enough promotional effort. Also, perhaps most important, that one very enthusiastic Lions' president was not free to direct the event again. Many times an event will not be a success unless there is a strong enthusiastic leader who can draw others to volunteer. Sometimes people assume that just because an event was a hit one year, it will be a hit the next year without the same amount of effort expended.

Undaunted, the East Brunswick Library continues to plan and execute successful fund-raisers.

How a Public Television Station Does It

All of you who live within range of a public television station know public TV "must eat" to survive. Besides the quarterly on-air membership drives and mailing list promotions, many plan special events. These events not only make money but also make the community more aware of the station. One successful public television station, KETC, Channel 9 in St. Louis, Missouri, has been in existence for 30 years. But it's only recently that the number of fund-raisers has increased dramatically.

A few years ago, the station established a Special Projects Council, "in essence, a Friends' group," to organize special events for the station. Now several events are held annually. One of these is an Autumn Winefest, usually held from 2 p.m. to 5 p.m. on a Sunday afternoon in the ballroom of a large hotel. Each year, the attendance has grown— from 600 in 1982 to 1,000 in 1983 to 1,500 in 1984. The public relations office of the station promotes the event and sells the tickets. In 1984 the tickets were $12 for Channel 9 members and $15 for nonmembers. The news release announced, "Over one hundred products representing nearly

Special Events Fund-Raising 61

thirty California and thirteen Missouri wineries will be available for an educational afternoon of comparison sampling."

Wine enthusiasts attending the Autumn Winefest not only enjoyed the wine with fruit, cheese, and breads and crackers but were also serenaded by La Belle Musique, a female string quartet. Each participant went home with a souvenir wine glass and a program describing all the wines sampled. The mounds of cheese and platters of fruits, bread, and crackers were all donated. The event was hosted by the California Wine Institute; the wines were donated. But most important was the fact that wine experts were in charge. They provided the information and education so there was less for the station to worry about.

Promotion

Although the special event/fund-raiser was not held until the first Sunday in November, the news release from the station went out at the end of September. It told the whole story, giving information concerning the cost of the tickets and how to order them, along with the information that people had to be 21 years or older to attend; the release also credited the Friends working on the fund-raiser. Later this information was attractively presented in handsomely designed brochures which were mailed to those on the mailing lists. The local print media and, of course, Channel 9 gave the event plenty of publicity. Last but not least, the Friends committee members not only worked hard but used their clout in the community to pull off this successful fund-raiser.

Another Channel 9 fund-raiser involved the celebration of its 30th broadcasting year. For the event the Plaza Frontenac hotel was turned into a luxury liner for "Nine's 30th Anniversary Ultra Cruise Party." Tickets were $75 per person; $150 would buy a benefactor seat at the captain's table.

Both sides of the KETC fund-raiser brochure showing all panels.

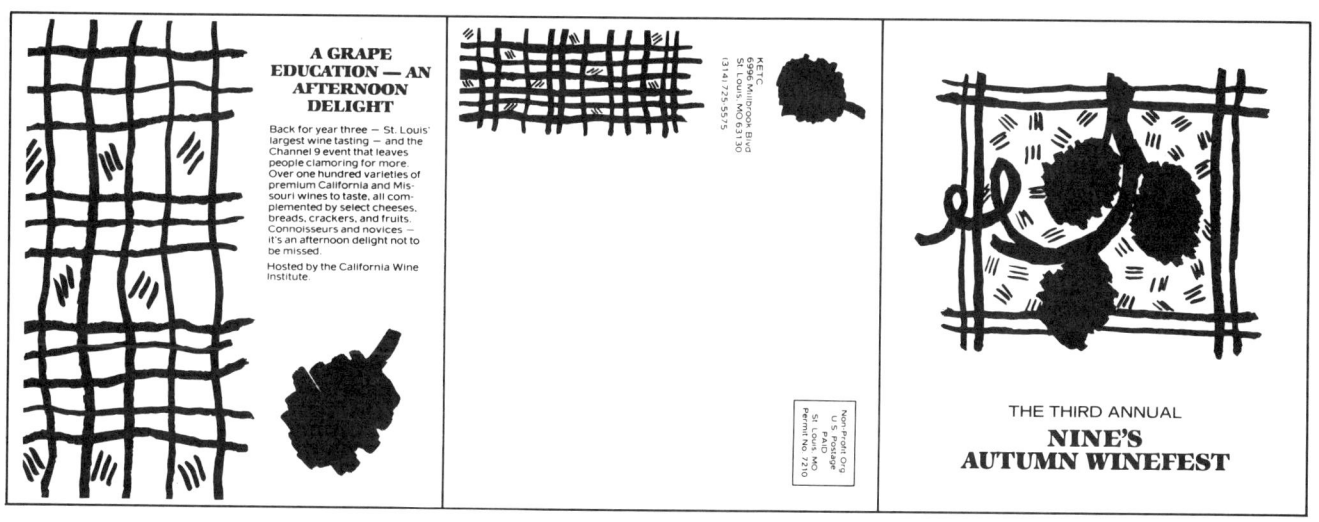

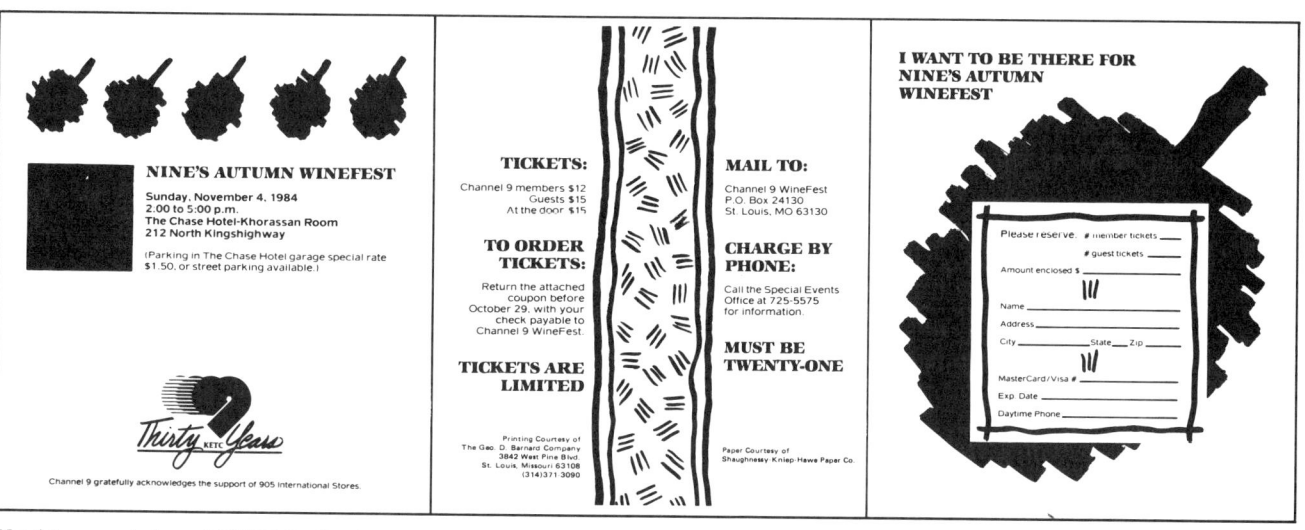

Used by permission of KETC-St. Louis.

"During the course of one week, Channel 9's programs take viewers all over the world and that's what we're going to do for those attending the Ultra Cruise Party," announced Pat Peck, event chairperson. "Exotic cuisines from the world's great ports are on the dinner menu. Entertainment will be diverse, going beyond the boundaries of the United States. The latest in men's and women's cruise wear will be exhibited as the evening goes along. Many shipboard activities, music, dancing are also slated for an evening designed to transport guests from the cold of January in St. Louis to the warmest spots on earth," announced the news release from Channel 9's promotion department.

This was a "first" for the station in many ways. It was the first time such an event had been attempted, and it was the first time the station tried to attract community/corporate leaders to lend a hand in their fund-raising attempts. It worked.

"Our goal is to be a real part of the community by holding activities to attract many different groups," states promotion representative Cathy Rothstein. "For example, last year, we brought in Big Bird to conduct the St. Louis Symphony and this year (1985) we're doing a concert with a puppet troupe and the Symphony, and in the Fall we're holding an art auction."

Not all of the special events held by this public TV station are fund-raisers. Many are strictly community get-togethers designed to better their image and to make the community aware of their existence.

A Museum and Its Fund-Raisers

The Hudson River Museum sits beside the Hudson River in the city of Yonkers, New York. It was founded in 1919 and established in the Trevor Mansion, a historic Victorian which is part of the museum today. The museum underwent expansion with new galleries, a planetarium, and a library added in 1969. And, in 1984, it became the Hudson River Museum of Westchester, an independent educational corporation receiving major funding from the county of Westchester. Like most institutions, it works from an annual plan for fund-raising and audience development. Their annual giving plan is considered separate from their annual benefit, which usually has a theme and is held in June. A total of 10 fund-raisers are held annually.

A Cruise to Paradise

Somewhat similar to Channel 9's "Ultra Cruise Party" was the Hudson River Museum's "Cruise to Paradise." Members, patrons, and the general public were invited: tickets were $150 each with discounts for tables of six, eight, and 10. Because the museum itself is in a lovely setting and has the space, the "cruise" was held there. All boarded the "S.S. Hudson River Museum" at 7 p.m. and were served cocktails on the afterdeck and nouvelle cuisine in the Grand Salon. There was a wheel of fortune and fabulous prizes in the casino, with dancing and entertainment on the main deck. Formal cruise attire was required.

The idea for the theme came from the grand prize offered, which was a free cruise for two on the new luxury cruise ship *Seagoddess II*. The cruise trip was worth $7,000. Other door prizes included a weekend for two at the Harborview Hotel on Martha's Vineyard; a week for two at the Cheeca Lodge in the Florida Keys; a weekend for two at New York's Mayfair Regent Hotel with limousine travel and theatre tickets; a private jet ride to a gourmet luncheon on Lake Champlain in Vermont; and a Hudson River luncheon cruise for five couples aboard the Sloop Sojourner Truth.

Promotion and Benefits

Those on the museum's mailing list received an attractive invitation/brochure showing a yellow crescent moon floating in a sky of yellow and green with waves below of a deep green. The brochure continued with a cruise ship on the waves heading for "paradise!"

The event was coordinated by the museum council, and museum trustees were actively involved in selling tickets. The museum's director of development, Bonnie Rosenblum; coordinator of public affairs Laura Byers; and director Peter Langlykke are all heavily involved in the fund-raisers. In 1984, the museum cleared $56,000. In addition to having experienced promoters, the museum is fortunate to have corporate sponsors. Some sponsers, such as Bloomingdale's and Neiman-Marcus, have held museum benefits in their stores. When Conran's furniture store opened its newest store in nearby White Plains, the museum benefited from an opening day party. Eight hundred people

Used by permission of The Hudson River Museum.

came and paid $25 each for cocktails and hors d'oeuvres; the museum made $11,000.

Throughout the year, the museum holds weekend brunches for about 50 people. Usually there is a speaker who talks about the current exhibition at the museum. A bit of musical entertainment may also be included. The charge is $35 per person, with the museum clearing anything from $900 to $1,100 each time.

Another fund-raising activity is the museum's Heirloom Exchange Days, a four-day tag sale. The sale consists of a preview and auction conducted by a local auctioneer/appraiser/dealer who donates his/her time and expertise. The auction is a big job. The museum must hire truckers and rent storage space for the donated merchandise. But it's worth it and will probably continue as an annual event; $36,000 was made in 1984. You might call it a "Spring Cleaning Auction" because it is held in mid-April. Think about it as a possible fund-raiser for your group.

For those who think it all sounds easy and a fast way to make a few quick dollars, museum director Langlykke says, "I would say that fund-raising events are a difficult way to grab bucks but they do have the advantage of cultivating interested donor prospects and getting people involved in educational programs. They take coordination of the most rigorous type with extraordinary attention paid to detail," he adds. "We have a pattern that works well, although we always analyze, compare and evaluate." Good advice.

SHORT SHORT SUBJECTS

Of course there are many ways to make money for your organization on a smaller scale. Some are more fun-makers than money-makers. You must always remember that one of the prime reasons fund-raisers are held is to cultivate interest in your group, develop a mailing list for future events, and promote goodwill. And, if you make money too, that's great! Here are a couple of fun, successful ideas that you could certainly try without too much trouble.

Lawn Mower Race

They must be doing something right in Twelve Mile, Indiana, because they have been running the same community event and fund-raiser for over 20 years, and it's always successful. They call it the Twelve Mile "500" Riding Lawn Mower Race, and it all began in 1963 when one of the members of the Lions Club suggested the idea at a regular meeting. Debbie Dillman, correspondent for the Twelve Mile Lions Club, reports, "After the laughing stopped, they decided that it wasn't such a bad idea and to give it a try."

Twelve Mile, known as "The Biggest Little Town in the World," has a population of under 300 people. The Lions Club was interested in holding a special event that would keep everyone "at home and bring the community together for the Fourth of July." It did. Patterned after the Indianapolis 500 auto race, the Lawn Mower Race has an appropriate set of rules created by the Lions Club. The race course is 12 miles long, and the speed limit is 12 m.p.h. This event is the major fund-raising project for the Lions Club, usually drawing between 3,000 and 4,000 people. Race entrants have come from as far as 200 miles away, but most come from a radius of 25–30 miles. Men, women, and youngsters over 11 years of age may enter. Nearly a third of the population of Twelve Mile serve as volunteers on this event, and the only person paid is the scorer.

The Twelve Mile "500" has had some exciting incidents through the years, but luckily there have been no serious accidents. There have been wet muddy tracks and dry hot tracks for the riders, but they still keep coming back! One driver had to get out of the race when he had a bad wreck which bent the axle on his mower. He wasn't hurt. Another time, a mower caught fire; it was the first time in the history of Twelve Mile "500" racing that any lawnmower went out of the race because of fire. It's a fairly safe race; it seems the worst that happens to drivers is a collision with hay bales which are located at various turns of the bumpy track.

In addition, there's a Twelve Mile "500" beauty queen contest and other special events held all weekend long, including a variety show in the park, pre- and post-race parades, and a "greased pig contest" for children 12 and under followed by a firecracker '6' foot race (6.2 miles). The weekend concludes on Sunday with a community worship at Plank Hill Park followed by a community square dance in the park that night. About $2,500 is raised annually from the lawnmower race. The program books raise the bulk of money, since the ads that appear in them are plentiful. There is an entry fee of $10 for the race; admission charges to the race are $1.50 for adults, 50 cents for children ages six to 12, and free for children under six.

Jello Jump

They called it the Cherry Blossom Festival in Barberton, Ohio, and one of the highlights was the local Jaycees' "Jello Jump." The Barberton Jaycees "borrowed" the idea from another Jaycee unit. Contestants paid a fee to jump into a vat of cherry gelatin. Why would anyone want to jump into a vat of gooey gelatin? To win the prize. The idea was to dive into the vat and retrieve a numbered disk which was matched up to one of a set of 50 keys. Each contestant then lined up and tried to fit his/her key into the grand prize—a brand new car, donated by a local car dealer.

A humorous note about the vat of gelatin. The Jaycees had their troubles making it. The vat was five feet deep, five feet across, and 10 feet long. Many methods were tried to set the gelatin, but none were successful. So, in most cases, the contestants actually jumped into a vat of cold, wet cherry water! According to Marty Luxeder, a member of the Jaycees, "That didn't seem to bother the contestants."

Another fund-raiser held in Barberton was the musical chairs event, which drew adults as well as children. There was nothing big about this event, but it certainly did create a lot of laughs and fun. The 50 contestants played the game outdoors, and the music came from a record player just like the old days. The prizes were small items donated by local merchants. This was just another way for a small town to make a bit of money and, most important, promote goodwill.

The last tale in this fund-raising chapter is just that.

A Short Tail

Some people are prone to say no matter who holds power in the town, that Washington, DC, "has gone to the dogs." Well, in 1985, it literally did go to the dogs! Lucky Reagan, Kiltie Weinberger, Digger Mondale, Cody Wick, Duke Domenici, Junket Aspin, and Coconut Gore, just to mention a few, lent their barks and tails to a fundraiser for the Capital Children's Museum.

Washington churns with benefits, and some people must have sniffed and snorted when this one, the Capital Canine Follies and Fair, was announced. But if two-legged creatures can have fun raising money for a worthy cause, why not the four-legged kind that bark and chew bones? A letter went out from cochairdogs Jasper and Muffin Meese, the schnauzer and poodle who curl up in the attorney general's home, to their 37 canine committee members.

The letter was a gem. It opened with this observation: "Certainly this is the most luminous gathering for canines ever assembled, with the possible exception of when Thomas Jefferson's dog dined alone." There was more. "We are all quite familiar with the charity cycle, particularly how it churns in Washington and so you will be thrilled to note that we are not calling together any dreary committee meetings nor are we asking any of you to sell tables for $10,000. However, as committee members you have specific duties to adhere to: You must be nice. No canine chaos allowed. Although there will be veterinarians and the OTHER kinds of doctors on hand, no incidents please."

The afternoon fair, held in mid-May on the grounds of the Capital Children's Museum, offered more than a dozen booths with food (for humans) and monogrammed collars, leashes, and custom-made clothes (for dogs). The dogs got into the act by entering the contest at the fair. A panel of judges, headed by White House press secretary James Brady, rated the canine celebrities on such traits as the "floppiest ears," "saddest eyes," and "most beguiling bark." In the "Dog-Eat-Dog World" competition, it was the Democratic dogs against the Republican dogs for the most blue ribbons. There was even an "Ambassadogeral" competition between such canines with diplomatic papers as Countess Chloe Wachtmeister of Sweden and Sweet Pea Gotlieb of Canada.

Lucky Reagan, who divides her time between the White House and Camp David, was the honorary patron of the affair. Chesty VII, the Marine Corps mascot, was proclaimed the honored guest. He escorted his friend, General P.X. Kelley, the Marine Commandant. It might have been a day that Washington went to the dogs, but it was for a worthy cause! The media lapped it up.

As you can see, the events in this chapter have a lot of "fun" in their FUNd-raisers. Never forget humor when planning events of any kind. Probably one of the most important ingredients in fund-raising events is the planning process. Do it carefully. Remember, in most instances you will be dealing with volunteers for help. If possible, have a paid staff member in charge of coordinating the whole show. Volunteers mean well and want to do the best for you. But you or a staff member must be orchestrating the event. I can't repeat two things enough: "Never assume anything and don't attempt to do more than you can handle." Begin small and then move on to bigger game. If you already have a successful annual fund-raiser and everyone loves it, why change it? Keep up the great work, but always be on the lookout for some new ideas.

In Chapter 8, "One More Time (Over 100 Additional Exciting Ideas)" you will find many more successful fund-raising ideas. As you can see, most have a lot of fun in successful FUNd-raisers. Never forget humor in your planning. Probably the most important ingredient is planning, because your staff will be dominated, in all likelihood, by volunteers. They need detailed plans and plenty of fun if their interest and concern is to be maintained. And they need you or a paid staff member to orchestrate the event. Two commandments to hold close: never assume anything, and don't attempt more than you can handle. Start small; then move on to bigger things. And, finally, always be on the lookout for new ideas.

RESOURCES

Ardman, Perri, and Ardman, Harvey. *Woman's Day Book of Fund-Raising*. New York: St. Martin's Press, 1980.

Dermer, Joseph. *How to Write Successful Foundation Presentations.* New York: Public Service Materials Center, 1977.

DeSoto, Carole. *For Fun and Funds: Creative Fund-Raising Ideas.* Englewood Cliffs, NJ: Prentice-Hall, 1984.

Drotning, Phillip T. *Putting the Fun in Fund Raising—500 Ways to Raise Money for Charity.* Chicago: Contemporary Books, 1979.

Flanagan, Joan. *The Grass Roots Fund-Raising Book—How to Raise Money in Your Community.* Chicago: The Swallow Press, 1977.

Kurzig, Carol M. *Foundation Fundamentals—A Guide for Grantseekers.* New York: The Foundation Center, 1980.

Margolin, Judith B. *The Individual's Guide to Grants.* New York: Plenum Publishing, 1983.

Petersen, Sheila. *Successful Community Fund-Raising.* Napierville, IL: Caroline House, Inc., 1979.

Schneiter, Paul H. *The Art of Asking—A Handbook for Successful Fund-Raising.* New York: Walker & Co., 1978.

Chapter 6
Games, Contests, Festivals, and Fairs

♠ The World's Largest Games
♥ Animal Contests
♦ Food Festivals
♣ Thematic Festivals

People love games and contests...some like to participate while others just like to watch. There are thousands and thousands of contests, festivals, and fairs held all year long that result in a great deal of fun for people all over the world. Why not join them? In this chapter you will find many ideas to consider, chuckle at, borrow, or discard as "too crazy for me!" It's up to you. Remember, always think of your community first and what will go over well there. But don't be afraid to try something new and adventuresome.

THE WORLD'S LARGEST GAMES

R. H. Macy's department store in New York City claims to be the "world's largest store." So, it would be natural for them to hold "The World's Largest Games." The highlight of the day was "the world's largest chorus line of tap dancers," who were going to attempt to break the current world record. In 1981, Macy's entered the *Guinness Book of World Records* when 2,023 dancers tapped their way down 34th Street to Macy's. Then in 1982, a new record was set by a group of 2,647 dancers in Australia. In 1984, Macy's was determined to get the title back. And they did with a total of 3,450 tapping enthusiasts!

Shuffling Off

You can imagine what a job it must be to assemble over 3,000 tap dancers on one block in New York City on a Sunday morning. The dance call was for eight in the morning. The first 3,000 registrants each got a spiffy T-shirt ("Record-Breaking Tap Dancer") and a hat. Aspiring dancers arrived from Manhattan, Brooklyn, the Bronx, Queens, Staten Island, Long Island, Westchester, and New Jersey, Connecticut, Virginia, Maryland, and Florida. A dance captain lined them up in rows of 25 and taught them a simple dance routine. There were tiny tots as young as 15 months old and grandmothers with silver hair and silver tap shoes.

The spectators cheered them on as they practiced. Finally, at noon, the official tapping began. What a sight! Visualize 3,450 tap dancers dancing away to "Give My Regards to Broadway" on a New York City street. The photo tells it all.

Used by permission of Macy's New York.

The media loved it as well. "Entertainment Tonight" and Cable News Network covered the event, and local print media like the *New York Post* featured the story as well as the wire services. Even radio stations from as far away as Colorado told the story of the record-breaking tap dancers! It was a natural for the media. The smiling and exhilarated tap dancers went home with their souvenir T-shirts and hats, and comments such as, "That's the closest I'll ever get to Broadway!" were heard often. Macy's public relations department submitted the results to the *Guiness Book of World Records* and then promptly began plans for a repeat in 1985! The 1985 dance event was called "Tap-O-Mania," and it set the world's record with 3,565 men, women, and children tapping away. At the finale of the 1985 "Tap-O-Mania," 5,000 balloons were released into the sky in celebration.

The Games

The day was not over yet. Calling it a "Block Buster Block Party," Macy's invited kids and their families to join them and some celebrity guests in an afternoon of big games. Soap opera stars David Oliver (Perry Hutchins) and Jane Cameron (Nancy McGowan) of "Another World," Robert Curtis Brown (Alec Kendall) and Page Hannah (Adair McCleary) of "Search for Tomorrow," and Eddy Earl Hatch (Tucker Foster) of "As The World Turns" served as celebrity hosts.

All were invited to put together a gigantic jigsaw puzzle illustrating the fantasy world of Rose-Petal (a cartoon character) Place. Families worked together to join the 13,500 jigsaw puzzle parts. Each piece was about five inches square. The puzzle when finished measured 3,648 square feet. This event was sponsored by Hallmark Cards, and the game was copyrighted by David Kirschner Productions.

If puzzles weren't your speed, then there were plenty of other games to play. Sponsored by DC Comics, Inc., the "Super Powers Action Maze" drew plenty of action, as youngsters climbed through a secret tunnel into a bat cave, walked on a balance beam, jumped through Wonder Woman's lasso, and met their idols: Wonder Woman, Batman, and Robin. Parents snapped pictures of their children with the comic favorites.

"The Get Along Gang Great Train Race" was another fun event for children and was sponsored by American Greetings. Would-be train engineers pumped miniature railroad hand-cars in a fast-track race to the finish line. An oversized version of the Little Red Caboose was side-tracked and ready for the kiddies. Once aboard, they were greeted by Montgomery Moose, Dottie Dog, and some of the other "Get Along Gang" friends, all popular children's cartoon characters.

Rainbow Brite and her friends challenged children ages five to 12 to a game of action and agility called "Star Hop." Mattel Toys sponsored this event. There were many other games played such as "Snag a Shark," "Care Bears Tree Climb," "Kiddie

MACY*S

WORLD'S *Largest* GAMES

Macy*s Sixth Annual World's Largest Games

Come on along! Come on along to Herald Square on Sunday, August 19th from noon until 4:00 PM (rain date Sunday, September 16th).

Join the young and the young-at-heart in this World's Largest Back to School Extravaganza. It is a Block Buster Block Party for all our beloved Citykids and their families.

Come and greet those dancin' feet at noon on 34th Street as Macy's assembles 2650 aspiring tap dancers to form the world's largest chorus line.

Then as the last tap of the Time Step is heard, round the corner to Herald Square and put together the world's largest jigsaw puzzle of over 13,500 pieces. Toss a hoop or a bean bag. Search for the real peanut. Create music with Macy's Tin Pan Junk Band. Meet Batman[TM], Snoopy[TM] and other favorite cartoon characters, and let us entertain you with the Young Artists of Ballet Hispanico and a variety of talent on Macy's Mobile Stage.

-2-

Macy*s believes that there's a lot of fun in learning, so learn while you play at The World's Largest Games. There's something for everyone and it's all free. The games and prizes are for children 12 years and under. The entertainment is for the whole family.

Helping to make the day a wonderful success for all, volunteers from the Police Athletic League (PAL) and Big Brothers of America will assist Macy employees who have contributed their Sunday in celebration of New York's Citykids.

For further information contact: Judy Cohn (212) 560-4060
Carolyn Klein (212) 560-4660

Used by permission of Macy's New York.

Peanut Hunt," "Tots Shoe Scramble," "Tin Pan Junk Band," and "Toss Games." Two of the games, "Kiddie Peanut Hunt" and "Tots Shoe Scramble," could be successful ideas to borrow for children ages four to six. (In the Kiddie Peanut Hunt, a kiddie wading pool is filled with water, and lots of real peanuts and some fake Styrofoam peanuts are thrown in. Kids have to find the real ones. Note: All children's games should have adult supervision.) In the Tots Shoe Scramble, children try to find their shoes, which have been mixed up with the others and piled in a heap. Once the kids have found their shoes, they run to the finish line.

If a participant got tired of playing games, s/he could enjoy the free entertainment. Throughout the afternoon, there was live entertainment from Macy's Mobile Theatre. The Calabash Dance Company treated the folks to break-dancing demonstrations. There was a Rose-Petal 'N Friends Revue. The Young Artists of Ballet Hispanico danced in the colorful tradition of Hispanic dancing. People swayed to the rhythms of the Police Athletic League's steel band, and there were clowns, mimes, jugglers, and favorite cartoon characters such as Strawberry Shortcake, Happy Moodie, Garfield, Batman, Rose-Petal, and Betty Boop. A unique treat of magic was offered in Anthony Carter's Magic Machine.

Comments

Macy's runs a big show, and not all of us are able or want to duplicate it all. But we can borrow many of the ideas. Their ultimate purpose was to create a small-town block party with games and contests. It just happened to be right in the middle of New York City. Why not try it for your group or organization? People are basically the same, whether they're from New York City or Gillette, Wyoming.

Even an organization the size of Macy's couldn't do it alone. They involved their community, including the Mayor's Office of Special Projects and Events, the New York Police Department, the Police Athletic League, Big Brothers of New York City, American Greetings Corp., Bobbs-Merrill Co. Inc., DC Comics Inc., Hallmark Cards, and others. The professionals in the public relations and the special productions departments of Macy's organized and publicized the events, and that took some doing. The attractive press kit they prepared told the whole story for the media. Nothing was left to chance. They even announced a rain date...just in case. It was a fair day, and all had a great time.

ANIMAL CONTESTS

William Schaefer, the mayor of Baltimore, Maryland, will probably never be a totally happy man. He wants "his city" to be the best at everything. No matter how many ways the city's problems are solved and no matter how many different and unique ways his staff think of to entertain the people of Baltimore, he's more than likely to say, "That is NOT ENOUGH." In his 10 years in office, he's made many changes and improvements in the city's character. On the light side, his Mayor's Office of Adventures in Fun creates and runs many festivals and contests for the people of Baltimore. Many of them are similar to other contests held in the country, but in Baltimore, they try to do it with a great deal of panache while retaining that small-town flavor. Here are three of their winning events, all involving animals.

Preakness Frog Hop

Since Mark Twain's tale of the most famous frog-jumping in "The Celebrated Jumping Frog of Calaveras County," frog-jumping contests are held annually in every part of the country. Probably the biggest is the International Jumping Frog Jubilee in Angel's Camp, California. Baltimore has been jumping frogs since the 1960s and officially began its Baltimore Frog Hop in 1974 in War Memorial Plaza in downtown Baltimore.

Their promotional flier, "A Toadally Unfrogetable History," informed readers about frogs and how they came to be jumping in Baltimore. They even supplied an information fact sheet which explained how to catch a frog (not a toad), feed a frog in captivity, house a frog, and build a fly trap (the better to feed your frogs with!). There was nothing slick in the graphics of the flier or the paper stock, just a good homespun look and text. The rules sheet for the contest listed the sponsor and stated that the winning frog and its jockey would get a chance to "represent Baltimore and Mayor Schaefer at the International Frog Jump in Calaveras County, California."

Turtle Derby

Claiming that Baltimore residents were the only ones in the country to race turtles, the mayor's office expressed interest in organizing a National Turtle Derby to be held in Baltimore either in July or August, to be called the Chesapeake Turtle Derby. The city of Baltimore holds at least 10 races at the War Memorial Plaza each June and has run a total of 45 turtles so far. No "dime-store" turtles are allowed; turtles must have shells at least three-and-a-half inches long.

Fortunately, the people who enter these contests also have a sense of humor. One of the 1984 turtles entered was called "Michael Jackson." The real Michael Jackson may be a winner in his field, but the turtle with his name came in dead last. The mother of another turtle jockey jokingly declared that her son's turtle, which had been entered and had lost in several past derbys, might end up in a pot of soup after this year's event. Not coincidentally perhaps, the 1984 sponsor for the turtle derby was Turtle Wax, Inc.

Hog-Calling Contest

A hog-calling contest in a big city? I wondered about that too. Well, why not? Just about anything is possible anyplace if people are willing to take the time to create, and have a sense of humor.

The 1984 contest was announced in a pale-pink flier written by Michael J. Baker, a naturalist with the Department of Parks and Recreation, which cosponsored the event:

> "One can sit for hours thinking of novel ideas for a new event to hold in Baltimore's War Memorial Plaza. Over the years, Baltimoreans have been treated to cultural shows, backgammon and chess tournaments, Turtle Derbys and Frog Hops at the Plaza, each a product of the Mayor's Office of Special Projects. The Special Projects squad is always looking for new ideas, too. Each suggestion is contemplated as to its practicality, how it can involve Baltimore's citizens, how well it promotes the City and just exactly how much fun it could be for all involved. Early June 1976, such a suggestion came along. A downtown worker suggested that the Mayor's Office hold a hog-calling contest. Although it was one of the most unusual ideas the office had received, [they] nonetheless decided to give it a try. The only problem was to figure out exactly what a hog calling contest was. The Inner City setting prohibited the use of live hogs for calling. With the usual large lunch time crowd in the Plaza, hogs on the loose would have created absolute mayhem. So the Mayor's Office decided to have hogs on display only. The contest itself would be judged by experts but it was soon apparent that finding expert hog callers was like finding needles in a haystack in a windstorm. A call was made to the Timonium State Fair personnel to locate experts for this contest. "After they stopped laughing, they gave us the names of two reputed hog-calling experts and wished us luck. We immediately contacted the two men and each chuckled softly before accepting (apparently the idea was funnier than we thought)."

Sponsors were enlisted and each donated, appropriately, either a ham or a food certificate. To complete the prizes, piggy banks (later renamed "hoggy banks") were purchased and made ready for presentation. And, finally, on July 26, 1976, the 1st Annual Baltimore City Hog Calling Contest was held.

An overflow crowd was on hand to witness what was billed as the biggest event since the Baltimore Turtle Derby. The health department supplied a swine flu information booth and the 4-H Club donated informational material and two hogs for spectators to view and learn about.

Sixteen contestants, ranging in age from 10 to 72 years old, competed for top honors as Baltimore's best hog caller. One by one, each with a different style, performed the ritualistic call, yelling "Sooooeeeee, here pig, here pig, here piggy, piggy." And yet throughout the hog calling and the crowd's seemingly ceaseless laughter, the two hogs slept quietly on, oblivious to their surroundings. In the photo you see the 1984 adult division's winner, Bessie Fite, holding her trophy and offering her award-winning call.

Used by permission of The Baltimore Mayor's Office of Adventures in Fun and *The Baltimore Sun*.

And, so it goes. A few things have changed since the contest began. A local radio station has been added as a sponsor and more prizes are given away. But basically, this annual event remains the same.

Comments

I think by now you have a sense of what the Mayor's Office of Adventures in Fun is all about. It seems they are doing a pretty good job and probably will be happy to share some of their ideas with you as they coordinate many other events besides the ones highlighted here. Most important, they involve spectators, contestants, merchants, local companies, etc. Involvement of others is the key to planning all special events. People like a good idea and will join in, especially if you are going to carry the weight of the production and promotion of the event.

Fun events, especially those that are highly visual, attract the media, since they can provide good photo stories for both the print and electronic media, and there's always the possibility of a good human interest story. Good soft news, something the media is always looking for, may not make the front pages or the top spot in the nightly TV news, but it could make for a light closing segment on the news. Baltimore not only creates fun events but promotes them well. Needless to say, though, Baltimore doesn't "hog" the limelight when it comes to hogs. Out in Kewanee, Illinois, they hold the "Hog Capital of the World Festival" over Labor Day weekend annually. With a committee of about 30 they plan a hog/pork chop barbecue (over 12,000 are cooked yearly), produce a hog festival parade with over 250 entries, and sponsor a mud volleyball contest with 560 participants! They also involve the local community and merchants and companies. Another example of big city ideas that can be scaled down to small group use.

FOOD FESTIVALS

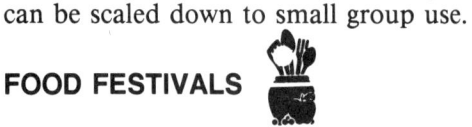

People are in love with food and people love to celebrate food. Cookbooks are devoured. People like to watch cooking demonstrations, taste foods, exchange recipes, and even make fools out of themselves over food.

If you're eager and able, and you've the stomach for it, you can enter a hot dog–eating contest held annually at Nathan's in Coney Island, New York. If smelt is your choice, then head up to the state of Washington for a smelt-eating contest in March each year. Maybe chili peppers are more your style...then eat away at a contest held in Rosamond, California, or travel to Illinois or Connecticut for an annual oyster-eating contest, or motor on down to Louisiana for a frog-eating contest in Rayne. If none of these ideas appeal to you, try cherry or pumpkin pie–eating contests, milk-drinking contests, or even a Bohemian apple-eating contest. (A Bohemian apple is an onion, and down in Victoria, Texas, they present huge trophies to those who can consume the most!)

It seems that if people are not cooking and eating food, they're using food as a catalyst for a festival. Digest the forthcoming ideas—just about all of them could be adapted with good results. And what would a section on food be without recipes? For the happy cookers, I have also included some winning recipes. Enjoy.

Popping in St. Louis

I remember as a child popping corn over the big black stove in the kitchen, using my mother's aluminum pot. Popcorn has come a long way since then. It was a popular movie food and still is more than ever, but now people are into "gourmet popcorn." There's even a Popcorn Institute to help you plan a popcorn event. Many interesting things can be done with this very American food.

For example, KETC, Channel 9, the public television station in St. Louis, Missouri, was planning a kick-off for their fall festival, "TV Worth Staying Home For." They called it their first "Popcorn Bowl" and held it in Kiener Plaza on the first Wednesday in October 1984 between 11:30 a.m. and 1 p.m. to catch the lunchtime crowds and shoppers. "Local radio personalities will battle in fierce popcorn competition," their press release read.

Popcorn is too soft-core for a "fierce" competition, but it was fun, anyway. Nine events—Popcorn Balance Race, Popcorn Toss, Popcorn Mystery Quiz, Popcorn Dash, Popcorn Stringing Contest, Popcorn Throw, Popfest Balloon Contest, the Nine Hop, and the Popcorn Eat-a-Thon—were held. Here are some of the details of the games used that day in case you would like to try them at your event.

- Popcorn Balance Race. Balancing one piece of popcorn on a spoon, walk a nine-foot course. The first person to get nine pieces of popcorn into a container in the shortest amount of time wins.
- Popcorn Toss. First person to toss nine pieces of popcorn into his/her mouth wins. Each person is given one cup of popcorn.
- Popcorn Mystery Quiz. How much popcorn would it take to fill Busch Stadium (not including the stands)? The answers were written on cards, then read.
- Popcorn Dash. Using a paper cone as a scoop, walk a nine-foot course. The first person to fill a bucket to a premeasured line wins.
- Popcorn Stringing Contest. The person who makes the longest chain in five minutes wins.
- Popcorn Throw. In two minutes, from a distance of three feet, the person who gets the most in a container wins.
- Popfest Balloon Contest. The first person to get nine pieces of popcorn into a balloon, inflate it, and tie a knot in it, wins.
- Nine Hop. Holding a paper cone filled with popcorn, each person must trace a pattern of nine while hopping on one foot. The person who spills the least amount of popcorn wins.
- Popcorn Eat-a-Thon. The person who eats a premeasured amount of popcorn in the shortest amount of time wins.

Crowned the "Grand Popcorn Champion" and appearing on Channel 9 live was Bill White of radio station WMRY. That's Bill pictured after he accepted the popcorn crown for a day and the royal popcorn sceptre. Master of ceremonies Jackie Dankner, a local media personality, bestowed the honors.

Used by permission of KETC-St. Louis.

Comments

Admittedly a promotional gimmick for the TV station's new fall season, this still was a good community outreach effort. It involved well-known local radio personalities from at least a dozen radio stations in a fun-filled few hours on a main street in town. And it got the word out about the station's new fall season using a well-known commodity, popcorn. Everyone can relate to popcorn; you either love it or hate it. They added more color with an antique popcorn wagon. Both the wagon and the popcorn were donated by a popcorn supply company.

A Popcorn Festival—Valparaiso Style

Now in Valparaiso, Indiana, they really mean popcorn business when they hold their annual popcorn festival each September. With 1,000 volunteers, the Greater Valparaiso Chamber of Commerce attracts about 75,000 people each year! That's a lot of popping. Orville Redenbacher, the "king of popcorn," developed his now-famous popcorn in Valparaiso, his hometown. Looking for some way to bring recognition and entertainment to this city, the mayor and the chamber of commerce dreamed up the annual popcorn festival, and it's still going strong, adding new activities each year. Orville lends his support, too: "In all of my travels, I've never known a city to have as much fun with popcorn as they do here in Valparaiso where it all began."

And fun it is. Everyone in town joins in and supports the festival. The local YMCA, churches, merchants, bankers, teenagers, and children, local university, arts groups, theatre groups, schools, and youth organizations all contribute time, talent, and/or money. It is a well-organized effort with many committees formed to help out. The organizers produce a money-making program book filled with local advertising and a listing of all of the events with a pull-out map showing where the events are held. Now, we're not talking about a half dozen special events—more like 18 prefestival doings; on festival day, there are nearly two dozen more things to do and enjoy.

Beginning in the latter part of July, prefestival festivities are held to warm up everyone for the great popcorn festival. Prefestival events include such programs as:

- "Get Poppin"—popcorn amateur show
- Women's Popcorn Open Golf Tournament
- Popcorn Queen Contest
- Men's Popcorn Open Golf Tournament
- Popcorn Ball (dinner and dance)
- Pop-Ball Co-Ed Softball Tournament
- Popcorn Art Contest and Window Display Judging
- B-Ball Popcorn Tip Off Tourney
- Popcorn National Derby Rally Race
- YMCA Art Fair
- County Seat Plaza-Popcorn Rodeo Days

During the "official" festival week, there are more preliminary events before the big Saturday, called "Orville Redenbacher Popcorn Tent Events." Events included a Grecian Fest with food, dancing, and music by the Porter County Greek Orthodox Church; a fun-day-with-the-cutest-baby contest; a cake decoration judging and ice cream social; and a Serbian festival with food, kolo dancing, and tamburitza music provided by members of the St. Sava Serbic Orthodox Church.

After all of this, one would wonder how the people of Valparaiso would have the energy for one more day of popcorn celebrations. But they do. At the 1984 event, the early risers greeted the sun at a flag-raising ceremony held at 7:15 a.m. on the Saturday Popcorn Festival Day; a Popcorn Panic (a five-mile race) began at 7:30 a.m. For the even younger set, there was a "Little Kernel Puff" kiddie run later on in the morning. For the children who just wanted to play, there were kiddie carnival games and rides.

During this period, the popcorn festival parade was held. There was a petting zoo and pony rides for children sponsored by the Montessori School from 11 a.m. to 7 p.m. Children were also treated to *Androcles and the Lion*, a play presented by the Memorial Opera House Theatre Guild. There were three showings.

The day ended officially at 8 p.m., but the hours in between were also filled with an amateur talent show, food booths, arts and crafts booths, a popcorn gospel fest, a Pop-N Round square dancing, popcorn bowl downs at a local bowling alley, helicopter rides, a popcorn sock hop and rock stage, and various other kinds of entertainment. And, if a person got weary, the YMCA rest area was open.

The following day, popcorn lovers got up to participate in their choice of three events: an antique show, a bicycle BMX moto-cross or a popcorn criterium (a bicycle race for licensed and novices). The last two weekends offered the Kernel Klassic in the Fitness Barn and the Popcorn Bowl football game. Yes, free popcorn was available just about any place you were at. There was even popcorn ice cream!

Comments

To publicize this festival, the committee produced a simple annotated festival broadside which was available in just every part of town. They also printed bumper stickers using their festival logo, and even created their own Popcorn Festival stationery. The whole series of events had a nice hometown flavor...just what they were aiming for. Since so many people do love popcorn and find it a nutritious snack, I thought you might like to have one of the recipes from the festival.

Pizza-Pleaser Popcorn

5 qts. unsalted popped popcorn
½ lb. pepperoni sausage, thinly sliced
¼ cup (½ stick) butter
½ tsp. ground oregano
½ tsp. salt
2 tbsps. grated Parmesan cheese

Keep popcorn warm in a 200°F oven. Fry pepperoni till crisp. Drain on paper towels. Melt butter. Stir in oregano and salt. Combine popcorn and drained pepperoni. Pour seasoned butter over popcorn mixture. Toss well. Sprinkle with cheese. Makes 5 quarts.

Used by permission of the Greater Valparaiso Chamber of Commerce.

Think of ways you can celebrate popcorn. Pick a month when things might be dull. Pop a few events such as a "Guess How Many Popcorns in the Jar" contest; hold your own "Best Popcorn Recipe Contest" (print the winning recipes and have samples available for all to try); hold a "Popcorn Movie Series" showing nothing but oldies from the 30s, 40s, and 50s and serve free popcorn. It's endless. You'll think of more.

Brussels Sprouts

I, personally, would never have thought of celebrating brussels sprouts, mainly because I am not too fond of them. But thousands of people love brussels sprouts, especially the Northern California Sprout Growers' Association, who joined forces with the Santa Cruz Beach Boardwalk for their Annual Brussels Sprouts Festival each October. An entire weekend is devoted to the celebration of brussels sprouts. Probably the most popular event is the brussels sprout tasting sessions held on the boardwalk by many of the local restaurants who provide the various taste-tempting brussels sprouts delicacies. Would you believe you can taste sprout-on-a-stick, sprout water taffy, sprout cotton candy, candy sprout on a stick, sprout chip cookie, sprout pizza, sprouts and cheese, deep fried sprouts, sprouts soup, sprouts kabob, guacasprout dip, sprout tostada, gyros with sprout dressing, and nachos with sprouts and cheese sauce? A "Gourmet Tasting Chart" was provided to each taster which stated, "In most cases, gourmet food is in the palate of the beholder. This is especially true with brussels sprouts. Therefore, to help judge how the various sprout items appeal to you, use this special tasting chart as you indulge. Be sure to taste the deep-fried sprouts before the sprout water taffy and clear your palate between tastings..."

Good advice. Sprout tasting went from 11 a.m. to 7 p.m. The first 5,000 families were treated to free sprouts between the hours of 11 a.m. and 5 p.m. Every half hour, beginning at noon, sprout cooking demonstrations by chefs from local restaurants were presented in the boardwalk's colonnade area. The entire boardwalk was sprouting with entertainment (jugglers, music, etc.), sprout games ("sprout toss" and "shoot out sprout"), face painting, a sidewalk sale, a garage sale, an arts and crafts fair, an ice carving display, and much more.

An attractive program booklet filled with information and ads was designed by a local production firm. One of the articles in the booklet, "The Curious History of Brussels Sprouts," explained the origin of brussels sprout growing in California. Claiming that 90 percent of the nation's brussels sprout crop is produced in the central coast region of California, the article said, "...in 1919, the industry began as John DeBenedetti planted a 20-acre plot of sprouts near Pigeon Point on the central California coast, replacing an artichoke crop previously grown there."

And so it went, and now about 30,000 tons of brussels sprouts are produced each year in the Santa Cruz region. That's something to celebrate! According to the sprout growers, a serving of five to six sprouts is only 33 calories. To tempt your appetite, they also provided recipes in their booklet. Here's one.

Belgian Cheese Pie

1 pint fresh (California) brussels sprouts

½ lb. bacon, cooked, drained and crumbled

1 cup grated processed American cheese (about ¼ lb.)

4 eggs, separated

2 cups milk

1 tsp. salt

1 tsp. dry mustard

¼ tsp. pepper

1 9-inch pastry shell

Cook brussels sprouts covered, in boiling salted water 10–15 minutes, until just tender. Drain and chop. Combine sprouts, bacon, cheese, egg yolks, milk, salt, mustard, and pepper. Mix well. Beat egg whites until stiff but not dry. Fold into sprouts mixture. Turn into pastry shell. Bake in moderate oven (350°) for 50 minutes. Makes one 9-inch pie.

Used by permission of the Northern California Sprout Growers Association and the Santa Cruz Boardwalk.

Comments

The Santa Cruz Boardwalk is certainly a visible place because of all of its year-round promotion and special events. They do more than celebrate foods. They keep in touch with the community and neighboring regions with their attractive bimonthly newsletter, which not only contains a listing of their special events but also bits of information about the boardwalk and its employees and some excellent photos. They are constantly in touch with the local media. Many of the radio stations have remote programs from the boardwalk when a special event is occurring. Many of the events they create can be revised to suit your needs and interests. Just plan and promote your way.

Carrot Festival

Moving over to another part of California, you will find yourself in Holtville, where they've been celebrating carrots for over 37 years! It's a small town. How small? Well, they have only two doctors serving their area. What is big is their pride in their carrot production. They claim to be the "Carrot Capital of the World." The whole town joins in the annual Carrot Festival. With a population of "close to 4,500," Holtville harvests carrots from December through May, and ships them all over the United States and Canada. The festival takes place in February. This information is printed on picture postcards sold in town.

"Get the community involved," is what Mrs. Marty Morris of the Holtville Chamber of Commerce tells would-be festival planners. And Holtville certainly does. Local merchants, farmers, youth organizations, schools, fire and police departments, and service organizations all participate. It is *their* annual event. For one week, carrots take top billing in town. "Cooking with Carrots" was one of the headliner events at the festival in 1984. The first three days were devoted to a junior carrot cookery contest (Little Chefs) at the Civic Center, a junior high carrot cookery contest, a senior high carrot cookery contest, and a microwave carrot cookery contest. Judging and tasting by the public went on at all times, and prizes were awarded on the third day.

In addition to the cooking competitions, other activities included a midway of games and fun and a special Rotarian luncheon on Friday with visiting Rotarians as the special guests. Saturday morning began with an arts and crafts fair which ran all day. Also held were a fine arts show at the Civic Center and a student art show, hosted by the Women's Club. Everyone turned out for the Carrot Festival Parade at 10 a.m. and "Run in the Sun" 10K and two-mile runs. A wrestling tournament was held at the high school following the race. The "ladies of the United Methodist Church" served a Mexican luncheon in Holt Park after the parade.

On Sunday, activities began with a Carrot Festival Tractor Pull at 9 a.m., and at 1 p.m. there was a livestock competition (swine judging, sheep judging, and beef judging, with 4-H and FFA members participating). The midway fun, art shows, and arts and crafts fair continued. Needless to say, it was a successful jubilee with all kinds of activities, concluding with a Fourth of July picnic in the park and fireworks display.

For the cooks who are reading this book, here's another prize-winning recipe to add to your collection. Marguerite Bernardi was the "sweepstakes winner," second place in the main course division in 1983, for her "Carrot-Stuffed Chicken Rolls with Apricot Sauce."

Carrot-Stuffed Chicken Rolls
with Apricot Sauce

5 large broiler-fryer breasts (about ¾ lbs. each) split, skinned, and boned
¼ cup chopped green pepper
3 tbsps. soy sauce
2 tbsps. corn starch mixed with ¼ cup water
2 eggs, beaten
oil for deep frying
2 cups buttermilk baking mix
1½ cups diced carrots
1 cup chopped green onions
1 cup minced shrimp
2 tbsps. oil
1 tbsp. instant chicken bouillon
salt and pepper to taste

Place chicken between pieces of waxed paper and with mallet or broad side of a cleaver pound thin. Dredge in baking mix; set chicken and baking mix aside. In large skillet, sauté onions and green pepper in oil until tender. Add carrots and continue cooking until just tender; add shrimp, soy sauce, bouillon, and corn starch mixture; cook and stir until thickened. Place 2 tablespoons of filling at one end of each breast half; roll up and secure with picks. Dip in egg mixture, rolling in remaining baking mix. Heat oil in fryer to 400°. Fry rolls 2 at a time for 10 minutes or until golden brown. Drain, keep warm in 300° oven until serving time. Serve with apricot sauce. Makes 5 generous servings, 2 rolls each.

Apricot Sauce

¼ cup apricot preserves
2 tbsps. each cider, vinegar, and soy sauce
½ cup packed brown sugar
½ tsp. dry mustard

Combine all ingredients in small saucepan. Stir over medium low heat until sugar dissolves. Serve warm or at room temperature. Makes about ⅔ cup.

Used by permission of the Holtville (California) Chamber of Commerce.

Comments

This is the story of a small town that makes the most of its most important commodity, carrots. Since the residents live, eat, and breathe carrots, why not celebrate them? For over 37 years, this festival seems to have bound the community together and provided an opportunity for all to do something special once a year. Although most of them are not professionals in the field of public relations and promotion, they have certainly learned a great deal just by doing. A good-looking program booklet, jam-packed with listings of events, historical notes and photos, ads by farmers and merchants, and recipes, is evidence of that.

Carrots can be celebrated by all. You don't have to grow them to exalt them. Just about everyone eats carrots. Some like them raw, and some like them cooked. Hold your own "best carrot recipe" contest and publish the winners in a booklet. Make it a fund-raiser. Don't stop there. Have a childrens' craft workshop making carrot people and other carrot objects. Hold a carrot cooking demonstration program. Gather nutritional information about carrots and include it in your cookbook. Hold free eye examinations (with services donated by a local eye doctor or optometrist) and give a carrot to each person who takes the test. You've got the idea; now it's your turn. And, if you don't like carrots, read on for garlic and bubble gum!

The Sweet Smell of Success

Gilroy, California, was described by the late American humorist Will Rogers as "the only town in America where you can marinate a steak by hanging it on the clothesline." Located in one of California's richest agricultural centers, Gilroy claims to be "the Garlic Capital of the World." The town produces about 90 percent of the garlic consumed in the United States. Learning about a tiny French town that drew thousands of people to its annual Garlic Fete, Gilroy was inspired to do the same. In 1979, they held their first annual Garlic Festival and have been doing it every year since. It is held in late July for three days in the town's oak-and eucalyptus-shaded Christmas Hill Park. What was begun by a few residents has now grown into a nonprofit corporation, the Gilroy Garlic Festival Association, Inc. The goal of the festival group is continuous support of community projects, charitable groups, and service organizations. In 1984, some 3,000 volunteers from 112 nonprofit groups worked 31,000 hours to stage the sixth garlic festival.

The celebration of the "scented pearl" is not only profitable but fun, tasty, and attractive to people of all ages. Food is very much the most important ingredient of the weekend, but there are arts and crafts booths, golf and tennis tournaments, a garlic queen pageant, a Tour De Garlique bicycle tour, a 10K Garlic Gallop, and a Garlic Squeeze Barn Dance as well. There are also four performing arts stages scattered throughout the creekside park area as well as roaming musicians. You can enjoy anything...country music, oom-pah bands, rock groups, big band sounds, jazz, and even mariachis strolling and playing. Over 200 booths, many of them food stalls which feature such goodies as garlic calamari, fettucini with pesto, and even garlic ice cream, beckon the stroller!

The highlight is the Annual Great Garlic Recipe Contest and Cook-Off. Cash prizes and national recognition serve as incentives for the participants. In 1984, over 900 entries were submitted from around the country and Canada. The entries were judged by professional home economists; from them, 10 finalists were chosen to participate in the cook-off, which was held during the festival. The finished dishes were scored on the basis of appearance, flavor, excellence, and good use of the garlic by a panel of nationally acclaimed food authorities. All of the recipes become the property of the Gilroy Garlic Festival Committee, and over 200 have been gathered in *The Garlic Lovers' Cookbook*, which can be purchased in either paperback or spiral. Included in the new revised edition is the 1984 Gilroy Garlic Festival Recipe Contest winner, created by Mrs. Beverly Stone.

Grilled Angler with Garlic Beurre Rouge

½ cup fruity olive oil
5 tbsps. lemon juice
4 cloves fresh garlic, peeled and slivered
1 bunch fresh cilantro (or coriander leaves) chopped to make ½ cup, reserving some whole leaves for garnish
Salt and freshly ground pepper to taste
6 six-ounce angler fillets, about ¾ inch thick (or any firm-fleshed fish)
¼ lb. sweet butter
¼ cup sweet red onion, chopped
2 small hot green chiles, finely chopped
1 tbsp. finely minced fresh garlic
1 lb. ripe tomatoes, peeled and chopped
Lemon wedges

Mix together olive oil, 4 tablespoons lemon juice, slivered garlic, ¼ cup chopped cilantro, and salt and pepper to taste. Add fish fillets and marinate for one hour or as long as overnight. Meanwhile prepare Garlic Beurre Rouge. In a frying pan over medium heat, melt 2 tablespoons butter. Sauté onion, chiles, and minced garlic until soft, stirring. Add tomatoes and the remaining one tablespoon lemon juice. Cook, stirring, for 10 minutes. Remove from heat and add salt and pepper to taste. Stir in remaining ¼ chopped cilantro. Slowly stir in remaining butter to melt. Barbecue fish over low glowing coals about 7 minutes or until done to your liking, turning fish once. Remove to warm serving platter. Top with Garlic Beurre Rouge Sauce. Garnish with lemon wedges and reserved cilantro leaves. Makes 6 servings.

Used by permission of the Gilroy Garlic Festival Association, Inc.

Comments

The *Los Angeles Herald Examiner* called the festival "the ultimate in food fairs." "The bulb's biggest booster since King Tut" was what *People* magazine had to say. *The San Francisco Chronicle* announced, "It was a rollicking good time."

As you can see, they got plenty of good press from local and national print media, including *The Wall Street Journal*. Food magazines hailed the event also. But even with all the national acclaim, small-town conviviality still dominated the festival. Besides promoting the town's garlic to over 125,000 festival attendees, the town benefited in another way. The festival committee, in exchange for the use of the local park, makes permanent additions to the park's community recreation facilities, which are enjoyed by the townspeople all year around.

So, borrowing an idea, beginning small, and then embellishing it until it became a national festival put Gilroy and garlic on the map! Why not celebrate garlic in your community? You don't have to be in the center of its growth to be a celebrant. After all, garlic is familiar to all. It goes back to ancient times when bunches of garlic were used by the Greeks to mark the crossroads leading to game grounds to lure god and mortal alike. Certainly most of us are familiar with its many medicinal uses. Have a garlic recipe and cook-off contest. Possibly have one set of local celebrities vie against another in the cook-off. Print the recipes in a book and fill it with garlic lore, then sell it as fund-raiser. Think of the many ways you can promote garlic...and then sense the sweet smell of success!

Pastaville USA

The weather is usually very cold in Minot, North Dakota, around mid-November, but the people there are warm in spirit as they celebrate their annual International Durum Forum. What's durum, you ask? It's the wheat that pasta is made from, and it is produced in huge quantities in North Dakota. Sponsored by the Durum Growers Association of the United States, the Minot Chamber of Commerce, and Ward Co. Crop Improvement Association, the "festival" is primarily for the farmers, grain buyers, and semolina processors. This is serious business. But on the other hand, the people of Minot call their town "Pastaville USA" and choose this time to celebrate pasta, in which durum is the prime ingredient.

Craig Bennell and his associates at the Minot Convention and Visitors Bureau and others have created a series of special events to get the community involved and draw others to Pastaville USA. Although the business seminars and presentations are open to the public, the festival committee plans other events, such as a "Pastalympics" on Dakota Square from 9 a.m. to 3 p.m. for youngsters in grades two through six. The Minot Jaycees act as meet coordinators. The "Lasagna Leap," the "Noodle Jump," and the "Pastacle Course" are just a few of the activities that bring awards to the winners. For the more adult members, there's a "Rigatoni Run" which begins at 10 a.m. in Dakota Square and is sponsored by the local YMCA, Pepsi, and Happy Joe's restaurant. Athletes could store up on carbohydrates the night before at the Spaghetti Extravaganza held at the Magic City Campus High School from 4 p.m. until 8 p.m. Prices were $3.50 (adults), and $1.50 (children, ages seven to 12), and free for youngsters six and under. Several sponsors made this event possible.

Everyone, it seems, likes to break records or create the "biggest" anything! At noon in Minot's Town and Country Center, people looked at the "world's largest lasagna" prepared by the Optimist Club. It was four feet wide and 10 feet long! The lasagna was sold by the piece until all of it was gone.

Just for fun was the "Mr. Spaghetti Legs Contest," held at the center. Local male "celebrities" modeled their legs, while judges decided which legs most resembled spaghetti (i.e., legs that are pale and skinny, etc.). These good-natured contestants drew lots of laughter and applause. For spaghetti lovers (with bottomless pits for stomachs), the "Speediest Spaghetti Slurpers" contest proved to be a delicious one. Each year winners from previous years compete to see who is the grandest spaghetti slurper of them all! Two local credit unions sponsor the event. "Oodles of Noodles," a pasta sculpture contest and display for students in grades 4 to 6, is held in the Town and Country Center for three days. Awards are given to the best pasta sculpture display.

During this four-day forum period, many of the restaurants in the city feature special pasta dishes on their menus. All kinds of pastas are offered for sampling in the food court on Saturday. Pasta is everywhere.

Comments

This Pastaville USA celebration is very similar in many ways to some of the others. Again, there is much community involvement and careful planning in this event. Local merchants and community organizations work together. But the thing to remember about this event is that it is also a serious forum about durum. The Durum Crop Show is held at a local motel; there is a youth division for 4-H and Future Farmers of America members as well as a commercial division. The "fun" part of the durum forum complements the business part.

Certainly pasta is one of the most loved foods and a familiar sight on many household tables. So a celebration of pasta could be held anywhere, even Alaska! Just borrow some of the ideas from Pastaville, USA, and create some of your own. Remember, people love anything to do with food, so don't forget a spaghetti cooking and eating contest!

Bubble Gum

What child has not had an affair with bubble gum, and what adult doesn't remember his/her first big bubble? That's why I thought the summer reading game "By Gum!" should be included in this section of this book. I know you're not supposed to eat bubble gum, but it is a "food" and not a toy, as some people think! The children's librarians at Daniel Boone Regional Library of Columbia, Missouri, who sponsored this summer reading program, must have had fun dreaming this one up.

The library announced the program with a bright yellow bookmark made to look like a stick of "Wiggly's Furry Fruit Chewing Gum." It said: "Let the library stick up for you with Summer Reading...By Gum!....Chews your books with care and flavor your summer fun with special reading club activities...." The program included these "activities to gum up your summer: May—"Willie Wonka and the Chocolate Factory" movie at both library branches; June—Eyeball the gumballs!!! How many gumballs do you see? (This contest was held at both branches and on the bookmobiles); July—Bubble Blowing Contest (Are You the Fastest Gum in the Midwest?). A bright pink bookmark entitled "I Blew It at the Library" promoted the "Who's the Fastest Gum in the Midwest?" bubble-blowing contest for ages two and up. The times were set: 10:30 a.m.–11:30 a.m. for ages two–six, 1 p.m.–2 p.m. for ages seven–nine, and 2 p.m.–3 p.m. for ages 10 and up. Refreshments were served afterward to wash down all the bubble gum, and prizes were awarded.

The promotional highlight of the bubble gum summer works was the publication of *The Incredible No-Joke, No-Stick Bubble Gum Book*, compiled by librarians Debbie Schluckebier and Elinor Barrett. It supplied great facts and history about bubble gum, bubble gum etiquette, bubble gum blowing techniques, baseball cards that came with bubble gum, "books to blow bubbles by," recipes for making bubble gum, myths and beliefs about the pink stuff, how to make chew chains, etc. This tiny book has a gummy pink cover with pale pink inside sheets. It was an in-house printed production.

Comments

Although this was a children's program idea, it could certainly be modified to include adults. In fact, you might consider two ways to approach this celebration: Do it during National Bubble Gum Week (usually in mid-April) or include a bubble gum contest in your humor month celebration (see the "Strictly for Laughs" section of Chapter 4, "Thematic Programing"). Who can resist laughing or at least smiling at a bunch of adults blowing bubble gum?

This certainly would be a fun event to promote, and with a couple of good gimmicks, the media would be receptive. I can see all the picture possibilities. By gum, it could be a fun time.

There are thousands more food festivals and fairs throughout the country and the world. I have touched on only a few just to give you the flavor of what's happening and how you can be a part of it all. You will find a few more ideas in Chapter 10, "One More Time (Over 100 Additional Exciting Ideas)." Savor and enjoy. Since we've included a few recipes from some of the food fairs, we couldn't resist including just one last one, probably the most unique, a recipe for making your own chicle gum borrowed from the Daniel Boone Regional Library's "Bubble Gum" book. The resourceful librarians found this recipe in a book which is now out of print, *The Standard American Encyclopedia of Formulas*.

The Store Bought Kind

Chicle Gum: This is purified by boiling water and separating the foreign matter. Flavorings, pepsin, sugar, etc., are worked in under pressure by suitable machinery. Ingredients:

1 lb. gum chicle

2 lbs. sugar

1 lb. glucose

1 lb. caramel butter

First mash and soften the gum at gentle heat. Place the sugar and glucose in a small copper pan; add enough water to dissolve the sugar; set on a fire and cook to 244 degrees F; lift off the fire; add the caramel butter and lastly the gum; mix well into a smooth marble surface, dusting with finely powdered sugar, run through sizing machine to the proper thickness, cut into strips and again into thin slices. If your gum turns out too hard or too soft, change the proportions until it is right.

Or, forget the whole thing and pick up store-bought gum at the local candy store!

THEMATIC FESTIVALS

Thematic festivals and fairs are held to celebrate all sorts of things: a well-known literary or historical figure's birthday, a particular harvest, a season, whatever.

The forthcoming stories about Huck Finn days, The Wonderful World of Oz, Chinese New Year Festival, the Woolybear Festival, and the International Whistle-Off could just as well have been included in the thematic programing section of the book. But, I felt that, although they were built around specific themes, it was their uniqueness as festivals that made them worthy of inclusion in this book.

Huck Finn Days

The year 1985 was deemed by many to be "Mark Twain Year" because it was the 150th anniversary of Twain's birth and the centenary of his book *The Adventures of Huckleberry Finn*. Here were two very good reasons to celebrate.

Hannibal's Celebration

The most natural place for the celebration was Hannibal, Missouri, where Mark Twain (Samuel Clemens) grew up. (Actually, he was born in Florida, Missouri, about a 45-minute ride from Hannibal.) Twain used several Hannibal locales as the background to many of his famous stories, including the whitewashed, wooden two-story home that was the setting for *Tom Sawyer* and the small islands near the town, like "Jackson's Island," where Tom, Huck, and Becky were trapped with Injun Joe. (A steamboat called the "Mark Twain" takes tourists around the island.)

That might be enough for a short visit, but for a special celebration, you must have more to offer. And Hannibal did. The special events began on May 4 and ran through September 8, 1985. Entertainment was high on the list, with daily street performers, Central Park bandstand concerts at noon and 4:30 p.m., theme center stage performers at 2 p.m. and 7 p.m., Main Street puppet theatre, and an "Everybody's Parade" one weekend morning. There were fireworks every Friday and Saturday night. Knowing that most people come to events with families, the celebrants set up a family activity center with 1800s games, frog-jumping contests, fence-painting competitions, youth performers, a storyteller's tree, and an arts and crafts exhibition.

Other highlights included a National Riverlife Music Festival with the emphasis on jazz on June 14–15, blues on June 26–27, swing on June 28–29, Dixieland on July 19–20, and bluegrass on August 15–17. On June 23, the St. Louis Symphony played the "Mark Twain Suite." The Jaycees held National Tom Sawyer Days with all kinds of events from July 3–7. The American Sternwheelers Riverfest Regatta was held July 11–14. There was even a rock weekend on August 2–3 with "Rollin' on a River." From August 31–September 2, "Hometown American Days" were commemorated, and on November 30, actor Hal Holbrook appeared in his one-man show, *Mark Twain Tonight*. The Hannibal celebration was the most publicized, and more than likely the biggest of the Mark Twain birthday commemorations held in 1985.

Twain's Connecticut Connections

Two cities in Connecticut also lay claim to Mark Twain. Twain lived in Hartford on Farmington Avenue for 17 years. The attractive house still stands and plays host to visitors the world over. It is a Victorian mansion and probably not a place Huck Finn would feel comfortable in. A "fancy place" with many rooms, this house was purchased during Twain's rich period and was decorated with elaborate furnishings, many from castles in Europe. Twain never managed to write anything in this house, but he did create the characters of Tom and Huck there.

In 1985, in commemoration of the 100th anniversary of the American publication of *The Adventures of Huckelberry Finn*, the Mark Twain Memorial Society presented opening performances of William Perry's *Adventures of Huckleberry Finn*, filmed for the Public Broadcasting System at the New Canaan Playhouse on June 28. The film was shown at the United Artists Theater in Manchester, Connecticut, from June 30 through July 13.

There were special summer workshops and a Pudd'nhead Wilson Day Camp for youngsters at the Mark Twain Memorial Center during July and August. In September, the Women's Committee sponsored a "Mark Twain in the West" tour. A dramatization of *Huckleberry Finn* was presented on Connecticut Public Radio in November. "Huckleberry Finn," a lecture by Dr. Shelley F. Fishkin, professor at the University of Texas, Austin, was offered at the Mark Twain Memorial Center in late November. On November 26, the center held a party celebrating Twain's 150th birthday.

In 1908, Twain moved to a mansion near Redding, Connecticut, where he died two years later. The house burned down in 1923. But Redding remembers those Twain years fondly. On Memorial Day, 1985, the town had a Mark Twain float in its annual parade; on July 7, there was a concert and a play by the Mashed Potato Players. In remembrance of Tom Sawyer, a fence was whitewashed on the town green. The Mark Twain Library displayed Twain memorabilia, including some of his books, photographs, a walking stick, and a lap desk.

Elmira's Claim to Twain

"For every page that Mark Twain wrote in Hartford [CT], he wrote 30 pages in Elmira [NY]," says Holly Hewitt, director of tourism for the Elmira Chamber of Commerce. Needless to say, Elmira is proud of its Twain connection as well. In celebration of the 150th anniversary of Mark Twain's birthday, the town promoted a Mark Twain Festival Summer in 1985 and declared that an annual festival would take place in Elmira thereafter.

Calling their area "Mark Twain Country," the chamber of commerce explained their Twain connection, this way: "Twain married Olivia Langdon of Elmira and spent many summers at the Langdon's Quarry Farm which overlooks the Chemung Valley. Here the author penned his most famous works, including *Tom Sawyer, The Prince and the Pauper, A Connecticut Yankee in King Arthur's Court, Roughing It, Life on the Mississippi,* and *The Adventures of Huckleberry Finn.*

During the Elmira celebration, there were parades with Mark Twain floats, exhibits in the county museum, and, in September, a weekend "Festival of Cats" in honor of the greatest cat lover in American literary history. "Mark Twain owned 19 cats at one time," Hewitt told a *New York Times* reporter. "Once, when he didn't have any, he rented three from a farmer."

The Chemung County Chamber of Commerce planned nearly 60 different Twain events from May through September 1985, concluding with a special Mark Twain birthday celebration, a variety show of drama and music held at the Clemens Center in Elmira on November 30. What would a Huck Finn celebration be without a Huck Finn river race? The Chemung River served as the course, and there were three races: Junior Class Race, Tanglewood Challenge Race, and the Huck Finn Open. The Huck Finn Open was probably the most entertaining. It was open to any seaworthy vessel including rafts, rowboats, bathtubs, sailboats...anything not powered by an internal combustion engine or electric motor. If you inquired about the Twain doings in Elmira, you were certain to receive at least 12 different pieces of promotional material! Located in the Finger Lakes region of New York State, Elmira may be considered a small town, but it certainly does a *big* Twain celebration and promotion.

If you were looking for something a bit more academic while in Elmira, you could have turned to Elmira College, which had its own commemoration, "Elmira College Celebrates Mark Twain." This celebration began in April with a workshop on "The Teaching of Huckleberry Finn," bus trips to Connecticut Mark Twain sites, Elderhostel courses on Mark Twain, and literature lectures on Mark Twain from experts in the field. Twain's wife, Olivia, attended the Preparatory Department of Elmira College from 1859 to 1860. His niece, Ida Langdon, was a professor of English literature there from 1920 to 1942 and emeritus from 1945 to 1964. Twain's father-in-law, Jervis Langdon, was a member of the executive committee of the board of trustees at the college.

Mark Twain, had he been vacationing in Elmira in the summer of 1985, might have shied away from the goings-on for his 150th birthday.

Used by permission of the Chemung County Chamber of Commerce.

Vendors were out in full force offering Twain-related fare. The League of Women Voters of Chemung County re-created Aunt Polly's "Apple Pie Kitchen" and sold Tom Sawyer's favorite dessert by the slice. The Horseheads Historical Society offered sweatshirts with cartoonist Zim's caricature of Twain and replicas of the head of Twain which appears on his monument in Woodlawn Cemetery, a bas-relief designed by sculptor Ernfred Anderson. The Chemung Chapter of the Daughters of the American Revolution had Mark Twain notepaper for sale, the Arnot Art Museum offered a variety of Mark Twain Country souvenirs, and the Chamber of Commerce offered Mark Twain Country bumper stickers and buttons.

Used by permission of the Chemung County Chamber of Commerce.

California's Twain Connection

Bishop, California, seems to have no tangible connection to either Mark Twain or Tom Sawyer or even Huck Finn. But for the past 16 years, the Bishop Chamber of Commerce has been holding "Huck Finn Days" in this small California town just for the fun of it. A river runs through the town, and residents thought it would be a great idea to use the river in some sort of celebration. The chamber of commerce formed an "idea" committee, which came up with "Huck Finn Days."

The committee officially called it the "Huck Finn River Festival." Contestants rode their inner tubes, rafts, kayaks, or canoes down the Owens River through Bishop. Open to all ages and sexes, the race drew from 200 to 300 entrants and about 9,000 spectators cheered on the sidelines. All enjoyed a barbecue afterward. There was an entry fee of $8 for adults and $5 for children. (This included race entry, decoration, and Western barbecue.) "We don't make money on this. We just break even," said Ellen Titus of the Bishop Chamber of Commerce.

At 10:30 a.m., canoe and kayak entrants began the race; at 11 a.m., the other entrants followed. There were prizes for the best raft design and the best-decorated tube entry. It usually takes about an hour to an hour and a half to complete the race. There is nothing too historical or literary about this Huck Finn celebration, but he is remembered by all in this outdoor event. Although small in size, the town promotes this event and others in a big way. Fliers are created and distributed; news releases are sent out regularly; mailing lists are updated and used; locals are involved and lend support; and a monthly newsletter informs them all on what's happening in Bishop.

Used by permission of the Bishop Chamber of Commerce.

Comments

You too can celebrate Mark Twain, Tom Sawyer, and Huck Finn anytime you want. A birthday celebration is the most eventful, but you could simply hold a Tom Sawyer frog-jumping contest or Tom Sawyer fence-painting day in conjunction with some other 1800s games and contests for a family day festival in the summer or fall. Or, go cultural. Have some book reviews and discussions of Twain's books; show some of the movies made from his books; hold an old-fashioned covered dish supper along with some of these activities. The sky's the limit. If you missed out on Mark Twain's 150th birthday, celebrate his next one...or wait for his 200th!

The Wonderful World of Oz

"Follow the yellow brick road to the Detroit Main Library and spend Christmas in Oz! See all the original Oz books and their sequels! See posters from the Oz stage plays and movies! See models of the Emerald City, Dorothy's farmhouse and the witch's castle! See a Christmas tree decorated with Oz ornaments! ... Plan a holiday visit to Oz at the Detroit Public Library!" read the public service announcement sent out by Detroit Public Library public relations director Jim Dance.

Sound enticing? Six thousand adults and children thought so and came to the opening of the library exhibit on December 7, 1983, between 5 p.m. and 7 p.m. The opening coincided with the annual "Noel Night" in the Cultural Center (made up of the library, the Detroit Institute of Arts, and the Detroit Historical Museum). The choice of Christmas for the Oz exhibit and programing was particularly appropriate, since the tradition of "a new Oz book for Christmas" was established in the 1900s when generations of children came to expect a new volume of the ongoing series under the Christmas tree every year.

The Main Library of the Detroit Public Library is a large and beautiful building, with 19 exhibit cases. Every one of them was jam-packed with Oz memorabilia: 14 original books by L. Frank Baum, record covers, toys and other collectibles based on the Oz characters, Oz on stage and in the movies. Over 300 books, illustrations, and artifacts, assembled in conjunction with the International Wizard of Oz Club were also on display and would be through January 14. The exhibits were just part of the *big* Oz show!

For the opening, members of the nearby Greenfield Village Players, who were staging *The Wizard of Oz* in December, roamed the library in costume, greeting youngsters and giving them certificates good for free French fries, donated by a hamburger chain. There were representatives from the International Wizard of Oz Club on one of the floors near the exhibits, answering questions about the display materials and about the club. Children 12 and under were invited to "Guess Who I Am?" as the actors in Oz costumes passed by. Children won a "lucky penny" for right guesses. The children's department ran an "Ozzy" boutique selling, among other things, paperback books, toys, notepaper, and encyclopedia raffle tickets.

There was more. The Renaissance Brass Quintet performed twice during the opening night's gala. The Recreation Players presented a vest-pocket version of the *Sound of Music* in the Friends' auditorium. There was a "December" photography show by Robert Kangas in the photogallery. Jim Dance, the library's musical PR director, played the organ continuously (with a few breaks!) in the Cass Concourse of the library. And, yes, there were refreshments. It was a big night!

Comments

Of course, everything has to have a beginning. Jim Dance had read a small item in the local newspaper about a year before the library's Oz event about the International Wizard of Oz Club. He wrote to the club and asked if they would be interested in putting on a display of members' books and memorabilia. The next thing he knew he was being inundated with first editions and all kinds of collectibles. Even the news media contacted Dance. Through the club's contacts, a film company in Seattle, Washington, which at that time was making a new *Wizard of Oz* feature cartoon, wrote and offered the library (for sale) an animated library public service announcement with Oz characters, which they had originally done for the Seattle Public Library. The Friends of the Detroit Public Library came up with the needed $1,500, and the local TV stations duplicated the tape and ran it at no cost to the library.

The library also sent out the usual stream of news releases and got good coverage. They produced in-house promotional bookmarks, fliers, and posters about the "Christmas in Oz" special events and exhibits on bright green and red paper. The library does not have a newsletter, so it is dependent on the local newspapers to run its calendar of events. The library does mailings to special interest groups and Friends and distributes the rest of its promotional materials in-house, through the library system and other institutions such as the Detroit Institute of Arts.

An interesting aside to this story is that, during the 40s and 50s, the library made headlines by refusing to stock the Oz books on the grounds that there were so many better contemporary children's stories being published. But times and tastes change, and now the Detroit Public Library recog-

Used by permission of the Detroit Public Library.

nizes *The Wizard of Oz* as an authentic children's classic and has approved as much of the series as is presently in print in paperback editions, for inclusion in its children's room.

According to Dance, the Oz promotion produced thousands of dollars' worth of good publicity and cost only about $500 (spent mostly for printing and postage). How long does it take to plan an event like "Christmas in Oz"? "It took 14 months in the planning," said Dance. "But, we've also been known to put one [a special event] together practically overnight," he added. "Looking back at some of DPL's special events that I would modestly call successful, I would say they were so because to be creative is often to be cooperative," stated Dance. "For some of our best projects, we didn't need major grants, just a little incidental money squeezed out of our regular budget because we had cooperation."

The Detroit Public Library works with many clubs, organizations, and educational institutions on many projects. One year the fall event had an Italian theme and the cosponsorship of the Italian Consulate. The library's role in this special event was to celebrate Pinocchio's Centennial, which effectively tied in the literary with the ethnic. Another fall, they saluted "1929, The Last Glad Year" and planned the library's observance around the best-sellers of the 1920s. Their neighbor, the Art Institute, participated by holding a special exhibit of 1920s fashions, and the Historical Museum put together a photo show of Detroit scenes and people of that period.

A piece of concluding advice from Dance: "It is generally better to do a smaller-scale activity on your own premises than a large-scale activity away from it where your identity may be lost, such as in a civic arena."

The theme of *The Wizard of Oz* is such a universally appealing idea and one that can be adapted by just about anyone. Create your own yellow brick road and Oz Festival!

Chinese New Year Festival

Ethnic fairs and festivals have been popular for years. Your community need not be large or be of a particular ethnic origin to celebrate with an ethnic fair or festival. It does help if there are some resource people, either in your community or from a nearby area, who can provide guidance. But, you can do it without any resource people except you, your committee, and your enthusiasm! I remember my first festival. Our district PTA group sponsored a "Foods around the World" event, and a cookbook with all the recipes from the festival was published (on a mimeograph machine) and sold. All of us who were members chose a particular country and made a particular dish from that country, and then invited our families to an evening tasting celebration. This was a minor event but very successful in a community that had many ethnic groups.

I have always loved the pageantry of the Chinese New Year celebrations held throughout the country, especially those held in San Francisco and New York City. Our community, East Meadow, is about 30 miles from New York City; the Chinese population is quite small. But, I know our community. Give them an interesting event and they'll be there!

Luckily, I had a head start because I was already taking Chinese cooking lessons from a young Chinese woman who owned an Oriental food and gift shop in our community. So I was able to arrange a wok cookery program with my instructor, Zen Leung. Knowing that one day I planned to have a Chinese New Year Festival at our library, I had been squirreling away all kinds of newspaper clippings about activities in the city and on Long Island. From this pile, I learned about the Sumi-E East Society of America, which had a chapter on Long Island. Their purpose is to foster and encourage an appreciation of Oriental brush painting. Contact was made, and I arranged for them to exhibit their members' works for the month with an opening/reception on the first Sunday in February. This would be the lead program or event.

My luckiest find was the Chinese Culture Center of Long Island, and what a bounty of programs came my way through them! I wanted a Lion Dance on the same day of the art opening/reception. Also, to appeal to the teenagers in the community, I planned a Bruce Lee movie night with a Kung Fu demonstration with Shifu Tonny Kusmotono and his students from the Chinese Center. In his limited English and with the aid of a translator, he also presented a short talk on this martial art. For $100, I got both the Lion Dance and the Kung Fu demonstration. But all of us in the community got much more. I found the people in the Chinese Center to be interested, helpful, and most friendly. In fact, we got to be such friends that a group of us joined the center in their official New Year's celebration at the Mah Jong restaurant, where we experienced our first authentic Chinese New Year's dinner. It was quite an experience.

The Chinese celebration program went like this: One Friday night, the film *The Good Earth*, with Paul Muni and Luise Rainer, was shown to a full house. Many of the younger members of the audience had never seen this classic. Through one of the local professors, I learned about a Chinese experimental theatre group, and they too came and performed one evening. Not too many of the public were familiar with Chinese music, and since East Meadow was not too far from Chinatown in Manhattan, I was able to contact the Chinese Music Ensemble. They performed on a Friday evening at our library, and not only did they introduce the people to Oriental music, but to instruments totally foreign to the audience. The ensemble members patiently answered many questions after the concert. It was a unique experience.

The wok cookery program was in the daytime, and those attending enjoyed tasting the many wok dishes created. The recipes were mimeographed and distributed at the program and on the main floor of the library during the month.

For fun and fortune, the library also held a month-long "Guess How Many Fortune Cookies in the Jar" contest. People love to count jelly beans, pretzels, peanuts, apples, what have you. Thousands of people played the guessing game. The winner was a man by the name of...Fred Lee! His prize was a wok set donated by Zen Leung, our cooking instructor. Lee, who is from a neighboring town, thanked me with a letter and a copy of his favorite Chinese recipe.

Comments

The Chinese New Year Festival celebration was widely promoted, and the media, newspapers, radio, and local television were more than generous. They liked the gimmicks in the programing, especially those having to do with the Sunday art opening. I knew an art opening would attract a certain kind of audience; we were also having a brush painting demonstration during the afternoon. But I decided to add two other features to appeal to families: the Lion Dance and the serving of rice cakes and brewed black tea as part of the reception. The Lion Dance was performed before the brush painting demonstration. Dancers continued up the stairs to the main floor of the library where people were reading, browsing, and doing serious research. Although it was a rather noisy intrusion, most people stopped and watched and applauded.

The community talked about this ethnic month for weeks and hoped it would be repeated. And why not? After all, half of the work was already done. I had unearthed a wonderful directory of Oriental talents and resources. But, it's best to wait a few years sometimes before repeating an event. In 1986 I opened up my files and planned another celebration of the Chinese New Year with some of the same attractions...plus some new ideas I've discovered. In 1986, the films *From Mao to Mozart* and *The Karate Kid* were shown. The Chinese Music Ensemble returned for another concert. Another martial arts program was held for the teens. A book/discussion night was added with a speaker, Gloria Yuin, talking about Bette Bao Lord's novel, *Spring Moon*. Another daytime Chinese cooking program was presented with printed recipes given away, and one lucky person went home with a complete Chinese dinner cooked by the program presenter. And, people, thousands again, played the "Guess-How-Many-Fortune Cookies" in the jar contest. The prize to the winner was a Chinese cookbook and a box of fortune cookies. The Sumi-E Oriental brush painters held another art show at the library, and this time we served Chinese almond cookies along with the brewed black tea. But, alas, the one thing missing was the Lion Dance. For several months, a member of the Chinese Culture Center tried to round up enough teen members to again perform the Lion Dance for us. Not enough volunteers were to be found. Since viewing the Oriental brush paintings, many people became interested in taking a brush painting workshop at the library. This, too, was provided on a Monday night. In 1986, we found a whole new audience for our programs, plus some of the community who had attended the first celebration.

One of the extras for the 1979 celebration was the publication of a Chinese restaurant guide combining Long Island and Chinatown restaurants. The list was compiled by two members of the community, Janis Wong and Zen Leung. In 1985, the library arranged two separate Chinatown bus trips. Both groups toured a Chinese fortune cookie factory, ate dim sum in a Chinese restaurant, and shopped in the many Oriental food and gift stores along Mott Street. Our Chinatown guide, Marilyn Buccola (see, you don't have to be Chinese), is also a Chinese cuisine expert. She also did our Chinese cooking program in 1986.

Since the time the first Chinese New Year festival was held, many people in the community have traveled to China, and there has been much written about the country and its culture. Our display cases exhibited Chinese artifacts and collectibles from the collections of a former library board member who is a tour escort for China trips. The interest exists in just about any community. You may not have a Chinatown nearby or even a Chinese community member, but the information and the ideas are there. Implement them to suit your purpose...and, don't stop at China. There's a whole wide world to celebrate!

Woollybear Festival

Since there are thousands of festivals and fairs and this book was not meant to include them all, I'd like to conclude this chapter with brief descriptions of two festivals. They represent some of the varied festivals and contests from which you can take ideas.

Whether or not you're interested in the weather and its forecasters, you might enjoy the annual Woollybear Festival held in Vermilion, Ohio, usually on the last Sunday in September. A woollybear, for you city folks, is a caterpillar, and according to my informants from Vermilion, they are indigenous to all of the United States and spend the winter in the larval (caterpillar) state. In spring, they munch on plantain weed, their favorite food, then spin a cocoon and emerge as pale-yellow tiger moths in the summer. Folklore says that if the rust-colored band in the middle of the woollybear is wide, it "portends very little snow in the winter ahead. If the black or dark-brown on the ends of the caterpillar crowd the rust-color into a narrow stripe, that presages a heavy winter." So they say.

In other words, fat and fuzzy caterpillars are said to forecast a very cold winter, while skinny caterpillars herald a mild winter. The most likely cosponsor for such a Woollybear Festival would seem to be a local television weather forecaster. In the 1984 festival, Dick Goddard of Cleveland's WJKW-TV (Channel 8) was the person. He even distributed funny "Official Dick Goddard Woollybear Watcher-TV 8" stickers for people to wear.

So, what do you do at a Woollybear Festival? A lot. Although the festival officially opened with a big parade at 1:30 p.m., there were some preliminary events such as the annual Kiwanis Woollybear Classic 10K run. From 11 a.m. to noon, the Woollybear 500 Caterpillar Race preliminaries were held. Bill Boehm's Singing Angels entertained on stage at noon. At 12:30 p.m., St. Helen's Unicycle Drill performed with the circus calliope in the town square; there were various band concerts in other parts of town.

The parade featured 10 high school bands plus the University of Akron Marching Zips, kids in woollybear costumes, radio and TV celebrities, bagpipe bands, and the usual clowns and horses. More entertainment came on stage when the Cedar Point Amazement Park Revue performed at 3:15 p.m. A short time later, the judging for the King and Queen Woollybears was held, plus animal woollybear look-alikes. At 4:30 p.m., the finals of the Woollybear 500 Caterpillar Race were held. At 5 p.m., people gathered at Schwenson's Bakery for the woollybear cake decorating judging plus chocolate chip cookie judging. The rock band Hemisphere entertained during this period.

This five-hour festival drew over 98,000 people. There was no charge for admittance. Food was provided by area service organizations (volunteer fire department, etc.), and souvenir booths were staffed by the local PTA groups and others. If you wanted to spend a few dollars, you could, but the fun came for free, and somewhere along the line, on the stage, the official Woollybear Festival folklore forecaster, Leon "Bad News" Bates, gave his weather outlook for the winter. The whole festival is a good excuse for people to get together for one last time "before the snow flies."

International Whistle-Off

This is a "melodic whistling competition," and it draws contestants from the United States, Mexico, Canada, Sweden, England, and Australia. The first "whistle-off" was held in 1977 when a computer firm envisioned a contest between whistlers and a whistling computer. After a year's hiatus and the elimination of the computer, the Carson City (Nevada) Chamber of Commerce knew a good thing when they heard it. They declared it an annual event.

The headline on their news release for 1984 read, "Whistlers from All over the World Pucker-Up for Annual Competition." There was a limit of 60 contestants; they competed in any of the four categories: Solo Classical Music, Solo Contemporary Music, Solo Novelty Whistling, and Dual Competition. You were allowed to use your hands or fingers. It was a two-day event held on the last weekend of September. Preliminary competitions were held all day Saturday until 5 p.m. From 9 a.m. until noon on Sunday, the preliminaries continued; the exciting finals began at 1 p.m. and ran until 4 p.m., when the winners were announced and the Grand Champion was chosen.

Admission to the event was free; spectators brought blankets and chairs or sat on bleachers or park benches to watch the whistlers perform. There was plenty of food and drink for sale and lots of entertainment in between whistling. In 1984, well-known blind whistler Fred Lowery was there. Whistle-Off audiences were also entertained by Dr. Horatio Q. Birdbath, who was given his name by Spike Jones, the zany bandleader of the 1940s and 50s. "Doc" created the shriek for Cheetah of Tarzan fame and howls for Lassie and Bonzo in the movies. Whistler/singer Francisco Hernandez from Mexico also entertained.

They did a professional job of promotion. An attractive brochure listed the rules and regulations of the competition. The International Whistle-Off of the Carson City Chamber of Commerce had its own attractively designed stationery. They mean business in Carson City. They send press kits all over the country to all of the media. They also use paid advertising. But it still comes down to local support and involvement. Community support and involvement are the two most important ingredients in all special events, whether they are multimedia events or one-day fairs. There are contests, festivals, and fairs worldwide...be a part of the fun and creativity!

RESOURCES

General for Games, Contests, Festivals, and Fairs

Dollar, Ken; Reichl, Ruth; and Subtle, Susan. *The Contest Book.* New York: Harmony Books, 1979.

McWhirter, Norris, ed/comp. *1985 Guinness Book of World Records.* New York: Sterling Publishing Inc., 1985.

Wasserman, Paul, managing ed. *Festival Sourcebook*. 2nd ed. Detroit, MI: Gale Research, 1984.

The World's Largest Games

Public Relations. R.H. Macy's, Herald Square, New York, NY 10001.

Animal Contests

Baker, Virginia S., coordinator. The Mayor's Office of Adventures in Fun, 250 City Hall, Baltimore, MD 21202.

Food Festivals

Popcorn

Pierce, Roberta, coordinator. Popcorn Festival, 601 E. Lincolnway, P.O. Box 330, Valparaiso, IN 46383.

Popcorn Institute, 111 E. Wacker Dr., Chicago, IL 60611.

Rothstein, Cathy, director of advertising and promotion, KETC, 6996 Millbrook Blvd., St. Louis, MO 63130.

Brussel Sprouts

LaFrank, Glenn, public relations. Santa Cruz Boardwalk, 400 Beach St., Santa Cruz, CA 95060.

Carrots

Holtville Chamber of Commerce, P.O. Box 185, Holtville, CA 92250.

Garlic

Gilroy Garlic Festival Association, Inc., P.O. Box 2311, Gilroy, CA 95021.

Pasta

Pastaville USA, Box 940, 200 S. Broadway, Minot, ND 58701.

Bubble Gum

Caney, Steven. *Kid's America*. New York: Workman Publishing, 1978.

Hendrickson, Robert. *The Great American Chewing Gum Book*. Radnor, PA: Chilton Book Co., 1976.

Hiscox, Gardner D., and Sloane, T. O'Conor, eds. *Henley's Twentieth Century Book of Formulas, Processes and Trade Secrets*. New York: Norman W. Henley Publishing Co., 1955.

Hyde, Linda, public relations. Daniel Boone Regional Library, 100 W. Broadway, Columbia, MO 65201.

McLoone, Margo. *Sports Cards, Collecting, Trading and Playing*. New York: Holt, Rinehart and Winston, 1979.

Thematic Festivals

Huck Finn Days

Hannibal Visitors and Convention Bureau, 308 N. Main St., P.O. Box 624, Hannibal, MO 63401.

Hewitt, Holly. Chemung Chamber of Commerce, 224 William St., Elmira, NY 14901.

Mark Twain Memorial, 351 Farmington Ave., Hartford, CT 06105.

Titus, Ellen. Bishop Chamber of Commerce, 690 N. Main St., Bishop, CA 93514.

The Wonderful World of Oz

The International Wizard of Oz Club, 220 N. 11th St., Escanaba, MI 49829.

Chinese New Year Festival

Liebold, Louise, public relations. East Meadow Public Library, Front St. & East Meadow Ave., East Meadow, NY 11554.

Woollybear Festival

Goddard, Dick. WJKW TV, 5800 S. Marginal Rd., Cleveland, OH 44103.

International Whistle-Off

Wood, Leona. Carson City Chamber of Commerce, 1191 S. Carson St., Carson City, NV 89701.

Chapter 7
Publicity and the Media

- Some Thoughts on Publicity
- Mailing Lists and Promotion
- News Releases
- Press Kits
- Public Service Announcements
- Radio and Television Interviews
- Some Thoughts on Image
- Good Graphics
- Newsletters, Brochures, and Fliers
- Basic Tools for the Do-It-Yourselfer

Good public relations should be everyone's concern. But what is public relations? There are over 100,000 professional public relations practitioners in this country, and they don't all agree on one simple definition. I offer you one that has been accepted by many and repeated often. Denny Griswold, editor of a weekly newsletter, *PR News*, developed this one: "Public relations is the management function which evaluates public attitudes, identifies the policies and procedures of an individual or an organization with the public interest, and plans and executes a program of action to earn public understanding."

Want something simpler? Someone in the public relations field once said "public relations is doing good and getting credit for it." That's true, but it's a bit too simple. Public relations is communication. It's a persuasive action. It's promoting goodwill, and doing "good" and getting credit for it. It's responsibility. It's planning. It's evaluating. It's understanding and being aware of who your "public" is. You see, it gets more complex as you think and talk about it. The "field," I am happy to say, is filled primarily with fine and dedicated people. But then there is a whole tribe (who should be lost!) of people who claim to be "in public relations."

You don't have to be a professional in the public relations field to develop a positive public relations program for your company, organization, or club. If you are the one chosen to do the public relations, begin with a policy. Working with administrators, trustees, and anyone else on your staff who feels they should have input, develop on paper a public relations policy. What is it you are trying to do? What do you believe in? Who is the public you are trying to reach? How do you plan to reach them? Once your standards are set, you can then go on to plan a public relations program.

Some things to remember: Don't neglect evaluation. Even a good thing should be evaluated from time to time. When everything is down on paper, be certain that the employees know of any changes in your public relations program. If your employees deal directly with the general public, impress upon them from time to time how important their job is, that they are doing "public relations" each time they answer the telephone or deal with a patron or customer. However, suggest that they leave formulation of public relations policies to administration and the public relations department.

The public relations person or department should always keep everyone on staff informed about a new service or product or special event. Administration, in turn, should always keep public relations informed of any important changes in the company or its policies. The public relations person should not be the last to know. The media will wonder about your internal communications network if they contact the public relations person about a change in the company, and the public relations person doesn't know a thing about it! It happens, so don't let it happen to you. Communications should always be open, internally and externally, for a successful public relations program.

SOME THOUGHTS ON PUBLICITY

So, then what's publicity? Publicity is part of public relations, and its most important ingredient is the press or news release. Publicity is part of promotion. Promotion is similar to marketing. And marketing is a form of selling. So, when you send out a successful news release and the media picks it up and gives you air or print space, you've gotten free publicity—advertising you would normally pay for.

Of course, there's good news and bad news. It is the public relations person's job to turn the bad news around if possible or at least to present it in a more favorable light. Everyone loves good news; it's the bad news that takes special handling. You see examples of this every day in your newspapers and on radio and television news programs. Corporate officials, politicians, and government are best at turning bad news into good news...they can't afford not to. Think of yourself as a business; this way you will handle your public relations, publicity, and promotion in a professional manner. If you can, hire a public relations consultant, possibly just for a special project or to help you set up some guidelines. If you can afford it, you might want to have a consultant on a retainer. Check credentials. Lots of people say they can "do PR." Yet, many can't even write a simple news release. Or you can write news releases yourself by just following some simple rules and practicing.

In practicing good public relations and promotion, you learn to make the most of a good thing. Overlook nothing. If someone in your business community has promised to donate a sizable check to your organization, don't just send out a story stating this information. With camera in hand, you and the representative from your organization should go to the company and have a formal acceptance of the donation with both people in the photo. Your local weeklies will use the story and photo if it's good. Don't expect your daily newspaper to send a photographer and a reporter for a story such as this one. If you feel the event warrants it and you can afford it, hire a professional photographer who will then make up the proper black-and-white glossy prints needed. Once in a while, it's worth spending money on a photographer. It all depends on your budget.

Publicity is free, but remember, it takes time and money to get it. You do not pay for air time or print space, but you must write the release, make multiple copies, address and mail it, and even spend some time on the phone occasionally with editors or make personal appearances taking your copy directly to the media. If you are your own photographer too, it might pay to take some courses in news photography, or at least learn from an experienced photographer how to handle and use your camera. A good news photo can tell the story better sometimes then a full-length news story. Look at the popularity of television news—it's mostly visual. Leaf through your local newspapers and carefully examine the photographs and analyze why these particular photos were used. Read some of the stories in the newspaper, especially the "soft news" items. Soft news is when a local organization holds a duck-racing contest. "Hard news" is when a plane is hijacked. The hard news takes priority and usually makes the first three or four pages of the newspaper, unless the special event is a truly local special event. Small weekly newspapers will feature local events right on the front page; after all, it is not their job to compete with *The New York Times* or the *Los Angeles Times*. The local community is their focus, and the local newspaper should be your focus. However, sometimes your event is so spectacular that it makes the "big time."

Promotion is a combination of all of these factors. If you are practicing good public relations, getting good publicity, then you are promoting your cause or your company in the right way. Personally, I feel you can never promote enough. You never reach everyone you want with one effort. People forget. Their lives are busy. They need to be reminded. So, you tell them your story in many ways. Begin with your newsletter, if you have one. (This chapter includes a discussion of the hows of publishing a newsletter.) At least the people receiving it are on your mailing list and know of your existence. Then send out your news releases. If the event is part of an ongoing series, begin with a general story about the entire series and then feature the first event. This can go out anytime from one month to six weeks in advance. Follow this with two to three more news releases for the other events in the series. By this time, you probably have created brochures, fliers, and posters related to your event. If your budget allows, you have them distributed in-house and every place else you can in the community. If you have a Friends group, you might want to send them a personal invitation, which may simply be the brochure or flier. If the event revolves around a special interest subject, then you should definitely send out a mailing to local clubs, etc., whose purpose and interest is the special event you are presenting. Their membership will then hear about it and your audience will build.

MAILING LISTS AND PROMOTION

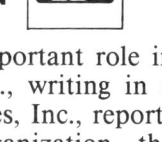

Mailing lists can play a very important role in your promotion. John J. Patafio, Jr., writing in a tipsheet from Nassau Mailing Services, Inc., reports that "according to the Gallup Organization, the average family (out of a sampling of 1,500) receives 9.8 pieces of advertising during a seven-day period." Direct mail is personal; if it's interesting, informative, and attractive, it will be read. Many organizations use *only* direct mailings for their fund-raising. With the right list, you can raise funds or promote an event.

I would like to cite two examples of good personal promotion and the use of mailing lists. Out in Orient, Long Island, there is a performing group called Theatre in the Works. Orient has a population of several hundred people and is at the end of the north fork of Long Island. You can't go much farther east before you'll be in the ocean. If you operate a theatre in such a spot, how would you develop an audience...and make a living from your theatre? The first thing you do is have a "side" business as your mainstay. Norman and Sandra Dietz are actors who decided to leave the city life and settle in a more serene setting. But they still wanted to perform and make a living. So they bought a town landmark, an ice cream parlor. They brought it back to life with some charming alterations and added a tiny stage in one corner. The Ice Cream Works operates from May through November. Theatre and musical programs are presented in two series, one from January to April on a monthly basis and the other in the summer months after the shop is closed on Saturday nights. During other months, they might take the show on the road. During the holiday season, Norman does Dickens's *A Christmas Carol* for six weeks to filled houses.

The Dietzes had built up a following when they were performing in New York City, and from that they developed a mailing list of over 2,000 names. Norman is the writer/creator of most of the dramatic and comic presentations. He is also the graphic artist, news release writer, promotional director, ice cream scooper, and cleaner of the unisex restroom. He is savvy to the whys and hows of advertising and promotion. He sends out news releases, mostly to local weeklies, *The New York Times*, and *Newsday*. His tiny advertising budget pays for small ads in the local weeklies. He designs the promotional brochures, which are used for the mailing list. The brochures are also available in retail establishments in neighboring towns. As you can see from the two promotional brochures, they are skillfully designed. One is a self-mailer and the other is a program (*Worksbill*).

The mailing list is composed of people whom Norman calls "our people," people who have come to at least one of their shows and filled out a mailing list card. The audience comes from all parts of Long Island and some from as far as New York City.

Theatre in the Works attracts a special kind of audience and Norman knows this, so his promotion and theatrical presentations are directed with these facts in mind. Norman says it best: "I think we have an operation that is unique, and I think one of our strong points is that our promotion, and our product, are both classy, aimed at people who like nice things and who find it difficult to find theatrical experiences that are personal and tasteful. Theatre for me is a party where I'm the host and the audience is composed of my personal guests. I think of Theatre in the Works as an occasion when friends get together and celebrate their friendship."

As you can see, the Dietzes have found their niche. Theirs is a very personal theatrical experience for the audience and them. Norman meets and greets people and bids them a personal farewell after each show. This is not Broadway, but the presentations are professional. The one thing Norman has learned from promotion is that you never sit back and rest. Norman is always looking for that extra something to add to the Ice Cream Works or the Theatre in the Works. In 1985, he added a gourmet hot dog to the menu and called it the "Fifth Avenue Frank"...and the mailing list is also growing!

You read about Sherlock and the piano player in the section "I Love a Mystery!" in Chapter 4, "Thematic Programing." Arthur and Joyce Liebman, the couple who presented the Sherlock show, also know they must be more than performers. To succeed, they must promote themselves. They have developed a mailing list by always having a guest book present when they perform, no matter how sophisticated the setting. And it works. They now have a large follow-

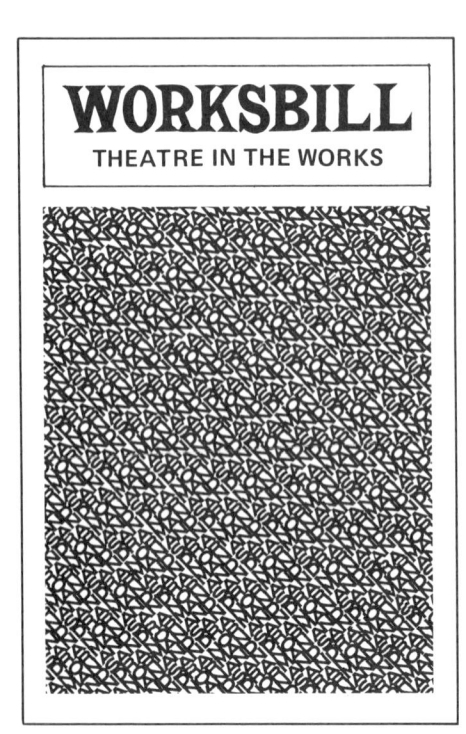

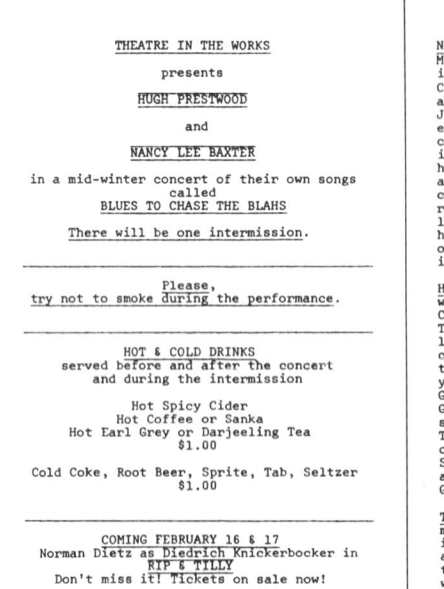

Copy and graphics by Norman Dietz. Used by permission.

Copy and graphics by Norman Dietz. Used by permission.

ing, partly due to their mailing list. And their booking schedule is constantly filled. Not only do they provide an entertaining program, but they also offer a complete promotional package. The package includes a program flier (you just insert your name, etc.); a suggested news release; biographical material about themselves; a black-and-white glossy photograph of them in costume; several appropriate mystery quizzes (camera-ready); and, if requested, a complete bibliography (prepared by Arthur). Realizing there can never be enough promotion, Joyce sends out news releases to the media whenever they are presenting a show "just to be sure."

An Evening With

SHERLOCK HOLMES

Time _____
Date _____
Place _____

Dr. Arthur Liebman, Ph.D.,
Presents

A Nostalgic Evening of Sherlockiana
As the Great Detective Reminisces About
His Life, His Times and His Most Memorable Cases.

An Entertaining and Informative Slide/Lecture with
Nickelodeon Piano Accompaniment by Joyce Ann Liebman

Used by permission of Arthur Liebman.

In conjunction with their Dracula night, the Liebmans hold a raffle at the program. The winner receives a pendant on a chain in the shape of a coffin which contains "authentic" earth from Transylvania, Romania, Dracula's hometown! The winner also receives a certificate of authenticity. The Liebmans play colleges and universities, libraries, museums, theatres, and senior citizen centers. They have traveled to Europe and Alaska doing their thing, mainly because of their promotional efforts and the use of a good mailing list. The Liebmans have also learned how to make use of the media.

NEWS RELEASES

All of this takes careful planning and timing. Remember that when you are dealing with the media, you are dealing with deadlines. Phone your local weeklies and find out when your news release should be in their hands to make next week's edition. Some newspapers have guidelines and tips and suggestions printed in a brochure. If you ask, they will mail it to you. The same holds true for some television and radio stations. Be informed so that you can better inform others. It will help to make your job easier. See the sample press release in this section; here are some simple rules to follow when preparing and sending out news releases.

- All news releases should be typed and double-spaced, with plenty of margin space for the editor's corrections or changes.
- The first paragraph should contain all the essentials of your story: who, what, where, when, and why. A good first paragraph should tell the whole story. Sometimes that is all the space you will get. So make it count.
- Use only one side of the sheet of paper. For page two, use a fresh sheet of paper. Type the organization name, address, and phone number with a contact person's name on the upper right or left side of the first page. Another suggestion: If your building has facilities for the disabled, add the disabled symbol in the upper-right-hand corner of the paper. If there is no smoking in your building, add that symbol also. If the story continues beyond one page, identify the story and the organization again at the top of each page.
- Try to keep your paragraphs and sentences short. Don't keep writing because the news release looks short. You've probably said it all!
- Photocopy your original news release if you are sending out many copies to the various media. Never send out carbon copies.
- Try to have someone else (preferably two people) proofread your copy before sending it out. In most cases, errors are seen by the writer only after the copy is in print. Fingers "slip" in typing. So, proofread carefully. *Never assume anything.* Check your facts, especially the names and dates in a story.
- Always use the full name of an organization or company, not abbreviations. You may know that K of C stands for the Knights of Columbus, but don't assume the editor or the readers of the newspaper do. Spell it out. The same goes with names of people in your story. Always use full names.
- Include photographs if possible. One picture *is* worth a thousand words. Some weeklies will use

good black-and-white "instant" photos. Black-and-white glossies are preferred. All photos should be in focus and have enough contrast for reproduction. Be certain to identify the people in the photo from left to right; front, middle, and back row; sitting and standing. It is preferable not to use too many people in one photograph. Editors prefer "action" photos rather than people lined up in a row doing nothing in particular. I personally like candid shots; most of my best were not set up. Creativity in news photography can also be developed with practice. Type a separate caption sheet for the submitted photograph. One weekly newspaper suggests this: "Rubber cement the lower part of the [caption] sheet to the back of the photograph so that the typed portion is facing the photo. When unfolded, the copy and picture face the editor."

Use a -0- or -30- or ### at the end of your release so the editor will know it's the end.

It's not necessary to have letterhead news release paper. Graphically, it looks better, and there is continuity in your look, your image.

[Boston Harborfest press release sample]

Used by permission of Boston Harborfest.

But what is more important is that you compose and type the release so it's readable and interesting and has all the correct facts.

PRESS KITS

Most professional public relations firms and consultants prepare a press kit for important stories. A press kit is simply a collection of materials (news releases, fact sheets, photographs, etc.) to help make the reporter's and editor's jobs easier when it comes time to cover the event. The fact sheet provides important information about the organization and why you are holding the event. It gives all of the pertinent dates, times, and titles of forthcoming activities and gives them the name(s) of people to contact for further information.

The best time to assemble your press kit is after all of your plans for the event are complete. No reporter or editor is going to use everything you send him or her. The press kit helps them develop their own stories and gives them leads. How much they use will depend on print space, the uniqueness of your event, and what kind of story you gave them. People love to read about other people doing things. Always look for a human interest angle. The media will. You might include a photograph, possibly one taken the year before if it's an annual event. If anything changes with your program plans, be certain to notify the media. You must be dependable.

You don't have to pre-order slick folders for your press kit. Just make the packet neat and attractive with everything as handy as possible. The cheapest kind of folder is a two-pocket file folder found in stationery or dime stores. If you have a company logo sticker, place it on the cover. In the left-hand pocket, place the fact sheet and photographs. In the right-hand pocket, put the news releases, in order of importance. You might want to write a cover letter and clip it to the front of the folder telling who you are and what the kit contains. It's always best to find out beforehand the name of the proper editor or reporter to send your press kit to so that you have more of a chance of it being read by the right person.

PUBLIC SERVICE ANNOUNCEMENTS

Nearly all radio and television stations allow time for public service announcements (PSAs). PSAs are like news releases, only they are much shorter and they are written to be heard rather than to be read. They range in length from 10 to 60 seconds. It may sound like a small amount of time, but you can say a lot in that short time and still get your point across! Here's an easy way to determine what time on air is: Twenty words are about 10 seconds. So, for a 20-second spot, you'll need about 40 words, and for a 30-second announcement, you'll need nearly 60 words. Since air time is highly competitive, you're more likely to get on if you write a good 10-second spot.

Handle the PSA like a news release, putting your name, address, phone number, and contact person's name on top of the release paper. You can do it right on your organization's letterhead paper and let them know if you are a nonprofit organization. First type in the number of seconds. Then be sure to type the words "PUBLIC SERVICE ANNOUNCEMENT" in capital letters right under your letterhead. Here you can also tell them the number of seconds the PSA is and the word count. Keep it simple and make each word count. Remember: the who, what, when, where, and why should always be answered, preferably in your lead sentence. If you submit a 60-second spot, the radio or TV station can cut it back to a 10-second spot. Just be grateful you're on the air and the facts are right. Always remember the words you are writing will be spoken. After you've written your PSA, read it aloud and have a few others do the same. After a while, you'll get the hang of it. Here are a few sample PSAs.

:30 PUBLIC SERVICE ANNOUNCEMENT
for Holiday Festival of Trees

Catch the spirit of the holidays at Hartford's Wadsworth Antheneum's 11th annual Holiday Festival of Trees. Starting Friday, November 30th through Sunday, December 9th you can see over 200 beautifully decorated trees, wreaths and gingerbread houses. Listen every day to glorious music and see fun demonstrations from the making of holiday breads to designing rag dolls. Attend special concerts on Sundays. Take the family to Family Night with magical entertainment for the children. Tree hours are Tuesday, Thursday and Friday 11 to 7; Wednesday 11 to 9; Saturday and Sunday 11 to 5.

WADSWORTH ATHENEUM,
Hartford, Connecticut

Used by permission of the Wadsworth Atheneum.

Here's the same information, only in a 10-second PSA:

:10 PUBLIC SERVICE ANNOUNCEMENT
for Holiday Festival of Trees

Catch the spirit of the holidays at the Wadsworth Atheneum's 11th annual Holiday Festival of Trees. Friday, November 30th through Sunday, December 9th. Tree hours are Tuesday, Thursday, Friday 11 to 7; Wednesday 11 to 9; Weekends 11 to 5.

WADSWORTH ATHENEUM,
Hartford, Connecticut

Used by permission of the Wadsworth Atheneum.

Here are two more PSA samples:

:10 PUBLIC SERVICE ANNOUNCEMENT
for Bop-Til-You-Drop Summer Readathon

Teens: Beat the summer blues and break out with the Albany Public Library's Bop-Til-You-Drop Summer Reading Contest. Remember: You cannot win if you do not play. Call four-four-nine-three-three-eight-oh for details.

ALBANY PUBLIC LIBRARY,
Albany, New York

Used by permission of the Albany Public Library.

:60 PUBLIC SERVICE ANNOUNCEMENT
for "Swingtime" Concert

It's "Swingtime" at the Albany Public Library. Hear the music of the twenties and thirties played and sung by Doc Scanlon's Rhythm Boys and the New Moon Swing Band. The free event begins at seven-thirty p.m. Friday, October ninth in the main library on Washington Avenue. For information, call four-four-nine-three-three-eight-oh.

ALBANY PUBLIC LIBRARY,
Albany, New York

Used by permission of the Albany Public Library.

If you took the time and counted the words in each of those PSAs, you would find not one of them hit the count right on the head. The numbers I gave you were just guidelines. If you have the time and talent, you may also submit slides with the television spots and taped music with the radio spots. And, if you have the facilities of an in-house video station and can produce your own spot with action and people, you'll have more to offer. But it's always best to check with your local television station to see if they will accept your tapes.

RADIO AND TELEVISION INTERVIEWS

There may come a time when you feel you have a terrific story to tell about a special event or program your organization is presenting and want to get it on the air in an interview or possibly on a talk show. Why not? If you live in a large metropolis, your chances are slimmer because of the competition. If you live in a more rural area, you'll have better luck.

If you, as the spokesperson for the group, are asked to appear on a local talk show or news show, you'll have some time to prepare, in terms of the way you dress and what you'll say. You might even want to bring along colored slides to help tell your story. But be certain that the slides are sharp and properly exposed. Keep them simple. And, if you need help preparing them, ask the television station's community affairs director for help. You would be surprised how many radio and television stations in the country are willing to work with community organizations. Community relations are important at all levels of promotion. Take the time one day to make an appointment to visit the local television or radio station. Ask questions, and then ask how you and the station can work together.

If somehow you are involved in an on-the-spot interview because of a special event or a news story related to your organization, relax and, as my daughter says, "Be mellow." Speak slowly and clearly. Be honest and don't say anything you do not mean. Your words will come back to haunt you. Be yourself and speak directly to the reporter if you're on camera unless you are told otherwise before the interview. The same applies to the radio interview, except that it won't be visual. This is when your voice and the words you use will be even more important. And, if things are rolling along great, don't hog the airwaves; give others a chance, especially if you're involved in a panel discussion. If you can, put important facts about the subject being discussed on small index cards and have them handy when talking on radio. If you make a blunder, don't die...smile and correct yourself. You're human and so are the professionals who work before the cameras daily; they, too, make errors sometimes. Always remember that you...the time you are on the air...are projecting your organization's image. Make it a good one!

Don't forget another facet of the radio station that you might want to try to use when you're having a super spectacular event, remote broadcasting. You might be able to convince the station that your event is so newsworthy that they'll set up a remote station at your location and broadcast from there for the day. Local radio stations welcome community involvement, and this would be a natural for them...a chance to do their usual program, plus interview local people attending your event. Who knows, they might come up with a great human interest story!

I've only touched on a few aspects of public relations, publicity, and promotion (more about this in the section of this chapter titled "Good Graphics.") Because there is so much more, enough to fill hundreds of books, I have recommended a few resources (see below).

As part of your overall public relations program, you should decide what your image is and what you want it to be. This might be a good way to begin your public relations program. It never hurts to reevaluate your look and image. The following sections of this chapter cover image building with some case histories and give some wonderful examples of good graphic design in newsletters, brochures, and fliers.

SOME THOUGHTS ON IMAGE

You project a certain image; so do I. It's projected in the way we speak, the way we look, the way we dress, the way we think, and how we act. Remember your mother or grandmother saying, "Don't wear that outfit when you go to the party; people will think that's all you've got"? At the same time, you were probably annoyed with the suggestion that you should change your clothes. Now you know that people do make judgments about you because of the image you project, even if the only criterion they have to judge you on is your clothes. In fact, many in business and in the public eye consult image makers. Your mother or grandmother was trying to be one way back then, and her unsolicited advice came for free! Nowadays, the image makers charge a hefty penny to tell you how to speak, walk, and dress. Because of the new electronic technology, the world has become more visual and the public has become a lot more savvy. Dale Carnegie was probably the forerunner of these modern-day image makers. Seminars are conducted in major companies throughout the country, and the image maker is paid anywhere from $1,000 to $2,000 for the day; if you would like the image maker to accompany you on a shopping trip, it could cost you a $100 an hour! (Mothers are cheaper.) Then there's the other image maker who, for about $350 an hour, will show you how to develop your own style in speech and manner. The image maker may be a former actress who will teach you how to relax, breathe properly, and "project your energy." A competent image maker would not want to change you completely but would try to accentuate your best points with a bit of polish or a down-to-earth touch. After all, not all of you want to have a slick look. Certainly you have smiled to yourself when a politician walked through the crowds during his campaign with his tie off and his shirtsleeves rolled up. That's just another image in motion.

A great deal more could be said about individual image, but let's turn instead to corporate image. Close your eyes. Try to envision Coca-Cola, McDonalds, Exxon, Mobil, Columbia Pictures, IBM, or the American Red Cross. In most cases, you will come up with a visual image. Lots and lots of money has been spent so that you, the consumer, will immediately conjure up a positive image of these people and companies. It takes careful and long-range planning. It is ongoing. Once an image has been established, you cannot sit back and rest on your laurels. The public is fickle. Look at what happened to Coca-Cola in 1985. Fearing they were losing much of their business to Pepsi's "New Generation," Coke came up with the "new Coke" and a big promotion to sell the product and the idea that "Coke is still it." A great majority of the cola-consuming public rebelled against the "new Coke." You just don't trifle with Mother, apple pie, the

American flag, and Coca-Cola. They wanted their "old Coke" back. Petitions were signed, letters written, threats made...and Coke listened. The "old" Coke is now back as "Classic Coke" alongside the "new Coke" on the supermarket shelves. Coca-Cola is spending lots of money to convince the public that *Classic Coke* is as symbolic to them as Babe Ruth, Orphan Annie, and the Statue of Liberty.

This is all part of image building. Image building begins "at home"—at your organization or company. You must believe and have pride in what you are doing before you plan your image building. You must also be willing to adapt your image to changing times and situations. Some people find it hard to change and want things to stay the way they are. G. Edward Pendray, former editor of *Public Relations Journal*, offered this statement as one of nine maxims in dealing with public opinion, "Change yourself. It's easier than changing the public."

Walter P. Margulies, president of Lippincott and Margulies, one of the country's top design consultants said in *Developing a Corporate Identity* that "The nostalgic and the quaint have no place in the world of corporate identity."

"That's fine for a large company, but we're only a nonprofit organization. Why should we be concerned with image building?" you might ask.

Image building should concern you no matter what kind or size of business you're in. You are in business even if your "product" is only a service. Public opinion is very important when you are seeking support for a new building, more funds for an existing program or service, a budget vote, or a plea for volunteers. If you have developed a particular (favorable) image through the years, you've won half the battle. Now, you must continue to work at it and reappraise your image in light of changes within you and the community.

GOOD GRAPHICS

Good graphics play an important part in conveying your image. Graphics is communication. With good graphics, you are communicating your story and your image. Sure, it's a show. So make it your "greatest show on earth" by learning and following some simple guidelines.

Certainly the best (and the easiest) way to ensure that you are using good graphics would be to hire a professional graphics designer to revamp your newsletter, brochures, letterhead, fliers, and in-house signage. Unfortunately, most cannot afford such a person, certainly not on a regular basis. However, some may be able to afford to hire a graphics designer as a one-shot consultant on a particular project. If so, make the experience something that will be lasting. Have the professional design a complete new look (if that is what you're after) in your stationery and anything that has to go before the public representing your organization. A new logo design might be the first step.

Logo

The word "logo" is short for "logotype." Most companies have a logo (also known as a trademark) which is considered part of their corporate identity. Much money can be spent on designing the proper symbol. Before you decide on a design, be certain all involved agree on the look you wish to achieve, the image you wish to project. Here are a few suggestions:

- Simplicity is best. Most logos will be reduced in size to fit on letterheads, brochures, fliers, newsletters, etc. So it's important to keep the logo simple so that details aren't lost in the reducing.
- Learn about typefaces. Consult your printer. You may decide to use only an interesting typeface in your logo without a drawing.
- If you cannot afford a graphics designer, don't attempt to draw the logo design yourself (especially if you are not an artist). Instead, tap a volunteer, an art student from a high school or college, or a local artist. Your logo design will be a welcome addition to his/her portfolio.
- Pay attention to color and paper choices. If you don't have a graphic designer, again, consult your printer. These selections will be as important as the logo design and something you will not be changing constantly. First and foremost, think of your logo design in one color even though you may ultimately decide on two or four colors. The more colors you use, the more expensive the job will become. You can get the effect of two colors by screening the color of your choice; the printer and/or designer will help you with this. Choose your "corporate" color and then follow through by using this color in all material to be printed for your company. For example, our library's "corporate" color is maroon. We use this color in our letterheads, business cards, in any papers facing the public whether we are using white or cream colored paper.
- Take the time to choose a graphic designer; it can be a difficult job. Your printer may have a subcontract deal with a graphic artist. Talk to people whose graphics you have admired. Collect the names of designers in your price category and make appointments to see them and their work. Show the designer samples of "good graphics" that you have collected. Give the artist a definite idea of what image you are trying to project. Don't tell the artist you want something "modern" when your taste is Victorian. But don't stifle the "creative juices" of the designer by telling him/her too much. An artist will produce several designs for you to choose from. Once the decision is made, the artist will create the finished design, order the type, prepare the mechanical, and specify the job to the printer. Check everything; after all, it's your

logo and you're paying for it. But don't show the design to too many people, ideally no more than three or four. Too many opinions can spoil a good idea. Have the courage to stick to your personal convictions.

On the next several pages, you will find examples of interesting logo designs used by both large organizations and smaller, less-well-off groups.

Boston Harborfest. Using a large star and stripes, the logo for this annual Boston celebration is very "American." The colors are red and blue and the paper for the news releases, press kit folders, and other materials is white. This is an example of Boston's graphic approach to show their part in American history.

BOSTON HARBORFEST

Logo used by permission of the Boston Harborfest.

Santa Cruz Beach Boardwalk. Using the sun and the ocean waves as the focal point in the logo design, the Santa Cruz Beach Boardwalk adds an attractive typeface to create a handsome logo. The four colors (red, orange, yellow, and navy blue) contrast well with the white paper on the boardwalk's stationery. Their note paper is white stock with the logo in orange. Their news release simply uses the logotype with navy blue ink on white paper. The beach feeling is certainly there.

SANTA CRUZ BEACH BOARDWALK

Logo used by permission of the Santa Cruz Beach Boardwalk.

Memphis in May International Festival, Inc. The graphic artist combined a simple, colorful graphic design with a handsome typeface, making the logo distinguished and identifiable. This four-color job (orange, yellow, and lavender with black typeface) on white paper has a bright and sprightly look. The logo design is used on the news release, stationery, business cards, press kit folders, and newsletter.

Memphis in May International Festival, Inc. ™

Logo used by permission of Memphis in May International Festival, Inc.

Lincoln Library. By just a quick glance at this simple logo, you have no doubts about the identification. Since its name and location, Springfield, Illinois, really tell it all, the logo design is incorporated into all of their promotional materials, stationery, and news release paper. No other color is used except for good old black and white, adding to the simplicity of the design.

lincoln library

Logo used by permission of the Lincoln Library, Public Library of Springfield, Illinois.

KETC, Channel 9. This public television station in St. Louis, Missouri, has redesigned its logo several times within the past 30 years. The most recent change came in 1978–79, when new management took over the station. According to Cathy Rothstein, manager of advertising and promotion, "Their first goal was to change the station image from rather dull and educational to dynamic, a place for great entertainment, etc. We started an image campaign, calling us 'The New Nine.' Part of that was a new logo, a new station magazine, a new on-air look." The number nine is used in a striking red/vermillion color; the typeface is in black ink; and the paper is white. Designed by Overlock-Howe Consulting Group for KETC-St. Louis.

Thirty KETC *Years*

Logo used by permission of KETC-St. Louis.

96   *Fireworks, Brass Bands, and Elephants*

The Hudson River Museum. Located on a hill overlooking the Hudson River in the city of Yonkers (New York), this museum uses a lively blue ink on white stationery in their logo design. The informal handscript design is used throughout all of their promotional materials. The color may vary, depending on the promotion and the piece. It's an identifiable and simple graphic image. The logo and stationery design are by Ivan Chermayeff, Chermayeff & Geismar Associates.

Logo used by permission of The Hudson River Museum.

The Popcorn Institute. Located in Chicago, the institute provides information about popcorn to the public. Its logo is its trademark, the little man with an ear of corn in one hand and an armful of popcorn in the other. On white paper stationery, the logo is in brown and golden yellow inks and the typeface is in reverse (white). On their news release paper, the logo design is bright red and the paper is bright yellow. It is eye-catching. Many newspaper food editors use this logo in popcorn feature articles.

Logo used by permission of The Popcorn Institute, 111 E. Wacker Dr., Suite 600, Chicago, IL 60601.

Smithsonian Institution. "Art TO Zoo" is an attractive newsletter produced by the Smithsonian's Office of Elementary and Secondary Education. The logo, "Art TO Zoo," was a corporate gift from Benton & Bowles, Inc., New York; it was designed by Sam Cooperstein. It made its initial appearance in 1980. The newsletter has a different designer/artist for each issue's layout. It is always printed in black and white.

Logo used by permission of the Smithsonian Institution.

Spokane Public Library. Originally designed for the public library's annual report in 1983, this handsome logo is on all library promotional materials, stationery, and news release paper. The pavilion covering the book in the logo is located in Spokane's Riverfront Park where Expo '74 was held. According to the library's public information officer, Lisa A. Wolfe, the logo ties the library to the Spokane community. The annual report logo is in black and white and the stationery is a burnt orange ink on a tan/gray paper, making for an interesting combination of colors. Staff artist Gerry Krueger designed the logo.

Logo used by permission of the Spokane Public Library.

The New York Public Library. Anyone who has visited or read about the New York Public Library knows of the two lion statues outside the building on Fifth Avenue. They are considered a landmark. What more natural logo for the library? The "marching" lions can be seen on news release paper, stationery, library guides, and brochures. The colors for the news release paper and stationery are deep burgundy, gray, and black inks on white paper. Nice contrasts and a light touch for an otherwise seemingly staid institution.

Logo used by permission of the New York Public Library. Copyright © New York Public Library.

Playwrights Horizons. An off-Broadway theatre which presents new plays by contemporary playwrights has achieved a graphic look that is immediately identifiable to members. Located in a newly developed "theatre row" on 42nd Street in New York City, the group uses the New York City skyline in its bold logo design. The skyline is in black ink and the words "Playwrights Horizons" are in red ink outlined in black. Red and black on white paper is the scheme used for all their promotional pieces. The logo design is by Holly Gewandter.

Logo used by permission of Playwrights Horizons.

These are just a few of the interesting and "good graphic" logo designs around. There are thousands more everywhere you look. Look, and then look some more wherever you go. There's a whole world of exciting graphic designs for you to discover and emulate. Choose your own logo design carefully. Then use it on everything you produce to spread your image. If after several years you feel the need for a change because your company or organization has gone through some change, don't be afraid to change your graphic look too. After you have found your image in your logo design, then rethink your newsletter (if you have one...or start one) and also remember that every promotional piece (brochure, letter, flier, poster, etc.) is part of your image. So make it a good one...consistently. On the following pages, you will find examples of good newsletters, brochures, and fliers. I purposely used some of the organizations with interesting logo designs in this section to show you that there is and should be consistency in your graphic design.

NEWSLETTERS, BROCHURES, AND FLIERS

Newsletters

For me and for many others in the public information field, a newsletter is one of the best ways to communicate with the public. Through the newsletter, you can promote your image by how and what you write. You can develop a rapport with your community. A newsletter gives the opportunity to sell your services and make the public aware of all the special events and programs available to them. If it's a regularly published newsletter that is jam-packed with good information, it will be a welcome item in the mailbox, something people will look forward to receiving. But it takes time to develop a good one. Brochures and fliers, I feel, serve as addenda to the newsletter. And, if you don't already have a newsletter, then it certainly should be considered. I never depend on just one piece of communication for spreading the word, whether it's an event or a service. An example: When I promoted the 1986 Chinese New Year month-long celebration at our library (see the "Thematic Festivals" section in Chapter 6), I gave it a whole page in the January/February newsletter. I followed with an annotated brochure with all of the events highlighted again. Then, each event had its own flier or brochure. Brochures and fliers can be particularly valuable if you have a new or ongoing service you want the public to be aware of. Certainly mention the service in your newsletter. But remember, the newsletter will either be filed away or more likely thrown away. The newsletter should merely serve (in this instance) as an appetizer for the service. The brochure or flier will contain the whole menu which could be for keeping. I feel you can never tell the public enough. So, brochures and fliers should stand on their own and serve a very important role in your communications program. Let's begin with the newsletter, and then we'll move on to brochures and fliers.

Starting a Newsletter

An external newsletter can be one of the most important ways to inform the public about who you are, what you're doing, and what you can do for them. Assuming you have justified the reason to have a newsletter, you must also know your audience. Who are your readers? It goes right back to knowing your community. Different newsletters for different people. In most cases, you will be the editor, writer, and graphic designer. The best way to begin is to look at and read other company/organization newsletters. Really read the text. Analyze the style of writing. Look at the photographs. Examine the graphics. Brainstorm ideas that can be adapted to your publication. It's always better to create your own image, even in a newsletter. Examining other newsletters should serve as a stimulus.

You may decide to publish a newsletter for one or more of the following reasons.

- Informing. Telling the community of a variety of activities, from what you've been doing to what you will be doing in the future.
- Educating. Giving the public real information they can use or referring them to sources or materials that you might have.
- Entertaining. If space allows and it's the approach you wish to take, you might include a humor column, some quizzes, or humorous anecdotes.
- Promoting. A newsletter is one of the best tools to use to publicize an upcoming special event, membership drive, support for your budget vote, Friends' activities, etc.

Those are just some of the reasons to start a newsletter. Once you decide to start one, you need to choose a format. Since it is a "letter," the recommended size would be 8½ x 11 inches. The length can be anything from a single sheet to an eight-page piece (any longer and it becomes a magazine). To make the newsletter part of your corporate identity, you might consider using your logo design in the nameplate or banner. If you have the funds, you could hire a graphic artist to design a newsletter for you. The artist will also help you decide on the column format. Using 8½ x 11-inch pages, the three most popular ways are a one-column, two-column, or three-column format. Again, look at other newsletters and then make your decision.

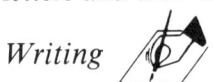

Writing

Newsletter writing reads best when it's concise and simple. Fewer words are always better than too many. Develop a style. Make it as personal as possible without being cute. Write one-to-one as though you are talking to someone. Feel insecure about writing? Don't fret; it is something you can learn to do. Two good books I heartily recommend are *The Elements of Style* by William Strunk, Jr., and E.B. White, and William Zinsser's *On Writing Well*.

Story ideas for your newsletter can be varied ranging from hard news to light features. Some ideas to consider include these.

- Building expansion, personnel changes, policy revisions, etc.
- A calendar of events with individual stories about some of the special ones.
- Stories written by and/or about the staff.
- How-to articles such as a consumer complaint letter or household hints.
- Service offerings and changes.
- Informative stories that relate to services your organization has to offer.

Those are just a few suggestions. You'll have your own. Putting a newsletter together is like being a reporter. You have to go out and get the news. It can be fun but sometimes a drag because some people don't know what a deadline is. In most cases, you will have to be the staff photographer also. After you have gathered all of the information, you will need to sit down and make an outline. If a new director has been hired, that should be your lead story. This should be followed by stories presented in order of importance and public interest. Look at other newsletters and then decide on your own approach.

Photographs

Photographs play an important part in a newsletter. Learn to use a camera—the simpler the better, unless you are a proficient photographer or can hire a professional. Be certain that there is enough contrast in your photos and don't try to get everyone in one shot. Fewer people with some action thrown in makes for a better picture. Most photos should be cropped to give a better image. For a special effect, you might want to bleed a picture on a page. To bleed a picture is to print it right off the edge of the page. Your printer should be able to help you with this if you don't have a staff artist. Remember, each time you use a picture, it costs money. Each photograph must be shot through a screen to produce a "halftone." Black-and-white glossy photographs work best, but I have used colored shots which, because they were sharp, reproduced well. When in doubt, consult your printer. Leave space under the photo for your caption. On your layout, using a nonphoto blue pencil, indicate where the picture is going and call it photo "A." Leave adequate space for the photo. If it is to be reduced, indicate how much reduction. Since this can get rather technical, why not leave that problem to your printer? I do. Do not write on the photograph. Tape instructions on the bottom of the photograph with masking tape.

Reproduction

There are several ways you can reproduce your newsletter. The cheapest way is on a mimeograph machine in-house. Your size will be limited and photographs will not print well. If you have an electronic stencil maker, you know the many creative opportunities it offers you. You can use line drawings and clip art on your paste-up. You can use headlines made with transfer type (rub-on letters). You can set up your newsletter in columns. Your paper quality may be a bit more limited, but you can use a variety of ink colors. Many mimeograph manufacturers will provide you with a simple paste-up and mechanical tip sheet or booklet. You can also purchase nonreproducible blue-lined layout pads for direct use for your typing and layout. Most people can learn how to do a simple paste-up and mechanical.

Probably the most used method of printing a newsletter is photo offset. The "quick printing" shops use this method. Most printers use this offset negative process. This means your paste-up pages are photographed by a camera and a negative is made. The printer can then touch up any smudges and "glitches." A metal printing plate is then made. What you give the printer is what you get when your newsletter is printed. So be certain your copy and layout are neat and crisp. Ask the printer for a blueprint proof. This is very important because this is where you might pick up mistakes not discovered before. And, it's just possible that the printer might make an error. It happened to me once. The printer had transposed the names of the library board of trustees in a photo caption and some of the men had women's names!

To create clean copy for your newsletter, a good electric typewriter is a must. It gives you an even touch and produces dark, legible letters. A carbon ribbon is the best choice. To make life even easier, use a self-correcting electric typewriter. *And*, if you're fortunate enough to have a personal computer with a word processor, you can create more newsletter magic!

What typeface to use? It does matter if you have a choice. Information about typography could fill many books, but here are a few simple suggestions. The typeface you use (in headlines and text) should be easy on the eyes and attractive to read, but the reader should not be aware of the typeface. You don't want to distract the reader from the text with some outrageous typeface. Typography can create a mood; it can be bold or quiet. It's up to you to choose. I use the Artisan 12 typing element in my IBM Selectric typewriter because it's clean, sharp, legible, and takes up less space per line than Letter Gothic or Courier would. To make a bolder point, I also incorporate the Orator type into the copy. I also use transfer type headlines or headlines produced on a simple computerized headliner machine, but all this is not necessary. You can create with the simplest of tools. Just learn the rudiments.

The third method of reproduction is typesetting. This is more expensive. Typeset material is usually better looking than typewritten (which would be your mimeograph and offset reproductions). You should follow the same rules for layout as before, but you won't need to have your copy camera-ready. Just give your copy to the printer, who will typeset according to your directions. You will have to decide the type size and the amount of space you want between lines. Perplexed? Relax. Pick out some sample typefaces and take them to the printer. You may be all wrong...but then, you may be all right. It's a learning experience, and it can be fun. If you have the time and interest, you will find the art of typography fascinating! After the type has been set, the printer will give you "galleys" or proofs which you must check for errors. Typesetting not only costs more, it also can take longer, so you must allow extra time and not run your deadline time too close. But, in the end, you do have more choices with typesetting. For one thing, you can have your type "justified" or "ragged." Justified type means that all the copy lines are set to the same length, giving you a neat right-hand margin as well as a neat left-hand margin. If neatness counts with you, then that may be your selection. Ragged type simply means that the lines of copy are in varying lengths along the right-hand margin. According to many graphics experts, the ragged right-hand margin reads better and can be corrected more easily. But, again, look at newsletters, books, magazines, etc., to see what appeals to you and why. When you have found a typeface you like for your newsletter, stick with it. It will become familiar to the reader, and familiarity is one of the goals of your newsletter, right?

More decisions await you in your newsletter production. The choice of paper and inks can be crucial. The paper selection should occur early in the process. It's important to choose the right paper. Of course, you're not "married" to it, but using the same color paper makes it a familiar piece to your readers. They feel comfortable with it. If you can afford it, spend a little extra on the paper. Want to learn more about paper? Paper manufacturers promote their wares avidly and have plenty of freebies. At the end of this chapter are listed some paper sources. They will send you all kinds of attractive promotional materials (many will give you great ideas for graphic design because they are that good!) and paper samples. They will refer you to a sales representative in your area. In most cases, the paper distributor will not sell directly to you because you are considered "small potatoes" to him/her. But, your printer can order the paper for you. When you decide on a paper stock, how many issues you will be printing per year, and how many copies per issue, the printer can order a large supply of "your" paper. It might be cheaper than buying it yourself. I do this with my printer. Most offset paper comes in sheets measuring 25 x 38 inches. Check it out. If you have an in-house printer, don't leave all the printing decisions to that person. It's your newsletter...be informed and involved in the printing. Ask questions...it's the only way to learn!

My personal suggestion for the choice of a newsletter paper is to go with a light color, something in the cream, beige, tan, gray, off-white range. Of course, you can use soft shades of green, blue, pink, and yellow, too. This brings me to the choice of ink color. I remember when my printing budget was larger; then I used two colors on ivory. One color was black (for the copy) and the other color was used for the nameplate/banner and headlines. It was an attractive combination and eye-catching. Now, I use an ivory paper (cheaper stock, but still good) and contrast it each month with a different color of ink. You must always consider the reproduction of your photographs in the colored ink. The ink may look fine with the line drawings and headlines and copy, but the halftones (in most colors) may look washed out. (Note: Many graphic designers frown on photos being reproduced in anything but black or brown ink!) Your printer or graphic artist can help you in the choice of ink colors. Those with more money can go to a four-color printing job, but it's really not necessary. In fact, even if you can afford it, I wouldn't recommend it. You don't want to appear too slick and turn off people. Paper and ink can be that influential.

If you wish, you can use the same paper and the same ink for each newsletter issue. If it's distinctive enough and interesting, it will be read. The choice is yours; make it a good one, but don't worry if you find it wasn't the right decision. You simply start over again and that can be an exciting experience!

Proofreading

I saved the worst for last. Actually, it's only worst if you neglect to do it. "It" is proofreading. When reviewing your written material, assume nothing. Just because you wrote it doesn't make it all correct. You're only human; errors will be made in spelling and grammar. Have at least two other people familiar with the newsletter read the copy after it is camera-ready. Make the corrections. Then, read it again. Check all dates and spellings of names and places.

Since none of you are professional proofreaders, you must always double-check each other; even then, errors will slip by. Most times, you'll catch the mistakes in the printer's proof, and if they're your errors, you'll make the corrections and pay for "author's alterations." It's worth it, and the changes will become fewer as you get better at proofreading. Since I actually do the camera-ready copy typing (I edit as I go along), I don't want to type the whole thing over if at all possible. So I ask the "proofreaders" to write the mistakes they find on another sheet of paper, identifying all with page number and line. I then type the corrections and cut and paste them in place. Sometimes there's an awful lot of cutting and pasting! Other times I've laughed when my assistant declared, "I can't believe it. I can't find one mistake!" It doesn't happen too often. Remember: Don't assume that because the newsletter is camera-ready copy the printer can't make a mistake. It happens. So, again, check your proofs.

Distribution

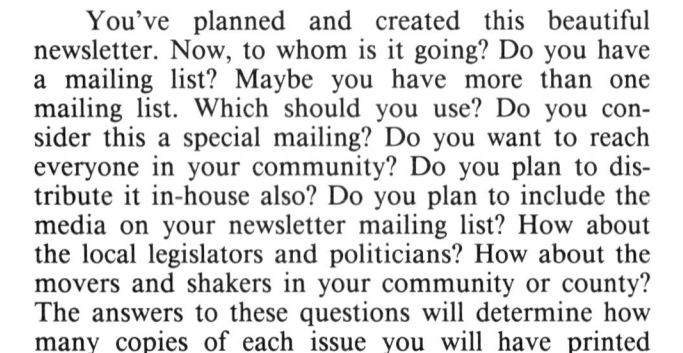

You've planned and created this beautiful newsletter. Now, to whom is it going? Do you have a mailing list? Maybe you have more than one mailing list. Which should you use? Do you consider this a special mailing? Do you want to reach everyone in your community? Do you plan to distribute it in-house also? Do you plan to include the media on your newsletter mailing list? How about the local legislators and politicians? How about the movers and shakers in your community or county? The answers to these questions will determine how many copies of each issue you will have printed and whether it will be a self-mailer.

If your newsletter is 8½ x 11 inches, it can be folded by your printer down to 8½ x 3⅔ inches, which is a bit smaller than a business envelope. If it's going to be a self-mailer, then you should reserve the bottom third of the last page for your mailing section. In the left-hand corner, you may wish to repeat your logo or nameplate design and add to this your complete address and phone number, hours of business (if pertinent), name of editor, and head officer of the organization. You might also reidentify whether it's a spring issue, etc. Leave ample space for the mailing label. If you are a nonprofit organization, have your nonprofit mailing permit number in the right-hand corner. If it applies, add the words "dated material" under the permit number. Don't forget, there should still be some white space left on the bottom of the mailer section. Use it by including an attention-grabbing headline and/or line drawing to draw the reader into opening the newsletter! It works.

Producing mailing labels has become easier with the advent of the computer. Just feed the names and addresses into the computer, place your roll of labels in your printer, and within minutes you've got your list ready to go. If your list is a large one and you can afford it, you may wish to have a professional mailing service handle the job. The mail is addressed, presorted, and taken to the post office. Of course, there is a nice tidy sum charged for all this. But it's worth it when it's a big job. Another approach is to type a master list and then photocopy the list onto sheets of gummed labels. However, someone must still place the labels on the newsletters. Still another choice is to use an addressing machine. Master labels are printed on cards or plates which can be used for years. However, someone must still type the labels and run the machine.

Most post offices require presorting of bulk mail. Check with your post office, and while you're on the phone, tell them the date your newsletter will be delivered to the post office. If it's a busy post office, the manager will appreciate the advance alert, especially if you add, "We've got dated material so we would like the newsletters to reach the community by next week." Get the name of the customer relations person and deal with that person only, if possible. Lost mail or late-delivered mail can make or break a budget vote or a fund-raising drive or an important meeting or special event.

Mailing lists can be developed, but they will take time. Have "I Want to Be on Your Mailing List" cards available in your building and in local museums, libraries, banks, stores, churches, temples, if you're looking for a very general audience. If you want to attract a more specific group, have cards at a table when you're holding a program or special event, include them in your newsletters as coupons, or submit the information to your local arts council's newsletter. You can use some of the names in your community directory if you have one, and you can even buy mailing lists. Finally, don't forget the media. It's one more way to keep them in touch!

Newsletter Samples

One of the best ways to learn is from examples. On the following pages you will find samples of good, working newsletters.

Arts Alive, The Stamford Community Arts Council, Stamford, CT. A combination newsletter and calendar, this attractive publication is printed on white Champion paper, Carnival Groove, with the text in black ink and the nameplate/banner in a different color ink each issue. Some of the headlines and graphics are also in the second color. It is published bimonthly and distributed by "mail, car, and foot." It features graphics utilizing clip art, original art, and excellent photographs. There is a pull-out calendar section and several news stories about forthcoming exhibits and events. It also has a few paid advertisers called contributors. It's a self-mailer with a nonprofit permit. Hilda Cook is the editor and president of the arts council. Circulation of 3,500. Sample used by permission of the Stamford Arts Council.

Perspectives, Wright State University, Dayton, OH. Lively in text and design, this newsletter is produced by the Office of Admissions. This issue is printed on white paper using three inks (bright orange for nameplate/banner, blue, and black). By reversing and screening colors, the newsletter gives the illusion of having many more colors. The paper varies. Sometimes it's a bright yellow with brown and orange inks or ivory with red and olive-green inks. Again, they reverse and screen inks to get a varied effect. It's published three times a year and is a self-mailer. Editors are: Carol Siyahi and Mindy McNutt Young. Design coordinator: Cynthia Poe. Designers: Theresa Almond, Joan Cornett, and Cynthia Poe. Sample used by permission of Wright State University, Dayton, OH.

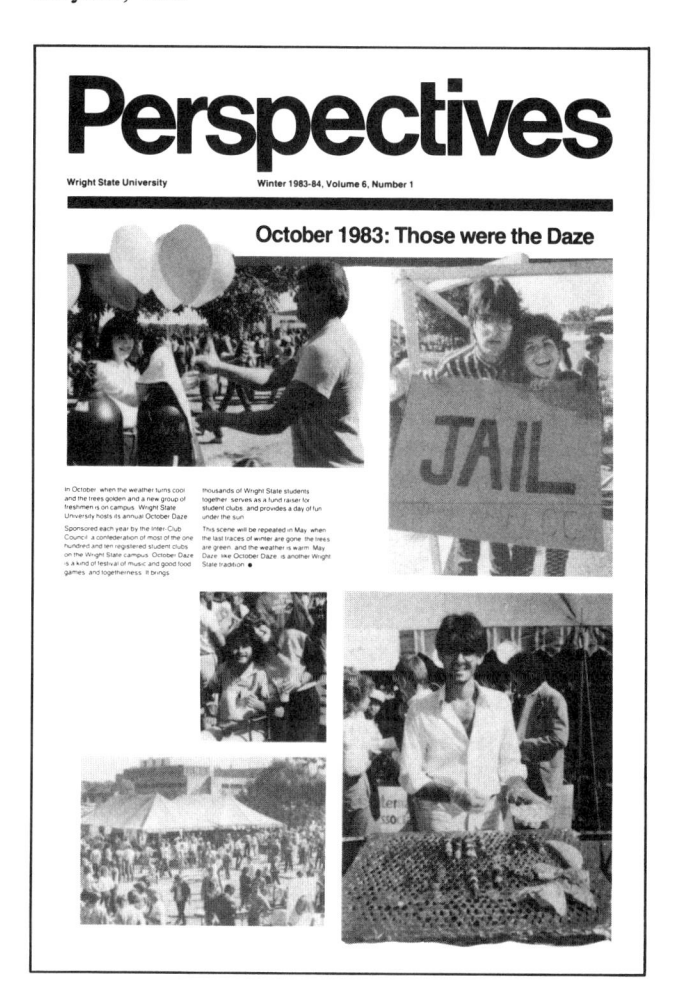

Annual Report/Newsletter, East Meadow Public Library, East Meadow, NY. Each May, the library incorporates an annual report with the newsletter. It's mailed to about 15,000 households, and the remainder are distributed in-house and on the Library-On-Wheels (bookmobile). Printed in black ink on white, coated litho paper, the annual report/newsletter features a different theme each year. "You're In Good Company" was the feature gimmick for 1985 and some of the "good company" were staff members. Inside were photos of six staff members along with brief biographical sketches. "Life Begins at 30" was the secondary theme which told about the library's recent 30th birthday in April (big birthday story appeared in March/April newsletter). This was followed by a picture story of the library's building expansion, bus trip information, children's summer reading game, Friends' fund-raiser photo story, and a "Bits & Pieces" section. Inside were: a photo of the board of trustees, their annual message and budget proposal, and a bold headline asking voters to "Vote Yes" for the budget. The back page had voting information with a map of the district, and the mailer portion had a headline (on the bottom), "Life Begins at 30...when you're in Good Company!" The library logo, address and phone number, hours, and director's name are all in the left-hand top area. The editor is Louise Liebold and the staff artist is Marion Rothenberg. Sample used by permission of the East Meadow Public Library.

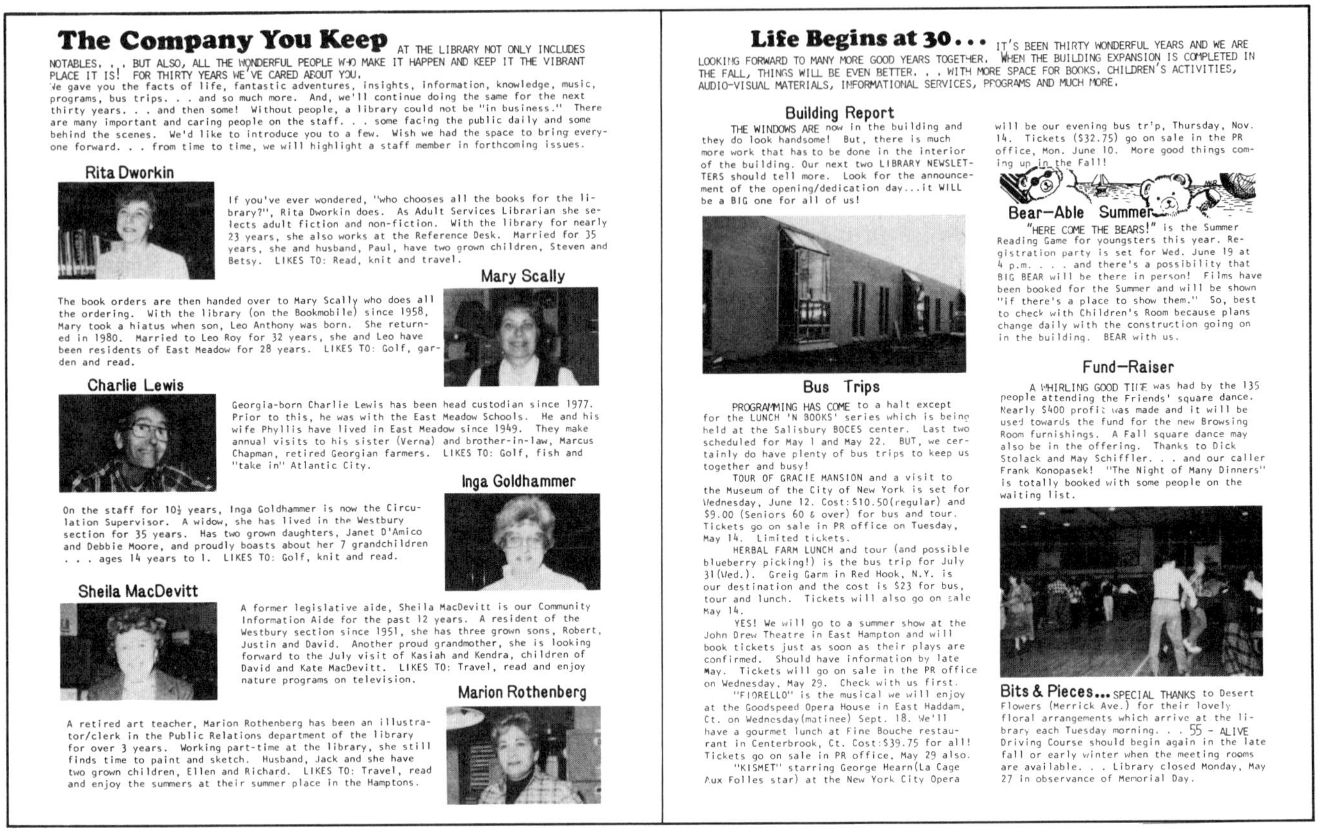

Art TO Zoo, Smithsonian Institution, Washington, DC. Created by the Smithsonian's Office of Elementary and Secondary Education, this black-and-white publication is jam-packed with great information and lively things to do. This particular issue deals with inventions and "turning dreams into reality." A special pull-out section in each issue features quizzes and craft projects. *Art TO Zoo* brings news from the Smithsonian to teachers of grades three to eight. It is published four times a year and distributed through schools, libraries, museums, parks, and zoos. Often it will include reading lists, one for children and one for teachers. Its layout and design make it inviting reading. Each issue is in black and white and usually features a different graphic designer, sometimes an in-house person and sometimes a freelance one. The editor is Dorothy Aukofer MacEoin and the designer is Joan Wolbier. Circulation of 50,000, free of charge. Sample used by permission of the Smithsonian Institution.

Ka 'Elele, Honolulu, HI. This is the Bishop Museum's monthly newsletter. It is an eight-page publication folded down to a 9 x 5½-inch self-mailer. The color is always an off-white. This issue has black and brown inks, an attractive combination. There is handsome artwork with a good overall design. Elisa Johnston, the public information officer, is the editor, and Mike Tamura is the designer. Six thousand copies are printed each time, and 5,000 are distributed through their mailing list. The remainder are distributed in the museum's reception area. Sample used by permission of the Bishop Museum.

Insight, The J.B. Speed Art Museum, Louisville, KY. This newsletter is printed on white paper with a different color ink for front page and inside headlines; black ink is used for text and photographs. This self-mailer is eight inches square as shown here. Folded twice, it opens to a 24 x 16-inch piece. It features stories about current and forthcoming exhibits, personnel notes, Friends' news and a membership application, a highlight calendar, and excellent photographs of paintings. Edited by Dr. Kelly Scott Reed, the newsletter was designed by Don Overmyer and continued by Alan Pardee. The newsletter is distributed monthly by mail to members and to other institutions. Price-Weber, Inc. designed the logo. Sample used by permission of The J.B. Speed Art Museum.

The Hudson River Museum, Yonkers, NY. This attractively designed bimonthly calendar of events is mailed to members and distributed in-house. It's not really a newsletter but a well-designed piece with bold headlines and interestingly placed photographs and artwork. There is no doubt as to what time period the calendar covers, as that information is in bold headlines on the bottom of each inside page. The self-mailer section is folded down (five times) to 10 x 4 inches. Unfolded, it measures 10 x 26 inches. A white offset paper is used with black ink for text and photos. A primary color is used for the banner and accents. Michael Bierut of Vignelli Associates did the design. Laura Byers is the editor. Sample used by permission of The Hudson River Museum.

104 Fireworks, Brass Bands, and Elephants

Brochures and Fliers

There are those who call a promotional flier a handbill. Well, no matter what you call it, it still comes out to be the same thing, a printed piece designed to sell, promote, or market your organization or special event. In most cases, fliers are used primarily for promoting events. They are also a good device to tell the story of a special service you have...simply and succinctly. Most of us find our mailboxes inundated with both brochures and fliers. Most of it is "junk" mail. But you must admit that you will take the time to read or at least glance at a printed piece if something in its graphic design, color, or copy catches your eye. That's the trick. Since the average household receives a heavy supply of such stuff weekly in the mail, your job is to create one of the pieces that is read, saved, and acted upon. Your promotional piece may be a fund-raiser solicitation, a membership drive call, information on a new service, or the publicizing of a special event or series of seminars. It has to tell the story simply and present the package in an attractive design.

The color of both the paper stock and ink plays an important role in your brochure/flier design. I favor bright colors for paper with black ink; but to contradict myself, my truly favorite combination is black ink on tan/gray paper. Just about all of the fliers and brochures in my office are done using an electronic stencil and mimeograph machine for the printing. Inks are changed often; many times two colors are used for a flier or brochure. This takes two paste-ups and a bit more time, but it's worth it, if that's the look you want. If you like pastel shades of paper, you can always jazz up the appearance by using colored inks that complement the paper. And, if you are printing by offset, which is the most popular method, you can always consider reverse printing with the background in one color and the type in another. And, don't forget the classic colors of black and white. Remember, the more copies you print, the cheaper the cost will be per copy. Just about any form of printing is better than photocopying. Here are a few suggestions to consider when putting together your promotional flier.

- Keep the copy short and simple.
- Get all of the pertinent facts on one page.
- Got a logo? Use it.
- Be sure the name, address, and phone number of your organization are in a prominent spot.
- Double-check that the date, time, and location of your special event are correct.
- Always think of the reader. When planning and creating a flier consider whom it is you are trying to reach.
- Use an appropriate line drawing or photograph to complement the copy and attract the reader.
- Leave plenty of white space on the flier. Don't clutter.
- Use bold headlines. Think of your flier as a poster. Design it so it has impact on the first look.
- Got the budget? Have your copy typeset. It looks better.

- Learn about papers. Cultivate a relationship with a friendly printer who can teach you a lot. Get samples from paper companies.
- Learn about typefaces and which ones best serve to enhance your image. Experiment.

Most of the suggestions presented here also apply to creating a good brochure, although a brochure may take more planning. While a handbill or flier might have a short life, a brochure could be something you wish to use for years or at least several months. The first thing to do is put down on paper what it is you're trying to communicate in the brochure and gather all of the facts you'll need. Then consider several other things. Is the brochure going to be mailed? Will it be a self-mailer or an insert into an envelope? If it's a self-mailer, it could be a variety of sizes. The format most used is the 8½ x 11-inch sheet folded twice, giving you three sections and bringing the size down to 3⅔ x 8½ inches. It's a handy size, as it fits into an envelope or someone's pocket or handbag easily. It also allows you varied design choices. Again, even though you may have a great deal to say, say it in as few words as possible. If you are using the 8½ x 11-inch format, you will want to zing it to them in your cover, the third of the page that, when folded, faces the reader first. It can be done by using interesting typeface along with a strong choice of colors. Or, you might wish to attract them with a line drawing or photograph accompanied by some strong copy. After all, your prime purpose is to get them to the second step: opening the brochure and reading it! Here is an example of a brochure produced by Playwrights Horizons which was mailed to current and prospective members. The mailing section (not shown) contains their name and address, nonprofit postage ID, and space for the member's name and address. When you turn the piece to open it, you are faced with catchy but simple copy: "Enjoy (the "E" is capitalized in red ink) Miami Beach, Nuns, Parties, Coney Island, Dining Rooms, Your Mother, Art Museums, Blockbuster Movies, Huck Finn, Vaudeville, Good Food, A Good Laugh, The Seasons, Changes." "Changes" is also in red. The rest of the copy is in black ink. The paper is white. Its simplicity attracts your eye and your mind. So you open the folded page, but not all the way because you are greeted with the headline, "Enjoy The Changes!" The words, "Enjoy The" and the exclamation point are in black ink and "Changes" is in red. Your eye then follows the top of the page, which you have opened, and the copy continues, "For fourteen seasons we've been creating the changes audiences and critics have acclaimed and we've got more in store for you! Celebrate the Changes!"

The strength of the design is in the way the copy is laid out, the omission of commas and periods, the size of the typeface, and the way the ink colors are used. The "F" in "For" is red and so is the word "Changes." Red is also the color for the

Enjoy
Miami Beach, Nuns, Parties, Coney Island, Dining Rooms, Your Mother, Art Museums, Blockbuster Movies, Huck Finn, Vaudeville, Good Food, A Good Laugh, The Seasons, Changes?

For fourteen seasons we've been creating the changes audiences and critics have acclaimed
&

Enjoy the Changes!

For fourteen seasons we've been creating the changes audiences and critics have acclaimed
&
we've got more in store for you!

Celebrate the Changes!

Used by permission of Playwrights Horizons.

"&" and "we've got more in store for you!" All the rest is in black. Since this is an informative membership drive piece, you will find all of the pertinent information about past season productions and what's in store for the current season attractively arranged using both red and black ink when you open the brochure. What makes you read this far is the design, the choice of colors, and the intriguing copy. It draws you in. It does the job.

They continue with the word "changes" in their "inside" text also. They tell you right out, "Plays that will change your life!" The letter "P" is in red, following the continuity in design and color. They never let up on the word "change." The text has headlines such as "Writers whose changes you'll enjoy," "Our season pass allows for changes," "What your change gets you," "Change you'll save!" "Our tickets for your change," "Our changes for your comfort," "Enjoy the changes as only passholders can." The brochure gets its message across in a simple and attractive fashion. It was designed by Neil Sandstad, and the copy was written by Paul Daniels.

Used by permission of the St. Louis Public Library.

The St. Louis Public Library consistently produces good graphic promotional pieces. Here are a couple of examples. For their series, "Outlaws, Indians and the Rest of the West," they created a poster which told it all in an eye-appealing manner. The paper was tan cover stock with the illustration and copy in black ink. Very striking. The copy was brief and easy to read. The illustration was by artist John Zielinski.

Used by permission of the St. Louis Public Library.

The Cabanne Branch Library in St. Louis celebrated its 75th birthday with a week-long series of programs. They produced an attractive poster featuring one of the guest speakers, author Maya Angelou. The illustration was by artist Jim Loveless. The slick-coated paper stock was white and the inks were lavender and black. In conjunction with this promotion, they also created a bookmark showing the front of the Cabanne Branch Library building using the same colors. A complete program brochure with historical facts about the branch library was also available. The same color combination and design prevailed. Again, continuity in look was evident.

U & lc (upper and lower case) is the international journal of typographics and is published by

ITC TYPEFACE DIRECTORY

ALPHABET SOUPS

International Typeface Corporation (ITC) for professionals and students. I find it an exciting, creative, and informative publication. ITC also has an educational center and gallery at its New York City headquarters. Many slide shows, based on past exhibitions, are available for rental for a two-week period. Subscription to *U & lc* is free by surface mail (see "Resources" at the end of this chapter). There is a charge for air mail delivery.

From time to time, *U & lc* produces special promotional pieces. In 1984, they created an entertaining and attractive typeface directory called "Alphabet Soups." In the introduction, ITC says:

> "Get out your stockpots, soup bowls and pica rules: here's the new ITC Typeface Directory. It's filled with alphabets and soups, so you can cook from it as well as create from it. You'll love it... We asked Mo Lebowitz to write and design this directory, using easy recipes and tasty types from our big collection. And Lionel Kalish's illustrations are the perfect garnish."
>
> "Keep this directory around. It'll come in handy whether you need a typeface or a lunch. Bon appétit."

The illustration on this introductory page shows a soup pot, two bowls and saucers, and a ruler. The booklet goes through the alphabet explaining various typefaces with yummy soup recipes for each page and typeface...it's a double learning experience! Reprinted here from the directory are two rather unique soups, "Asparagus Soup" and "Eggplant Soup." Note the typefaces, the layout, the illustrations, and all of that "white space." Also note that the type is in a ragged-right setting, a good format to copy.

Colden Center at Queens College in New York provides many entertainment series, and they do a heavy mailing of brochures and fliers announcing

Reprinted in the "Alphabet Soup" booklet, published by International Typeface Corporation. Used by permission of the International Typeface Corporation.

108   *Fireworks, Brass Bands, and Elephants*

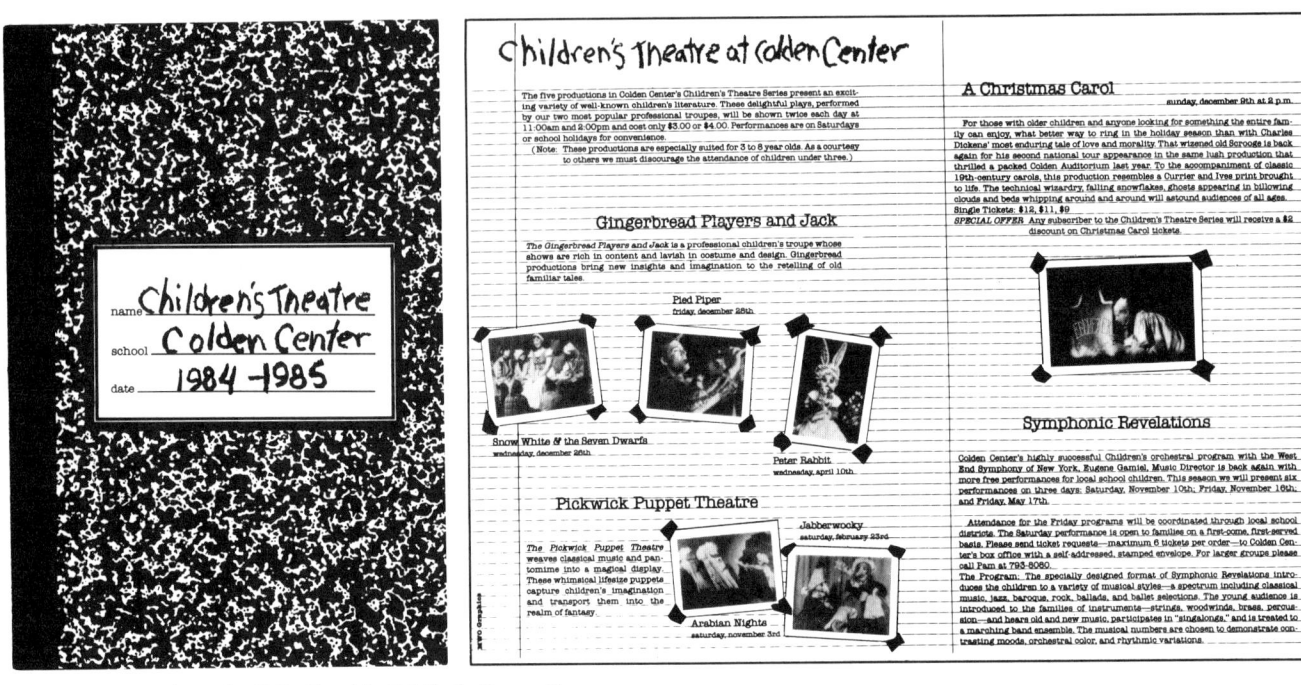

Used by permission of MWO Graphics/Mallorie Ostrowitz.

the events. To promote their children's theatre, they asked their design company, MWO Graphics, to create something appropriate and clever. Using the familiar black-and-white marbelized composition notebook format, artist Mallorie Ostrowitz produced this piece, which is also a self-mailer. Opening the brochure, you find lined pages as in a school notebook with the four theatrical productions highlighted in photographs. The photographs are pasted in, copying an old-fashioned photo album. The artist also used red crayon emulating a child's script for the cover headlines and some of the headlines inside the brochure. The text is in black and the headlines are in red. The paper is a white, coated stock. This simple graphic design proved very successful: The original edition of this brochure won first prize in the Graphics Competition of 1983 in the flier/mailer category sponsored by the International Society of Performing Arts Administrators.

Halloween is a fun time to do programing. The creative minds at the Salt Lake City Public Library in Utah hold an annual series, They prepare two pieces to promote the event. An oversized postcard "flier" with three familiar monsters tells the reader the time, date, place, and what's happening. It's printed on white card stock. The postcard side is white with black ink. Flip it over for the monsters, and you'll be faced with a bright orange background ink. The monsters are in black and white. Nice contrast. To complement the event, the library produced a reading list using the same monsters...this time in black and white only. The words "Creepy!" and "Spine-Chilling!" were added on the cover. Opening the brochure, the reader will find the detailed program information plus a bibliography of selected books, records, and tapes suitable for Halloween reading. The cover is white paper. The interior reading list is a bright goldenrod yellow-orange

Used by permission of the Salt Lake City Public Library.

with black ink. Staff artist Priscilla Vermilion was the designer/artist.

The Hudson River Museum is certainly consistent in its graphic design. The museum's logo is used in all of the promotional pieces produced. For the festival "A River for All Seasons," which was a year-long series with the summer programs beginning the day before the Fourth of July, a handsome annotated brochure was created which, when opened, could be used as a poster. Combining clip art with original artwork, the designer created the feeling of the river festival with an all-American flavor. The paper is a tan vellum and the inks are red and navy blue. This self-mailer is decorative and informative. The artist is Michael Bierut of Vignelli Associates.

Volumes could be devoted to highlighting the many exciting brochures and fliers produced to promote programs, special events, and services. Naturally, the best way to create these would be to hire a freelance graphic designer or have one on staff. However, most organizations do not have the budget to allow this. You can do it yourself. Learn a few simple rules, work with the necessary tools, discover the wonders of papers and inks, and then enjoy the art of creation! Whether it's a simple flier or poster or a detailed brochure, make it your best.

BASIC TOOLS FOR THE DO-IT-YOURSELFER

- A good electric typewriter or word processor with a good letter-quality printer
- Drawing board
- T-square
- Triangle
- X-acto® knife
- Nonreproducing blue pencil
- Eraser (art gum, plastic)

Used by permission of The Hudson River Museum.

- Fine-tipped felt pen black and, if possible, technical pens (Rapidograph®, Mars)
- Ink for technical pens (Koh-i-noor)
- Cleaner for technical pens
- A small jar of rubber cement
- Rubber cement thinner
- Ruler
- Small watercolor paint brush
- Masking tape
- Tracing paper
- Layout pads (lined) or white bond paper
- Vellum sketch pad
- Compass
- Stylus for rub-off lettering
- Workable fixative
- Templates
- Scissors

Your local art supply store will have a stock of necessary supplies and instant lettering catalogs.

RESOURCES

For Publicity

General

Associated Press. *Stylebook & Libel Manual.* 1984 ed. New York: Associated Press.
An up-to-date stylebook organized like a dictionary providing answers to such questions as when to capitalize a word and what an acronym is for a government agency.

Bortin, Virginia. *Publicity for Volunteers: A Handbook.* New York: Walker & Co., 1981.
A handy, down-to-earth book filled with tips and illustrated examples of good public relations, publicity, and promotion.

Cutlip, Scott M., and Center, Allen H. *Effective Public Relations.* 5th rev. ed. Englewood Cliffs, NJ: Prentice-Hall, 1982.
A widely used textbook in this field.

Kincaid, William M., Jr. *Promotion: Products, Services and Ideas.* Columbus, OH: Charles E. Merrill Publishing Co., 1981.
In textbook fashion, presents good information and illustrated examples of advertising, personal selling, sales promotion, and publicity.

Klein, Ted, and Danzig, Fred. *Publicity: How to Make the Media Work for You.* New York: Charles Scribner's Sons, 1985.

Lesley, Philip, ed. *Lesley's Public Relations Handbook.* 3rd ed. Englewood Cliffs, NJ: Prentice-Hall, 1983.
This book has 50 contributing writers and is considered to be a standard reference work for public relations practitioners.

Line, W.C. *News Writing for Non-Professionals.* Chicago: Nelson-Hall, 1979.
Tells how to write news stories; covers everything, including grammar and style.

Seitel, Fraser P. *The Practice of Public Relations.* Montpelier, VT: Perry H. Merrill, 1980.

Strunk, William, Jr., and White, E.B. *The Elements of Style.* New York: Macmillan, 1972.
One of the best; a classic.

Tedone, David *Practical Publicity: How to Boost Any Cause.* Boston: The Harvard Common Press, 1983.
In an easy-to-read format, this book presents practical tips and excellent examples of good publicity tools.

Zinsser, William Knowlton. *On Writing Well.* New York: Harper & Row, 1976.
A guide, written in an informal manner, on how to write nonfiction. Good reading.

———. *Writing with a Word Processor.* New York: Harper & Row, 1983.
Easy to read. Tells of a writer's experiences with a word processor.

PR Periodicals

PR News. 127 E. 80th St., New York, NY 10021.
Primarily for communications and public relations professionals.

Public Relations Journal. 845 Third Ave., New York, NY 10022. Public Relations Society of America. This monthly journal contains many helpful and interesting articles.

Public Relations Quarterly. P.O. Box 311, Rhinebeck, NY 12572.

Publicity Resources Primarily for Those in the Library Field

American Library Association. 50 E. Huron St., Chicago, IL 60611.
A good source for publicity items, bookmarks, posters, and other promotional materials for National Library Week.

Bryan, Carol, ed. *Library Imagination Paper.* 1000 Byus Dr., Charleston, WV 25311.
A quarterly newsletter with articles on public relations, programs, and graphics. It includes ready-to-use graphics.

Edsall, Marion S. *Library Promotion Handbook.* Phoenix, AZ: Oryx Press, 1980.
The definitive book in this field. Covers it all with many practical ideas and information.

Garvey, Mona. *Library Public Relations.* New York: The H.W. Wilson Co., 1980.
A practical handbook containing valuable tips and suggestions on library surveys, media relations, displays, programing, planning, and evaluation.

Library PR News. R D 1, Box 219, New Albany, PA 18833.

A handy bimonthly newsletter filled with informative articles, graphics, and resources for graphic supplies.

Rummel, Kathleen Kelly, ed., and Perica, Esther, ed. *Persuasive Public Relations for Libraries.* 50 E. Huron St., Chicago, IL 60611. American Library Association, 1983.
Chapters are written by experts in the library public relations field and cover just about everything including displays, staff relations, graphics, news releases, and special audiences.

For Image Building

Meyers, William. *The Image Makers: Power and Persuasion on Madison Avenue.* New York: Time Books, 1984.

Olins, Wally. *The Corporate Personality: An Inquiry into the Nature of Corporate Identity.* New York: Mayflower Books, 1978.
Written by a design consultant, this book takes the reader into the corporate world, explaining what it takes to develop an identity program.

Selame, Eleanor, and Selame, Joseph. *Developing a Corporate Identity: How to Stand Out in a Crowd.* New York: Chain Store Age, 1975.

For Good Graphics

This section contains reading materials and other excellent resources intended to stimulate, educate, and inform. Learning about graphic design and then actually trying to create your own can be very exciting. There are hundreds of additional resources you will discover on your own. Please don't forget television. Watch it with your eyes tuned in to graphics. With the increased versatility of the personal computer, you may find yourself turning to a word processor and a letter-quality printer for your printed materials. Computer graphics may be your next discovery! There are many computer books being published daily. Check them out at your library or bookstore. Finally, don't be intimidated. Find what works for you...and do it!

Books on Graphics

American Paper Institute. *The Cover & Text Book.* 260 Madison Ave., New York, NY 10016.
Examines the differences between paper used for covers and paper used for text.

Art Direction Book Company, 10 E. 39th St., New York, NY 10016.
An extensive, free catalog of books.

Evans, Larry. *Illustration Guide for Artists, Designers & Students.* New York: Van Nostrand Reinhold, 1982.

Glaser, Milton. *Graphic Design.* Woodstock, NY: Overlook Press, 1973.

Gray, Bill. *Studio Tips for Artists & Graphic Designers.* New York: Van Nostrand Reinhold, 1976.

Hart, Harold H., ed. *Compendium.* New York: Hart Publishing, 1976.
This book and the two following are from a series which contain a vast and diverse collection of illustrations in the public domain.

———. *Humor, Wit & Fantasy.* New York: Hart Publishing Co., 1976.

———. *Trades & Professions.* New York: Hart Publishing Co., 1977.

Hurlburt, Allen. *The Design Concept: A Guide to Effective Communication.* New York: Watson-Guptill Publications, 1980.

———. *Layout: The Design of the Printed Page.* New York: Watson-Guptill Publications, 1977.

———. *Publication Design: A Guide to Page Layout, Typography, Format and Style.* Rev. ed. New York: Van Nostrand Reinhold, 1976.

International Paper Co. *Pocket Pal: A Graphics Arts Production Handbook.* 1981 ed. International Paper Plaza, 77 W. 45 St., New York, NY 10036.

Laing, John. *Do-It-Yourself Graphic Design.* New York: Facts-On-File, 1984.

Levine, Mindy N., and Frank, Susan. *A Concise Guide to Graphic Arts & Printing for Small Business & Non-Profit Organizations.* Englewood Cliffs, NJ: Prentice-Hall, 1984.

McDarrah, Fred W. *Photography Market Place.* New York: R.R. Bowker.
This annual publication lists picture sources, organizations, equipment sources, and technical services.

Morgan, Hal. *Symbols of America.* New York: Viking, 1986.
A lavish celebration of America's best-loved trademarks and the products they symbolize: their history, folklore, and enduring mystique.

Silver, Gerald A. *Modern Graphic Art Paste-Up: The Workshop Approach to the Graphic Arts.* 2nd ed. New York: Van Nostrand Reinhold, 1983.

Graphic Layout and Design

Sutter, Jan. *Slinging Ink: A Practical Guide to Producing Booklets, Newspapers and Ephemeral Publications.* Los Altos, CA: William Kaufmann, Inc., 1982.

White, Jan V. *Editing by Design.* 2nd ed. New York: R.R. Bowker, 1982.

———. *Mastering Graphics.* New York: R.R. Bowker, 1983.

A how-to guide, a checklist, and sourcebook.

Periodicals

Print, 19 W. 44th St., New York, NY 10036.

U & lc, International Typeface Corp., 2 Hammarskjold Plaza, New York, NY 10017.
Free publication devoted to the art and design of typography.

Video

Pocket Pal—The Movie. International Paper Co., International Paper Plaza, 77 W. 45 St., New York, NY 10036. 18 min., color, 1985.
International Paper has updated *Pocket Pal*, the book, into a video which visually explains the process involved in producing a printed piece and deals specifically with new technology and the impact it has on the printing and graphics arts industries.

Paper Companies

Paper companies produce exciting graphic kits, posters, and designs promoting their papers. They're free for the asking through your printer or paper distributor or by writing directly to the company. Here are just a few. Specify that your query be directed to the "advertising department."

Appleton Papers Inc., P.O. Box 359, Appleton, WI 54912.

Hammermill Papers Group, East Lake Road, Erie, PA 16533.

Mohawk Paper Mills Inc., P.O. Box 497, Cohoes, NY 12047.

Neenah Paper, 1400 Holcomb Bridge Rd., Roswell, GA 30076.

Wausau Papers, Brokaw, WI 54417.

Graphic Arts Suppliers

Dover Publications, 180 Varick St., New York, NY 10014.
Publishes numerous inexpensive sources of cuts and illustrations. Their catalog is free.

Dynamic Graphics, Inc., 6707 N. Sheridan Rd., Peoria, IL.
A monthly clip-art service available on subscription basis. Ask for sample.

Graphic Products Corporation, 3601 Edison Pl., Rolling Meadows, IL 60008.
Clip-art, instant lettering, and all kinds of art supplies. Free catalog.

Harry A. Volk Art Studio, Clip-Art Booklets. Box 4098, Rockford, IL 61110.

Chapter 8
One More Time
(Over 100 Additional Exciting Ideas)

✓ Teddy Bears
✓ Noontime Fun
✓ For Sneezles and Weezles
✓ Book Sales
✓ Forgiveness Week with a Twist
✓ Foodstuffs
✓ Here's to Your Health!
✓ Alice in Wonderland
✓ Shoe Stuff
✓ Ethnic Celebrations
✓ Music Makes It with Teens
✓ A Woman's Place
✓ Film Fare
✓ Much Ado about Christmas
✓ Bits & Pieces
✓ Contests 'N Things
✓ Birthdays, Anniversaries, and More Festivals
✓ Bookstores
✓ Name Dropping
✓ Rubber Stamps

The next time you and your staff or planning committee are having a brainstorming session, try these next few pages for some clever, innovative, and fun ideas. The following ideas are not presented in any particular order; you could call this chapter a "grab bag" of programing and promotional ideas. The marvel of putting together a book such as this one is that there are so many creative events and promotional concepts out there; you must face the realization that you cannot put it all into one book. I hope you have been stimulated and encouraged by all that you have read before this and will be interested in these extra added attractions!

TEDDY BEARS

For a while, cats seemed to be getting the "best press" and publicity, but lately, teddy bears have taken the lead. Teddy bears might be considered more universal because just about everyone has had a teddy bear in his/her life. "The Great American Teddy Bear Rally" has become the Philadelphia Zoo's biggest annual event. It draws as many adults as children, with some 20,000 people attending. At its fourth annual event, held on a June weekend in 1985, contests were held for the largest, smallest, best dressed, and most unusual teddy bears. A contest was also held for the most talented (with some help from owners, I presume) and for "favorite" or "best loved" bears, whose wear and tear attested to their owner's love. A zoo veterinarian recommended remedies for "sick" bears on a prescription pad. Zoo staff in bear costumes wandered about. Children received bear masks and had their faces painted to match those of their furry friends. There were several guests at this event including the 66-year-old original teddy bear that inspired A.A. Milne's *Winnie the Pooh* and two live cubs. Visitors carrying stuffed bears got a dollar off their admission.

The Tucson (Arizona) Public Library holds a Winter Bear Party to which both children and their bears are invited. Refreshments are served, stories are told, and musical games are played. To inaugurate their summer reading game, "Here Come the Bears!" the East Meadow (New York) Public Library bear-costumed a high school thespian who met and greeted youngsters on registration day with a bear hug and free bear balloon. The Westbury (New York) Recreation Department loans teddy bears to lonely people of all ages.

NOONTIME FUN

Acknowledging that many brown-bag their lunch, some libraries, civic centers, and parks present lunchtime events to relax and entertain diners. The Suffolk County (New York) Office of Cultural Affairs offers concerts at the Suffolk County Center. One such event presented from noon to 2 p.m. was called "Brown Bag and Banjos." During July and August 1985, the Nassau County (New York) Parks and Recreation Department offered alternate Wednesday concerts at a local park for brown-baggers. Diners had to bring their own chairs or blankets. On Tuesdays at 12:15 p.m.,

"Noontime Concerts" are presented at the downtown library by the Detroit Public Library. Coffee is available for a quarter. The Friends of the Buffalo and Erie County (New York) Public Library present lunch-hour concerts and book talks, "Books and Music Sandwiched In," on alternate Mondays from 12:10 p.m. to 12:45 p.m.

FOR SNEEZLES AND WEEZLES

At the Library in East Brunswick, New Jersey, you can borrow a "Sneezle Sack" for a sick child from the children's department, complete with games, puzzles, paperback books, and other fun items. The parent or relative can phone in advance and a personalized "sneezle sack" will be prepared for the child. At the Plainedge Public Library in Long Island, New York, they call it a "Get Well Kit" and it includes records, puppets, jigsaw puzzles, puzzle books, paper dolls, and coloring books. The children's coordinators at the West Florida Library System promote their "Get-Well Kit" with a fun promotional flier that looks like a prescription pad. Its cover advises, "Prescribed by Children's Services, W.F.R.L. Dosage: Take as needed until well again! Keep this medicine within the reach of children!"

BOOK SALES

Most libraries, at one time or another, have held a book sale. Some of them have continuous book sales in some area of the library. Others choose a flashy way to sell off their old books. The Brooklyn (New York) Public Library holds its annual book sale by making it a special event, complete with live music, clowns, and magic acts. Not only is it a successful book sale, but it also promotes good community relations by using volunteers who pitch in and help. Friends of the Library in East Brunswick, New Jersey, hold their Annual Book Sale in Brunswick Square Mall and a "preview night" two days before the big day; admission is $2 (Friends are free). The sale is held on two consecutive weekday evenings and includes free puppet shows to keep the youngsters occupied. As an added gimmick, if you present the promotional flier at the sale, you get a free paperback of your choice with any purchase.

FORGIVENESS WEEK WITH A TWIST

There's nothing new about "forgiveness" week at libraries, but this promotional idea is rather novel. The Patchogue-Medford Library on Long Island (New York) knew they had to do something clever to get their library materials back from delinquent patrons. So they designed a Forgiveness Week logo which showed a smiling monk (complete with sandals and robe) holding a sign which said, "No Fines, No Fees, No Sermons." It gave readers a phone number to call, "Forgiveness Central," where they could get information and arrange for book pick-up service. Local merchants ran the Forgiveness Week logo in their ads in the weeklies that week. To encourage the "delinquents" even more, the library supplied another gimmick. Each person returning a book or other overdue materials had the opportunity to join the Forgiveness Week lottery. A "collection plate" was displayed in a prominent spot in the library where each person could write down his/her guess as to the number of overdue materials returned to the library during the week. The winner won a dinner for two at Friars Inn, a local restaurant. The library even had a life-sized cardboard monk on display in the library touting "Forgiveness Week."

FOODSTUFFS

Food plays an important role in many special events and programs. Just about everyone is interested in eating. The city of Chicago certainly does its share of special events promoting food and the joy of eating. Sponsored by the Mayor's Office of Special Events and produced by the Illinois Restaurant Association, a "Taste of Chicago" is a week-long celebration of food, entertainment, and fun. It takes place in Grant Park in the middle of the city and runs for one week early in July. The promotional flier offers the eater a "checklist planner for a ¾ mile of taste experiences." It lists the 84 restaurant booths and their menus where diners can treat themselves to just about anything from deep-dish pizza (many varieties) and New Orleans boiled shrimp to Polish sausage. This corporate-sponsored eating festival also offers entertainment on a daily basis. The entertainment is free, but the food is on sale, with nothing costing more than $3.50. Tickets are sold as "food coupons": A book of coupons is $5 and each ticket is worth 50 cents. No cash is handled at booths.

The city of Hartford, Connecticut, holds a similar food fair, "A Taste of Hartford," for three days in May. The fair draws crowds of 50,000 to 80,000. Fifty Hartford-area restaurants participate and offer visitors many choices from their menus, including French Quarter oyster roll, New England clam chowder, and white chocolate mousse. There are food and wine cooking demonstrations, entertainment such as strolling musicians from a local music college, and children's face-painting and games. These are free, but you must pay for the food at each restaurant's booth; prices range from 50 cents to $3.

Cooking programs are high on the list of entertaining and informative programs at libraries. The Akron-Summit County Public Library in Indianapolis ran a successful series of culinary programs in cooperation with a local utility company. The library supplied the cooks and printed materials (bibliographies, recipes) and the utility company supplied the sites, cooking equipment, and food.

Fund-raising and food also seem to go together. The Friends of the Atascadero California Library held a Lobster Fly-In. The group sold tickets for each live Maine lobster for $10, Blue Point oysters for $5.50 a dozen, and cherrystone clams for $3 a pound. Buyers planned BYOL (Bring Your Own Lobster) parties.

The New Orleans Public Library presented its annual report in the form of a menu a few years back. Its yearly summary of programs, services, and finances was spiced with such titles as "Appetizers" and under that, "Art Exhibit Quiche," "Women's Night Canape," and "Films du Jour with Chitterlings." "House Specialties" included "Consumer Information Jambalaya" and "Cassettes Julienne," and its entrees featured such goodies as "Book Theft Detection System en Brochette." Children's programs were listed under "Child's Plate," and the library's expenditures and budget were listed on a separate page under "Guest Check." The "menu" concluded with the message "Your New Orleans Public Library card welcome here. Take-out service available."

Old English feasts mark the Christmas season in many areas of the West. The Ahwanhee Hotel in Yosemite National Park has been celebrating with such feasts since 1927. It's the most sought-after and most expensive dinner. Ten thousand people vie for 1,000 seats; dinner is $83 per person. If you can't make it there, your choices are still varied, because many other events are sponsored by the Society for Creative Anachronism (SCA), a nonprofit educational organization dedicated to re-creating the atmosphere of the Middle Ages. It has 170 chapters in the West. (To learn about the organization and its events, write to Sandra Dodd, President, Society for Creative Anachronism, 8116 Princess Jeanne Ave., N.E., Albuquerque, NM 87110 and include a stamped self-addressed business envelope.) Here are just a few sanctioned feasts. In Phoenix, Arizona, the First Christian Church's Performing Arts Center becomes a medieval castle. Professional opera singers entertain, Renaissance instruments are played, professional stunt men stage sword fights, and 75 other entertainers perform. Costumed people serve the seven-course meal ($22.50 each). At the University of California, Berkeley, there's a Winter Revels, which is a night of "magical music, whimsical entertainments, and fabulous foolings" in the Student Union's Pauley Ballroom. Four hundred guests are invited to dress as a favorite fantasy or fairy-tale character. An eight-course meal features medieval breads, wassail, quail, beef, vegetables, flaming plum pudding, wine, and dessert. Student entertainers also perform. Tickets cost $20 each. At Fort Collins, Colorado, Colorado State University's department of music, theatre, and dance offers an Elizabethan madrigal Christmas dinner. A high lord and his lady, along with their 400 guests, are entertained by 60 costumed singers, dancers, gymnasts, and pipers. The food and entertainment costs $20 per person. There are many more such feasts in Montana; New Mexico; Oregon; Utah; Washington; and British Columbia, Canada.

HERE'S TO YOUR HEALTH!

Increased consumer awareness has heightened interest in health fairs. The Arlington Heights Public Library in Illinois called theirs "The Body Shop" and offered free blood pressure screening, hearing, vision testing, healthy refreshments, fitness trials, and computerized print-outs of nutritional information. The Onondaga County Public Library in Syracuse, New York, touted its health fair with "Be in the Pink! Take Charge of Your Health!" on a promotional flier printed on pink paper. Staff also offered the usual free health screenings and gave out free apples, cider, and orange drinks. The apples were supplied by the Western New York Apple Growers Association; the various information booths were staffed by representatives from local health-related organizations.

The East Meadow Public Library (New York) holds a series of four to six programs during alternate Februarys with such topics as "Children's Nutrition Workshop," "How to Choose a Doctor," "A Look at Everyday Neuroses," "The Intimacy of Anger," "Arthritis and Related Diseases," "Biofeedback Help," and "Phobias." In March 1985, Nassau Community College (New York) held a People's Health Symposium entitled "Men and Women: Old Questions, New Answers." During a week in March, they presented such programs as: "Sex and Power: The Psychopathology of Everyday Life," "Real Men Don't Relate: They Just Hold Everything In," and "Is Fidelity Obsolete?"

ALICE IN WONDERLAND

The Friends of the Bryant Library (Roslyn, New York) held a "Madhatter's Tea Party" one wintry Sunday afternoon. Stan Marx, a community member and founder of the Lewis Carroll Society of North America, made the introductions. The Royal Crown Players of Roslyn High School appeared in Eva La Gallienne's play, "The Mad Hatter's Tea Party." Tea and biscuits were served after the performance.

Using Alice in Wonderland as the theme, the Montclair Public Library in New Jersey ran a gala fund-raising event, "Digressions and Diversions." The event offered an auction of unique trips and gifts. The entire library was decorated to suit the theme. Book stacks had to be dismantled and books packed away for this successful Saturday night party. One of the fun gifts auctioned off was a "magic birthday party in the library for 25 children." Everything was donated, including staff time, and the library realized an income of $48,000 for its building renovation fund.

SHOE STUFF

Just about anything to do with celebrities draws people. Originally, the Pawtucket (Rhode Island) Public Library's Office of Community Services wrote to some celebrities asking for their old shoes to decorate the library's Christmas "Shoe Tree of the Stars." The staff had constructed two wooden trees and were going to decorate them with the donated shoes, plus autographed photos, complete with red and green plaid holiday ribbons. With so many stars responding, the library decided to auction off the shoes with proceeds going to support the library's programing budget. Stars who sent shoes, photographs, and other items included Brooke Shields, Richard Chamberlain, John Travolta, Ed Asner, Richard Simmons, and Marty Ingels. The auction netted $2,255. Sally Struthers's platform sandals brought the highest price, $700! The auction was moved to the armory because of the high attendance (400 people); the media gave it tremendous coverage with such headlines as "This library is well-heeled," "Area residents get a 'kick' out of celebrity's shoes" and "Stars bare their soles for library benefit."

ETHNIC CELEBRATIONS

People enjoy ethnic festivals and celebrations even though their family heritage may not be that of the country being celebrated. Of course, if you are having an Italian festival and also have a large Italian community, it makes the celebration that much more meaningful and encourages more participation. The Port Washington (New York) Public Library commemorated "American Italian Culture and Heritage Month" in October 1983. They worked with a Sons of Italy Lodge, the American Italian Historical Association, and the Center for Migration Studies in New York City. Enlisting the help of local artists, the library displayed 20 regional banners of Renaissance Italy with heraldic designs in authentic colors. On exhibit also was sculpture by Clemente Spampinato and "We Italian Americans," a photographic display highlighting American Italian history on loan from the Center for Migration Studies. Display cases featured artifacts, photos, memorabilia, and drawings relating to the Italian immigrant experience in America. There was a special Columbus Day program with readings and story hours featuring selections from Italian literature in English and some in Italian. The film *Christopher Columbus* was shown twice, the last time on Columbus Day. The films *La Strada* and *Christ in Concrete* were also shown during the month. Opening ceremonies featured local Italian dignitaries and a dance performance by the Orsogna Paese Mio Dance Group in authentic native costumes. Local academics presented programs such as "The Italian Experience in America," "A Survey of the Contributions of Italy to Western Civilization from Etruscan to Recent Times," and "Italian Art: The Classical Style and Spirit." In addition, an informative resource guide was published by the library, listing the library's collection of materials pertaining to the Italian American culture and history. It was a total celebration...the only thing missing was pasta and pizza!

Down the road a piece is the Great Neck Public Library, which chose to celebrate "Japan in Great Neck." The library worked with its Japanese community members, the Consulate General of Japan, the Japan Information Center, Japan Airlines, the Nippon Club, and others to offer the community a two-month Japanese celebration. The Great Neck Public Library was one of 10 in New York State to receive funding to participate in a special pilot project entitled "A Sense of Community: Diversity and Change." The presentations were varied and many: Japanese traditional dances, flower arrangement demonstrations, a tea ceremony, films and lectures, musical concerts, doll making, "Variations on the Theme of the Kimono," plus children's fun, film, and craft programs. A special Japanese art show was a part of the whole presentation.

Columbus Day was celebrated at the Tucson Public Library in Arizona one year with a totally different approach. Using the talents of their entire community, they opened a school festival with musical groups from high schools and junior high schools performing. This was followed by recognition ceremonies with speeches and music. Members of the Arizona Opera Company (sponsored by the Italian American Club of Tucson) sang arias from favorite Italian operas. Then the Good Steppers jumped in and entertained with an Afro-American dance, which was followed by Mexican dances by the Folklorico Infantil de Tucson. The University of Arizona Choral Group sang; the Intertribal Dancers of Tucson danced; and the Ododo Theater presented "Voodoo Blues & Hues." The day ended with the Arizona Civic Theater Roundtable discussion of the season's plays.

The Detroit Public Library, in cooperation with the city's Polish American Ethnic Committee, presented a Polish film series with funding obtained from the National Endowment for the Humanities. Their theme was "The Polish Experience through Humanities." The films offered were *The Peasants, Non Matrimonial Story, Death of a President*, and *I Am a Butterfly*. All the films had English subtitles. The Friends of the Detroit Public

Library held a Polish Book Sale the year before to sell Polish-language new and used books and magazines in the downtown library branch. The proceeds were used to maintain and upgrade the Polish language section of the library's foreign language collection.

MUSIC MAKES IT WITH TEENS

It takes perseverance, special interest, and time to create programs that will appeal to teenagers. Albany (New York) Public Library young adult librarians Carol Dratch Kovier and Sheila Kirven Talma seem to have hit on the right formula, because things are happening in the young adult department there! Beginning in 1982, these two music lovers started their music mania, and the teens in the community joined in the fun. "Use your own local talents first" might be a good slogan for programers, especially if your budget is a tight one. Carol and Sheila promoted (with the help of public relations director Fran Lewis) a Valentine's Day party for teens as "Meet Albany's Heart Throbs." They turned out to be Albany's best-known and -loved rock band, Blotto. "Live and in person," the band was allowed to sell recordings, and, being a witty and personable group, they spent a lot of time talking to teens, answering questions, and signing autographs. Blotto showed a tour video to the audience, and in turn, media librarian Bob Katz agreed to help the band make a music video.

This was the beginning of the music connection between the librarians and the teens. Since the initial event, Carol and Sheila have staged a wide variety of music-related events, which included live concerts by local amateur and professional bands, and "meet the D.J's" nights, starring personalities student polls indicated were favorites. In 1984, Carol started a "New Music" club. Teens could come to the library weekly and watch MTV or BTV or music videos and films from the library's collection. As the young people came more and more to the library for the musical events, they became more at ease and used other sections of the library frequently. The connection was made; Carol and Sheila continue to pursue other areas to keep the young people interested in the library. The "biggest hit" was their 1984 "Bop-Til-You-Drop Summer Readathon." Just to get a bunch of teenagers to join a reading club is a high mark of success! In celebration of the school year's end, Sheila hosted a party on the front porch of the library's Victorian house branch in the Pine Hills section of town. Teenage "poppers" were invited to perform. One hundred and five teens and a TV news crew came; the "poppers" were invited to entertain at other area libraries as well. The library's video department made a TV public service announcement using three of the "poppers" to promote the readathon.

How to attract young people to a reading game? Do something unique. Carol wrote to personalities important to junior and high schoolers.

> "The power you have to affect your fans is very real. We are therefore requesting your participation in our summer reading event, Bop-til-You-Drop Readathon. We are asking celebrities to donate photos, records, autographs or even personal items to offer as prizes to the teens who read the most books. Each student will give an oral report to prove familiarity with the contents of each story...."

Two hundred letters were sent, and no more than 30 responses were expected. The library was pleased when 80 musicians, actors, writers, sports figures, astronauts, and other celebrities were heard from! Here's how the readathon worked: Contestants registered at the branch or main library and listed five prizes they would like to win. They also listed the books they intended to read through the month. Four books on an appropriate level (no comic books or picture books), read and reported on (a special "report card" was used), made the contestant eligible for first choice of the prizes. The tempting prizes were on display at the main library and featured in newspaper, radio, and television announcements.

The real promotion began with the librarians' school visits in the spring. School visits are very much a part of their MO. Close to 100 teens signed up for the readathon and just about everyone read something! Sixty prizes were awarded at a party. Circulation figures for the two summer months skyrocketed—500 more books circulated at the main library than the previous year in the same time period. The high school senior who won top prize by reading 42 books received two free tickets to a Rick Springfield concert at nearby Saratoga Performing Arts Center. She not only visited with him backstage but also had her picture taken with him. Springfield, by the way, had just released a song he had written entitled "Bop Til You Drop." Before things quieted down too much, Carol and Sheila held a reading contest called "The Jacksons Read It." Prizes included certificates autographed by the Jackson brothers and Jackson albums donated by a local music store. They're still hitting all the right notes for teens at the library!

A WOMAN'S PLACE

Since the woman's movement began, more programs and events have been scheduled pertaining to women's lives and issues. The Indianapolis-Marion County Public Library (with a grant from the Indiana Committee for the Humanities and Indianapolis-Marion County Public Library Foundation, Inc.) presented a series of creative programs "exploring women's contributions in the humanities and arts." It was called "A Woman's Place" and ran for three months. Three major lectures were offered with authors Nora Ephron, Gerda Lerner, and Pauline Kael. A chamber music series featuring the music of Clara Schumann, Elizabeth Gould, Mrs. H.H.A. Beach, and Maria Szymanowska was presented. "A Woman's Place" dance concert, choreography and dance by women, was performed at the All Souls Unitarian Church by members of the Indiana University Dance Theater. "Expressions," an 11-week series of programs of music composed by women, was broadcast on WIN (FM radio). Several women academics gave talks on such topics as "Women Poets," "Contributions of Women in American History," and "Women and Stress." A series of films dealing with women's issues was shown each month, including such movies as *A New Leaf, Girlfriends*, and *Seven Beauties*. A handsome brochure annotated the events and there was a bibliography on women in art, music, history, literature, film, and science available at all library locations.

In the spring of 1985 at Sarah Lawrence College in Bronxville, New York, the offering was an all-day conference on "Working." After listening to two keynote speakers, the participants had lunch and then proceeded to two afternoon workshops. They could choose from among 32 different workshops, each of which ran for one hour and 15 minutes. The purpose of the conference was to "provide you with resources for further education and action" and was sponsored by the college's Center for Continuing Education and Women's History Program and the Westchester County Office for Women. Some of the workshops were: "Family-izing the Workplace," "Educating Children to Be Productive Adults," and "Getting Fired."

FILM FARE

When planning film programing, again, know your community. If you have found a successful pattern that works, stick with it, but don't be afraid to occasionally offer something a bit off-beat. Here are a couple of promotional ideas you might try. The Bloomington Public Library in Illinois "sold" its lunchtime film offerings with a promotional flier printed on a small brown bag: "Every Wednesday, Bring Your Lunch to the Library. Munch Your Lunch with the Bunch Film Program." The library's name was on the front of the bag with dates and times of film programs. The back of the bag had the library's address, phone numbers, and hours of service. You could take this idea one step further by filling the bag with popcorn and serving it at comedy movie festivals or series. Rubber stamp your organization's name on the bag or possibly the name of the food merchant who might have donated the popcorn.

The West Virginia Library Commission produced a popcorn bag a few years back which was imprinted with popcorn and the words "Things are always popping at the library" and "Yum, Yum, Yum, Yum" and "Film, Food, Film, Food, etc." Another promotional idea that was novel involved a mystery series at the Milwaukee Public Library. The brochure was printed in brown ink on beige paper stock and the title of the series was "Murder on the Menu." When you opened the "menu" you found the main courses: *Phantom of the Opera* (1925), *Secret Agent* (1936), *Sherlock Holmes and the Secret Weapon* (1942), *Topper Returns* (1941), and *Blackmail* (1930). The brochure, art deco in design, used copy in keeping with its menu theme, "Forest Home Library is serving up a 5-course tragedy of old time mystery films. Bring a bag lunch and watch a film over supper; we'll make the coffee. Tuesdays, 5:30–7 p.m. Come watch the villain get his just desserts."

Thematic film programs always draw audiences. Again, the theme to choose goes back to knowing your community. The Indianapolis-County Public Library held a series on Thursday nights called "The Way We Were: Films about the '60s." For culture and counterculture buffs they showed *Lenny* (1974). For music lovers the film *Woodstock* (1970) was offered. *Hearts and Minds* (1974) told the Vietnam story. Protest was covered in the showing of *The Return of the Secaucus Seven* (1980). And for retrospect, the film *A Small Circle of Friends* (1980) was presented.

Women have been the subject of many film festivals throughout the country. The Center for Unlimited Enrichment at Queens College of the City University of New York presented a free summer film festival, "Not for Women Only: Filmmakers Look at Women." Films were shown on six consecutive Wednesday afternoons at 1:30 p.m., and film critic Victor Gluck held a discussion after each film. Films included *I'm Dancing as Fast as I Can, A Doll's House* and *Red Desert* (Italian with English subtitles).

One thought to keep in mind: Don't try to compete with the local movie houses in your film programing. Not only is it not a good idea, but your budget probably won't allow it. Feature films are loved by audiences, and one of the cheapest ways to book a series is to do it cooperatively with others. Film programing does not have to mean feature films. Introduce the unique qualities of less well-known films and filmmakers. Invite a filmmaker and show his/her film followed by a discussion. You can't get that kind of film programing in a commercial house. The Port Washington (New York) Public Library on Long Island has been doing this type of film programing successfully for years. In most cases, they obtain matching grants. Look into your local, state, or county film agency. Also, if you plan a series in the humanities, you can apply for a mini-grant, as did the Ohoopee Regional Library in Vidalia, Georgia. Calling the series "Humanities on Trial," the library showed the films *A Man for All Seasons, Mr. Smith Goes to Washington,* and *They Might Be Giants.* An Episcopal priest discussed the religious theme in *A Man for All Seasons,* and two professors of political science and literature handled the other two films. The series cost $800.

One of the best resources for film planning is your public library. If it's a large enough library, it will have an audiovisual or media department which will have a collection of film catalogs. The audiovisual director may also help you in your program planning. There are some free sources for films. Check out the *Annual Educator's Guide to Free Films* (Educators Progress Inc., Randolph, WI 53956) for one. Also don't forget your telephone or utility company as a source (even though you'll have to put up with a few lines of commercial in the film). Good film programming takes creative thinking. Plan carefully.

MUCH ADO ABOUT CHRISTMAS

Christmas lends itself to much festive celebration. Two cities that do their share are Hartford, Connecticut, and Bethlehem, Pennsylvania. Actually, the whole state of Connecticut joins in the celebration, but Hartford is the site of an annual musical concert which is rather special. One hundred tuba players gather from all parts of New England under the direction of tuba virtuoso Harvey Phillips of Indiana University to play Christmas carols on the city's green one afternoon. They call the concert "Tubalation."

If your name was Bethlehem and it was Christmas time, you'd be lacking something if you didn't celebrate in a unique way. And they do just that in Bethlehem, Pennsylvania. *The Bethlehem Star* is the attractive newspaper distributed free and produced by the chamber of commerce. Calling itself "Christmas City, USA," Bethlehem uses its heritage and local architecture to set the stage for its special events. Going back to the earliest Moravian settlement there and its influence on the observance of Christmas, Bethlehem plans its holiday activities. Several hundred volunteers and animals present the Live Bethlehem Christmas Pageant annually at the Community Arts Pavilion. To inaugurate the festivities, a Christmas city lighting ceremony is held first. Visitors and locals can then take Christmas City Night Light Tours of the historic buildings in the city. They can also enjoy the Moravian Christmas Putz (a miniature display of Christ's birth), lantern tours, Christmas revels, and special musical presentations and candlelight services held during the month of December by colleges, schools, churches, and choral groups. The city also holds an annual "Musikfest" in August with the famous Bach Choir of Bethlehem and others performing. It's a nine-day musical treat.

BITS & PIECES

The Providence (Rhode Island) Public Library created two rather unique and interesting programs and exhibits with financial support from the National Endowment for the Humanities. Working with the U.S. Small Business Administration, the library presented a month-long exhibit and lecture series highlighting the best of over 24,260 inventions Rhode Islanders have created since 1790 and called it "A Lively Experiment." On display were over 100 items, from Betsy Baker's straw bonnet to G.W. Perry's steam generator. The lecture series included patent specialists, attorneys, and designers who talked about such things as "preparing for patenthood" and "how designers invent."

Magic seems to appeal to all ages. The Providence Public Library took magic and turned it into a month-long presentation, "ABRACADABRA!" The presentation included an exhibit of rare books, posters, catalogs, photographs, and an antique conjuring apparatus, all from the collection of magician John H. Percival, a Rhode Island resident. The collection, which was bequeathed to the library, makes Providence "one of the greatest repositories of literature on magic in the United States." There were several live magic performances, with an all-day magic show held on Halloween Eve, with some of Rhode Island's best conjurers onstage. The library worked with the International Brotherhood of Magicians and the Society of American Magicians to put together this event.

The Friends of the J.V. Fletcher Library in Westford, Massachusetts, told the world they loved their library. They designated February as "Love Your Library" month and proceeded to show all the ways they loved their library. First they displayed a colorful red-and-white banner out of one of the library's windows with the message "Love Your Library." But words were not enough. They showed the community all of the contributions they had made to the library in the name of love. Each item purchased by Friends of the library had a red heart sticker which read, "I was given to the library by the Friends of the Library. Are you a Friend?" During school vacation week, children were invited to take part in a treasure hunt to find all 20 of the hearts. The reward was a candy heart given just for the effort and a gift certificate to a local bookstore for finding all of them. A romance book sale was also held.

The Bryant Library in Roslyn, New York, began a new service called "The Bryant Calendar of Community Events" and threw a party to draw attention to the new service. The calendar is on permanent display in the library and shows at a glance what's happening around town and where and when the programs are. Hundreds of "Calendar Day" invitations went out to representatives of social, business, and civic organizations. Response was great. Over a free breakfast, each representative got the chance to speak briefly about his/her group's planned activities for the year.

An eye-catching graphic device on the cover of the University of Maryland's library directory brochure certainly makes you want to open the brochure and learn more. Called a "Self-Guided Tour through the Undergraduate Library of the University of Maryland," the brochure has the imprint of a human footprint in black ink complementing the vermilion typeface; the paper is white.

How many times have you received the same brochure or newsletter in the mail? "What a waste of time and money" might have been your comment. I like the addendum that Theater in the Park (Flushing, New York) puts on brochures they send out: "If you receive more than just one of these, please pass it on to a friend." The suggestion appears on the mailer section of the brochure, and even though it's in small print, it attracts your attention. I did just that...passed it on to a friend.

Sometimes you can use a little help with your programing. In fact, you wouldn't mind a complete package deal. Why not? The Columbia Public Library (Daniel Boone Regional Library, Columbia, Missouri) has a very active and creative programing schedule. One of their goodies was "Remembering 1924." The promotional flier touted remembrances of times past: "Flappers. Bathtub gin. 'Keep Cool and Keep Coolidge.' Babe Ruth. The first crossword puzzle book. Rudolph Valentino. Silk stockings. Speakeasies. Bobbed hair. 1924." They invited the community to "an exciting time to be young and exciting now to remember. Join us for a look back with pictures, music, sound, smells, and fun." The library got its 1924 program kit from a group called Bi-Folkal Productions, Inc. Primarily produced for older audiences, the group's slogan is "Sharing the remembered past." Some of the kits are: "Remembering Summertime," "Remembering Automobiles," "Remembering the Depression," "Remembering School Days," "Remembering Birthdays," and "Remembering Farm Days." Each kit is a package of program materials. For instance, the "Remembering Summertime" kit includes an 80-slide tape program called *Summer Is*, 25 copies of *Summer Album*, a booklet with poems, discussion starters, and sing-along songs; a cassette tape with sing-along songs and stories for discussion; a large-print skit script; scratch-and-sniff strips of summer scents; lots of things to touch and talk about (baseball cards, Band-Aids, a flag, a fan, strawberry huller, and more); and a program manual with ideas, activities, and related materials. (Bi-Folkal Productions, Inc., Route 1, Rainbow Farm, Blue Mounds, WI 53517)

Speaking of remembrances, did you know there's a group called the National Radio Heritage Association? Included in their activities is an annual Oldtime Country Radio Entertainers Festival. The festival features an amateur contest, an arts and crafts show to browse through between shows, and a Radio Reunion Extravaganza with many old-time radio stars. The stage is set up to resemble an old-time radio station. (Interested in doing a program on old-time radio shows or just learning more? Contact Nadine Dreager, 8 Gayland Dr., Council Bluffs, IA 51501.)

Hotels are into thematic weekends, and some are doing fun and creative things. Who wouldn't want to indulge in "The Chocolate Lovers Weekend"? The Hyatt Hotel in Schaumburg (a suburb of Chicago) has an imaginative general manager by the name of Helmut Brenzinger who dreams up fun weekends with the hotel's public relations firm, Ruth Rashman Associates. The hotel recently held its third annual Chocolate Weekend. Guests were invited to partake of all the chocolate goodies laid out in the Grand Ballroom. Freaking out on chocolate can be easy when there are over 40 exhibitors tempting you with all kinds of chocolate delicacies...candies, brownies, candy bars, cookies, ice cream, cake, liquor, fudge, and many different kinds of pure milk chocolate and dark chocolate. A psychotherapist was also on hand to lead a Chocoholics Anonymous session. In previous years, only 250 rooms in the hotel were reserved for the chocolate weekend. This past year, all of the rooms, 479, were sold for the event. A few weeks prior to the weekend, about 30 people submitted recipes for a contest whose grand prize was to be the winner's weight in milk chocolate morsels provided by a chocolate company in Milwaukee. The winning recipe was a "zesty chocolate chip meringue."

Not to be outdone by its "sister" hotel, the Hyatt in New Orleans dreamed up a delicious weekend for ice cream lovers. Just about the same kind of weekend was planned except it was all ice cream...sampling, cooking demonstrations, contests, exhibits, and other sweet stuff.

CONTESTS 'N THINGS

There are thousands of unusual contests held all over the world. A few of them are covered in Chapter 6, "Games, Contests, Festivals, and Fairs." Here I would like to mention a few more. A nice simple idea comes from the Plymouth (Massachusetts) Public Library. Cooperating with an ice cream parlor, the library asked youngsters to draw a picture of their dream ice cream concoction. The 10 best entries were invited to the ice cream emporium and given a chance to create and eat their very own ice cream dream!

Sometimes the winter can be so long and dull. Out on the east end of Long Island, there is a free weekly newspaper called *Dan's Papers*. Dan Rattiner likes to keep things interesting all year 'round not just in the summer months when all the summer people arrive. So, in one of his February issues, he invited people to a "I Survived the Winter Party" to be held at the Long Wharf in Sag Harbor on Saturday, March 30, from 6 p.m. to 10 p.m. Tickets cost $6 and entitled the buyer to different and fun ways to make a fool of him/herself, including a beard-growing contest which would begin on February 1, with the judging at 9 p.m. on the night of the party. So that entrants did not have a head start, they had to report to the offices of *Dan's Papers* at noon on Thursday, January 31, so that "cleanshaveness could be confirmed." Another contest was a chili-making contest, to be judged between 7 p.m. and 7:30 p.m. that night. The chili was to be brought to the party already cooked. A half-gallon pot of chili was required. If you had other special talents, you were invited to enter the amateur talent contest. You just had to tell Dan what you would be doing in advance. To spare the rest of the party-goers, you were limited to 10 minutes to do your thing. A good way to perk up an otherwise dreary winter.

Everyone seems to get into the spirit whenever there's a "Guess How Many Whatchamacallits in the Jar." You name it and people have counted them. During their Halloween Week celebration, the children's room staff of the Acton Memorial Library (Massachusetts) invited the kids to count the candy corns in the jar. Out of 250 youngsters who tried, one young man guessed the closest, with a count of 655—the actual was 667. His prize was the most recent edition of the *Guinness Book of World Records*. The Freeport Memorial Library (New York) showed some "poppin fun films" for children on Saturdays during the month of October. And just because it was National Popcorn Poppin' Month, they celebrated with a "Guess How Many Popcorns in the Jar" contest in the children's room. Looking for ways to play the same game? Try counting gumballs, pretzels, jelly beans, fortune cookies, candy kisses. You'll think of more!

With the popularity of the game Trivial Pursuit, tournaments of trivia are being held all over. About 150 people gathered at the State University at Stony Brook (New York) a while back to try their hand at a New York State Trivial Pursuit Challenge. The local Easter Seal Society hoped to realize $6,000 paid by the sponsors. There were 39 teams of trivia buffs who were sponsored by individuals and companies from the tri-state area. Competition was intense at the 10 tables in the school's gym. These people really knew their trivia.

Another favorite is crossword puzzles. You don't have to have a competition as elaborate as the Annual United States Open Crossword Puzzle Championship. Do your own thing. The Friends of the Dartmouth (Massachusetts) Public Libraries hold an annual Southeastern New England Crossword Puzzle Tournament. The participants strain over puzzles created by Massachusetts residents. Prizes are awarded and a luncheon is served by the Ladies of Allen's Neck Friends. There is a guest speaker. In the past, speakers included Eugene T. Maleska, puzzle editor of *The New York Times*, and Will Shortz, senior editor of *Games* magazine. It makes for a good fund-raiser. Or you might want to copy the students at Keene State College in New Hampshire, who tried to beat a world record by assembling what they said would be the "world's largest jigsaw puzzle." The puzzle had 15,000 pieces and covered more than 4,000 square feet.

If you're out to just have fun and do "wild and crazy things," here are a few unique ideas. Try an "Ugliest Umbrella Contest," as the folks in Oregon City (Oregon) did one March. There's always the National Tobacco Spitting Contest held in Raleigh (Mississippi) in June. Don't forget the National Cherry Pit Spitting Contest held in July in Eau Claire (Michigan). If you're the easygoing type, you'll probably love World Sauntering Day, celebrated in June at the Grand Hotel on Mackinac Island (Michigan). The idea is to discourage jogging and encourage sauntering. If you saunter, you get a certificate. Up to 1,000 have been issued during one celebration.

The folks in Spring Hill (Florida) really make feathers fly when they hold their annual World Champion Chicken Pluckin' Contest on the first Saturday of each October. They work with teams, and so far the women are ahead. Milk lovers should jump at this one. The Los Angeles County Fair in California holds an annual milk drinking contest at the end of September. The only catch is that contestants don't know ahead of time how they will be asked to drink the milk—it could be in a baby bottle or a bowl. Then you could try a National Marbles Tournament, such as the one held since 1922 at the resort town of Wildwood by the Sea in New Jersey. During the championship elimination games, young people play about 80 games of marbles before the champion is declared. If you're planning this one, there's a lot to learn, so you'd better know your marbles. You might also try a Frisbee, yo-yo, tug-of-war, watermelon seed-spitting, apple seed popping, apple core throwing, clamshell pitching, stone skipping, skillet throwing, pancake races, or Bohemian Apple (onion) eating contest.

Then you might want to try the "Scrambled Legs" contest; several schools have. Darlene Shiverdecker, librarian at Aiken (Ohio) High School sent fliers to the 60 male staff members asking them to participate in the school's contest, "Mr. Legs." The men's legs were photographed in color, naked from the knees down. All were on display in the library's display windows. Each vote cost one penny, and voter turnout was terrific. The contest ran for two weeks and $180 was raised. The winner was a teacher in an auto body class who earned $65 in votes. He was treated to a meal in a local restaurant.

BIRTHDAYS, ANNIVERSARIES, AND MORE FESTIVALS

Imagine if you were invited to a private birthday or anniversary party and there was nothing but dull speeches with no opportunity for fun. You wouldn't enjoy it; no one would. When celebrating the birthday of your organization or company, think people and then think fun. Try the unusual rather than the humdrum. Don't forget participation. People, even the shy ones, have more fun when they're involved. A few years back, R.J. Reynolds Industries, Inc., of Winston-Salem, North Carolina, threw the "world's biggest company picnic" for the company's 100th birthday. The guests, Reynolds Industries employees, their families, and company retirees, numbered 50,000. They used the local fairgrounds to hold the picnic. Seven tons of barbecued pork, 13,000 pounds each of fried chicken, potato salad, and cole slaw; 15,750 pounds of baked beans; 50,200 pieces of corn on the cob; 51,600 rolls and buns; 100,000 ice cream bars; 250,000 packages of potato chips and other snacks; and 10,000 gallons of soft drinks and punch were consumed. There was big-name entertainment, amusement rides for children, and plenty of music. The media gave the event plenty of attention. Many feature stories were run and the story about the "biggest picnic" reached places as far away as Japan. A film was even made about the picnic. Now, you may not be able to budget as gigantic a picnic as this one, but you could throw a birthday picnic on your own scale the next time an anniversary comes up.

The Chamber of Commerce in Lake Havasu City (Arizona) claims to have the country's "largest antique" and they celebrate its birthday each year with a big bash. The honoree is the London Bridge, which was transplanted to this Arizona city in 1971. There are foot races, water-skiing contests, dances, softball tournaments, and wrist wrestling matches. Of special interest are the medieval combat tournament and display (sponsored by the Society for Creative Anachronism) and the English costume contest for children and adults.

National monuments have birthdays too. To New Yorkers, the 100th birthday of the Brooklyn Bridge was a very special occasion. You didn't have to live in Brooklyn to celebrate the bridge's birthday. The staff at the East Meadow Public Library on Long Island loves birthdays, too, theirs and everyone elses. Parties are planned at the drop of a balloon, so it was natural that they should plan a series of activities around the Brooklyn Bridge's birthday. Knowing your community again proved most helpful in making plans. The community is composed of people from varied ethnic backgrounds; many are émigrés from Brooklyn. With a mini-grant from the New York Council for the Humanities, the library planned a series of events, beginning with a showing of the award-winning film *Brooklyn Bridge* and followed by a lecture and discussion led by a local (ex-Brooklynite) humanities professor. The next morning, a chartered bus took 53 people back to Brooklyn for a variety of activities. One of them was to walk the Brooklyn Bridge with guides from Brooklyn Rediscovery, a local historical and preservation organization, followed by lunch in the Park Slope section of Brooklyn and a guided tour of the Brooklyn Bridge exhibition at the Brooklyn Museum. The following Friday night, another humanities professor made introductory remarks for the showing of the movie *A Tree Grows in Brooklyn*. She also led a discussion after the film. Brown-baggers got a chance to see the film the same day from noon to 2 p.m. Another bus trip to Brooklyn was slated the following Thursday night to Barge Music, which is anchored under the Brooklyn Bridge. A chamber concert was the treat; the sight of the bridge lit up topped off the evening. The birthday party was held on the following Sunday afternoon with cake, entertainment, music, and dramatic readings. There was a Brooklyn Bridge art show, and a Brooklyn Trivia quiz and reading list were also printed. It was a memorable birthday celebration.

There were many celebrations for the centenary of composer Jerome Kern's birthday. A party and an unveiling of the new 22-cent performing arts stamp featuring Kern was held at the New York Public Library for the Performing Arts at Lincoln Center in January 1985. A group of composers, lyricists, and musicians played and sang some of his songs. Since New York City was the place of his birth, the city planned many more celebrations with many of his shows being revived just for this occasion. Why not plan a birthday celebration for Cole Porter, Jerome Kern, or other well-known composers with a series of musical programs? The composer need not have been born in your locale. Take Sinclair Lewis's birthday; he would have been 100 years old in February 1985. People celebrated his day in many places and in many ways. In his hometown of Sauk Centre, Minnesota, birthday signs were erected all over town. Sinclair Lewis T-shirts, mugs, crystal bells, and baseball caps were sold. Even a 14-cent Sinclair Lewis stamp was issued. Most of the 3,370 residents of Sauk Centre turned out for a flurry of events. After the birthday dinner, the community adjourned to City Hall for the unveiling of the Lewis bust, a talk by the postmaster on commemorative stamps, Ida Compton's reminiscences on her friend "Red," and the announcement of a $1,000 short story contest by the Sinclair Lewis Foundation.

The staff at the Daniel Boone Regional Library in Columbia, Missouri, are always up to some sort of fun and games. For their 25th birthday, they invited the community to a "Big Birthday Bash." They set aside the entire month of

March 1984 for celebrating. The big bash was scheduled for Tuesday, March 27, at 7:30 p.m. Before that date, they planned many other activities. For "The Joke's on Us," staff provided the public with a cartoon for their "That Was No Lady, That Was My Librarian" contest and asked them to provide a funny caption. The caption had to be funny and relate to the library; prizes ranged from a "warm handshake to a rubber chicken!" S.E.A.R.C.H. was played at the reference/information desk by third to sixth graders. They had to find the answers to such questions as "What was the weight of the largest birthday cake ever?" or "When is Michael Jackson's birthday?" Young people were instructed to bring a towel and a change of clothing when invited to the next event, a pie-throwing and water balloon party in the Friends room and parking lot. There were three age categories for the Second Annual Kids' Cook-Off. Kids ages six–eight, nine–11, and 12–15 were asked to make their favorite cake, pie, or sweet treat and decorate it for the library's birthday. On the *big* day, the public was encouraged to make a birthday card (supplies provided) in the front lobby. There was a book-stacking contest for preschoolers with a juggler entertaining in between stackings; cake was served during the day in the Friends Room; a book-stacking contest for all ages was held in the afternoon; a balloon-blowing contest was held on the front patio for all ages; and lest you think it was nothing but fun and games, William Least Heat Moon, author of *Blue Highways*, spoke and autographed books at the program that night. The good times continued the next day.

BOOKSTORES

Sometimes you get your best ideas from areas outside of your working environment. All such ideas need is a little alteration to suit your needs. When you're in the commercial field, competition is keen; it's even more difficult when you're a small group surrounded by large organizations.

A Different Drummer Books serves the suburban community of Burlington (outside of Toronto, Canada) and is run by partners Al Cummings and John Richardson. People know of their existence there because of many things, but primarily because of their mailings, which keep people informed. They have an imaginative newsletter, special promotions, and well-created promotional fliers. Humor is a very important part of their operation. For example, they designed one lemon-yellow brochure, to announce, "We pull out all the stops for our fourth annual lemon sale! Our lemons may be very sweet bargains for you, no matter what some sour-faced publishers think." Their post-Christmas sale was announced this way: "The Official We Hate Winter Sale." They hold events at their bookstore and at the local country club. For over seven years, they have been holding book/author breakfasts on Tuesday mornings in March, April, May, October, and November. The fee for the breakfast covers promotional costs; all the tickets are sold within 24 hours. Their whole operation and approach is creative and consistent. They do well because they do march to a different drummer.

Sometimes it pays to specialize, but that too can present problems. You then have a limited audience and you must prepare a specialized promotional approach. However, it can be done and done successfully, as Joel Fram has shown with his two Eeyore's books for children stores in New York City. One store is located on the East Side, the other is on the West Side of town. What makes his operation successful is that he really knows children, their reading habits, and their likes and dislikes. He has competent and interested employees. He's covered both sides of town. He offers a Sunday morning story-telling hour conducted by himself, his staff, and many times, children book professionals. From this attendance list, he arranges author's appearances and special events. He has craft and puppet shows, story-writing contests, book fairs, and even folk concerts.

Often, especially in a library setting, you may be asked to set up a display. After hitting the books on the subject, you might try taking the time to explore retail establishments, especially innovative bookstores. One such place is Cover to Cover Booksellers in San Francisco. Their displays have won many awards, and it's all due to the creative thinking and design of Joan Vigilotta, who manages the store. For a window promoting baking books, Cover to Cover obtained loaves of bread from a local bakery and just slipped the baker's business card in the window. The bookstore had their props and the bakery got free advertising. Vigilotta found that many of their regular customers "had discovered that their tastes coincided with those of individual staff members." They would come into the store and share books and recommendations or simply discuss books. What came next was a "staff favorites" window. Sometimes it was one staff member's choices and another time it was a collection of staff members' choices. Extra little touches in window display can make the exhibit grab the viewer. Cover to Cover's calligrapher added a special touch to the prize-winning "Looking Glass Window" by writing bits of text into the display. Quotations included "Why sometimes I've believed as many as twelve impossible things before breakfast" and "Buy me" (referring to the draught and cake which tempted Alice to eat them). According to Vigilotta, publisher's promotion departments will provide you with special materials for displays if you show an ongoing interest in mounting special promotions. You might get special props, extra book jackets, posters, author photos, etc. It's certainly worth a try to contact them.

NAME DROPPING

What's in a name? Certainly more than letters. How you word the title of your special event or program can be the most attractive draw. Sometimes it happens quickly in a brainstorming session; sometimes it takes a few days to think of a good title. Simplicity is still the best policy to follow, so don't get so cute and involved with words that no one knows what you're talking about. Here are a few good examples.

The people at Clark County (Nevada) Library District do have a way with words. Promoting an art, music, and dance afternoon with their first annual arts festival, they called the day "It's an Affair of the Arts." They invited local volunteers and community members involved in the arts to a buffet reception on a Sunday evening during that same month and called it "An Affair to Remember." The promotional pieces for these events were printed on a white, coated paper stock using hot pink and gray inks. "Rustle Up Some Readin" was the name of their summer reading game at the Clark County Library District. Youngsters ("Tumbleweed Tots, Vegas Varmints, and Red Rock Rangers") were invited to join "that crusty Rattlesnake Rose and the Readin' Rustlers for a larrupin' good summer at the YPL Corral." A program on tips on dog care, showmanship, and grooming at Clark County was promoted as "Dog Gone It!"

The Chemical Bank in New York City ran a series of seminars for consumers planning their financial future and called them "Fiscal Fitness." The Houston Public Library in Texas calls their Tuesday lecture series "Tuesday Talkies." Their Wednesday program series is called "Lunch Bunch." To make a classical concert offering more attractive, they called it "The Classic Experience: Musical Recipe, One Part Roquefort and Two Parts Rachmaninoff."

The Detroit Public Library is clever with words. Their travel/slide programs are called "Getaway Series." "The Game's Still Afoot" was the title of a book list for "Sherlock Holmes: Cases Old and New." The Lincoln Library in Springfield, Illinois, titled its list of recommended reading materials for those restoring old houses "Homework." Most apropos was the title "Bully Birthday Cake" when the American Landmark Festivals presented a birthday celebration/fund-raiser in commemoration of Theodore Roosevelt's 125th birthday at his New York City birthplace on East 20th Street.

Lore has it that America's favorite food, the hamburger, was first invented in Hamburg, New York, 100 years ago. In the summer of 1985, the town of Hamburg invited the world to a three-day "Birth of the Burger" celebration. It all began with the Hamburg Holiday Inn offering a 100-pound hamburger, which the chamber of commerce claimed was "the biggest in western New York." This was followed by an All-American Hamburger Parade, a celebrity softball game, and, of course, there was a hamburger barbecue. The motto of the town is "On a Roll in Hamburg, New York."

RUBBER STAMPS

I had a bit of trouble figuring out where to slot this bit of information. It had to be in the book, since it was about one of my favorite things, rubber stamps. I have been playing with rubber stamps for years, in my professional and personal life. Rubber stamps are fun and add a personal touch. Graphically, I feel rubber stamp art is pretty nifty, as long as it's not overdone. I'll try to control my enthusiasm.

I had been using rubber stamps for quite a few years when I discovered *The Rubber Stamp Album* by Joni K. Miller and Lowry Thompson, in 1978. I contacted the publisher and was promised a copy of the book to begin the plans for my program (still unnamed). I also got the addresses and phone numbers of the authors. By this time, the idea was worked out. There would be a "Stamp Out Art!" Sunday at our library. It also would be a sort of contest. People of all ages would gather and create their very own rubber stamp art which would be matted and then mounted on the meeting room walls, creating an instant art show. Lowry Thompson would be one of the judges along with a local artist/teacher. Lowry brought along hundreds of rubber stamps and gave a 15-minute workshop. The rest of the rubber stamps were provided (free of charge) by the many rubber stamp companies I contacted. And as for the stamp pads, what self-respecting library would not have a full complement?

Even the promotion of this event was fun. My assistant and I created rubber stamp promotional fliers for the program; rubber stamp art was used in the library newsletter; and we even created a rubber stamp art "show" for the meeting room walls to promote the event. Taking the library's brown wrapping paper, we stamped away, creating a continuous sheet of rubber stamp art. We added, "On these walls will hang examples of rubber stamp art. Be part of it and come to our Stamp Out Art Sunday!" People from six–75 showed up; some came because of the promotional material in the library and the newsletter; and some heard about the event through media stories. A group drove in from New York City after reading about our rubber stamp day. The publisher supplied two gift copies of *The Rubber Stamp Album* as prizes. Two adult prizes were awarded for "best in show," and junior prize (a rubber stamp kit) was given to the best in the childrens's category. The "instant" art show was enjoyed by the public for the remainder of the month.

Since then, I have shared the rubber stamp program idea with a bookstore in Arizona which created its own version, and our children's room librarians held a "Rubber Stamp Family Sunday" several years later using the rubber stamps I had obtained for the initial program. Rubber stamps can also be used in graphic design. Watch out. Fooling around with rubber stamps can be like eating potato chips...you won't be able to stop at just *one*!

RESOURCES

General

Miller, Joni K., and Thompson, Lowry. *The Rubber Stamp Album.* New York: Workman Publishing, 1978.
Contains just about everything you might want to know about rubber stamps.

Rubber Stamps and Catalogs

Below are just some of the many rubber stamp outlets. You will find rubber stamps on sale in many gift and stationery shops. You can even design your own rubber stamps and have them made up.

All Night Media Inc., Box 227, Forest Knolls, CA 94933.

Bizzaro, Inc., P.O. Box 126, Annex Station, Providence, RI 02901-0126.

Imprint Graphic Studio, Box 2868, Carmel-By-The-Sea, CA 93921.

Inkadinkado, Inc., Dept. W, 105 South St., Boston, MA 02111.

Kidstamps, 1585 Maple Rd., Cleveland Heights, OH 44121.

Nature Impressions, 1000 Leneve Pl., El Cerrito, CA 94530.

The Rubber Stamp Catalog, P.O. Box 209, Bristol, RI 02809.

Chapter 9
Quotable Quotes

While putting this book together, I came in contact with many wonderful people who not only shared some exciting programs and special events, but also offered some thoughts and suggestions which I would like to pass on to you.

❝Let your imagination run wild...you can always pull yourself in if you have to because of budget restraints, time, etc., but you have to have a good, creative idea to give the event the extra push it needs.❞
—*Suzanne Dutilly,
Salt Lake City Public Library,
Salt Lake City, Utah.*

❝Don't rely on one technique. Be diverse, imaginative, eclectic. Plan your campaigns, stating your goals, expected outcomes, strategies for reaching diverse target publics, methods for evaluating the effectiveness of your efforts, etc. Be flexible, prepared to innovate and discard what doesn't work. Seek feedback from participants. Look for new methods and materials to do the promotional job more effectively.❞
—*Ed Walsh,
Westbury Recreation Department,
Westbury, New York.*

❝Programing is a wonderful part of the public efforts of historic sites because [it allows] the public [to] act or interact with the site in a looser way than they do in tours. News media respond well to something different, so we have had the best interest from them when we have been slightly daring in the program ideas.❞
—*Vera Stanton,
Minnesota Historical Society,
St. Paul, Minnesota.*

❝In the library, programming should be designed to promote the library's resources, to inform the public about what the library has to offer and how those resources can benefit them in their daily lives. Libraries need to put a lot more effort into promoting themselves; they need to learn how to sell themselves and the services they offer just like Proctor and Gamble merchandises soap. Only by keeping themselves constantly in the public eye can libraries hope to achieve the name recognition and the instant association with being the community information resource they are seeking. Let the community know where you are, what you are, and what you have to offer, and make sure that when they do come, that they get quality service that meets their needs and you will have gone a long way toward achieving a successful image.❞
—*Victoria Campbell,
Timberland Regional Library,
Olympia, Washington.*

❝Besides promoting library function, the most important role of promotion is to promote the library in such a way that the public's perception of it as an old-fashioned and stuffy institution populated by weird librarians removed centuries from real life is changed to an image of the library as an integral part of contemporary life.❞
—*Ophelia Georgiev Roop,
Indianapolis-Marion County Public Library,
Indianapolis, Indiana.*

❝Develop your ideas with those who must carry them out; make the plans well in advance; build in regular periods for checking on each person's implementation of responsibilities; design captivating materials; and don't be afraid to try something that seems offbeat. Some of our most successful programs seemed strange at first breath. Give an idea a chance to grow and look at it several times before going ahead or cancelling it. Sometimes an idea needs to be 'turned around' so you can look at its other dimensions before accepting or rejecting it, and that means allowing people freedom to develop it a bit.❞
—*Patricia H. Latshaw,
Akron-Summit County Public Library,
Indianapolis, Indiana.*

❝Aim for organized, honest, entertainment for those who are interested in exploring something for the first time; or for those who want to explore something with greater depth.❞
—*Ali Fujino Miller,
Museum of Flight,
Seattle, Washington.*

"Conceive it well and promote it vigorously."
—*Peter Langlykke,
Hudson River Museum,
Yonkers, New York.*

"Schedule your time carefully, it takes longer than you expect." —*Wendy Metcalf Roy,
North Vancouver District Public Library,
North Vancouver, British Columbia, Canada.*

"Have a *lot* of imagination, and *persist*! Ask help of those who are genuinely interested and involved in the event. Pool ideas. Trial and error has been our best course of action." —*Nadine Dreager,
Golden Age of Radio Reunion/Festival,
Council Bluffs, Iowa.*

"Remember your audience. Don't underestimate the importance of promoting your efforts."
—*Kelly Goodrich,
Tucson Public Library,
Tucson, Arizona.*

"Libraries have an obligation to excite as well as instruct. One way to accomplish this is through innovative programing. If you have an idea, do it, even if it's done on a small scale the first year. If it's good, it will gain support and grow."
—*Rosemary Medeiros,
Dartmouth Libraries,
South Dartmouth, Massachusetts.*

"Be enthusiastic about your project because it's contagious. Pay attention to details. Be very organized; especially plan deadlines for various items for yourself and others. Never take no for an answer, but be flexible. To be successful is to be persistent. Train your staff and library board to think good public relations." —*Iolani Domingo,
Edmonton Public Library,
Edmonton, Alberta, Canada.*

"Promote or perish/promote and prosper."
—*Frederic J. Glazer,
West Virginia Library Commission,
Charleston, West Virginia.*

"Enthusiasm is more important than money in the bank." —*Harold Smith, Jr.,
Dumas Cultural Commission,
Dumas, Arkansas.*

Index

Compiled by Linda Webster

Acton (MA) Memorial Library, 121
Adolescents. *See* Young adult programs
Advertising Age, 4
Aiken (OH) High School, 121
Airplanes, 37-40
Akron-Summit County (IN) Public Library, 114-115, 126
Albany (NY) Public Library, 23-25, 92, 117
Albany County (WY) Public Library, 54-56
Alice in Wonderland, 115-116
Allen, Bernie, 24
Ambro, Jerome, 21
American Picture Palaces (Naylor), 2
American Theatre Festival, 14-16
Angelou, Maya, 106
Angel's Camp, CA, 68
Animal contests, 68-70, 85. *See also* names of specific animals, such as Dogs, Teddy bears
Annual reports, 43, 101-102, 115
Architecture, 24
Arlington Heights (IL) Public Library, 115
Art institutes. *See* Museums
Art TO Zoo, 102-103
Arts Alive, 101
Arts councils, 4, 17, 20, 101. *See also* National Endowment for the Arts
Astor, Jacob, 21
Atascadero California Library, 115
Auctions, 13, 60, 63, 115, 116
Automobile industry, 25
Automobile races, 20-23
Aviation, 37-40

Bacon, Karin, 9
Baker, Michael J., 69
Baltimore, MD, 68-70
Barberton, OH, 63-64
Barrett, Elinor, 76
Baseball, 25, 50-51, 59-60
Baum, L. Frank, 80
Bears, 113
Belmont, August, 21

Bender, Betty, 43
Bennell, Craig, 75
Bernardi, Marguerite, 73
Bethlehem, PA, 119
Bibliographies. *See* Booklists
Bicycle repair, 6
Bierut, Michael, 103, 109
Bi-Folkal Productions, Inc., 120
Birdbath, Horatio Q., 84
Birthday celebrations
 Bronx Zoo, 9-11
 Brooklyn Bridge, 122
 Daniel Boone Regional Library, 122-123
 East Meadow (NY) Public Library, 6, 51
 musical composers, 122
 R.J. Reynolds Industries, 122
 Sherlock Holmes, 31-32
Bishop, CA, 79
Bishop Museum, 103
Bloomington (IL) Public Library, 118
Bonnemere, Eddie, 14
Book sales, 60, 114, 117
Booklists, 43, 44, 108-109, 124
Bookstores, 123-124
Bop-Til-You-Drop Summer Readathon, 92, 117
Boston (MA) Harborfest, 91, 95
Botanical gardens, 58-59
Brenzinger, Helmut, 120
Brewing industry, 24
Brochures. *See* Fliers and brochures
Bronx Zoo, 9-11
Bronxville, NY, 118
Brooklyn Bridge, 122
Brooklyn (NY) Public Library, 46-48, 114
Broward County (FL) Library, 26-27
Brown bag programs. *See* Lunchtime programs
Brussels sprouts festival, 72-73, 85
Bryant Library (NY), 115
Bubble gum festivals, 76-77, 85
Buchanan, E. T., 29

Budgets
 children's programs, 44
 promotion, 43-44
Buffalo and Erie County (NY) Public Library, 114
Bulk mailing, 100
Burlington, Canada, 123
Buttons, 16
Byers, Laura, 62, 103

C.W. Post College, 14-16
Cable television, 27, 59. *See also* Public television; Television
Calendars of events, 4, 103-104, 119-120
Campbell, Victoria, 126
Campbell County (WY) Public Library, 45
Capital Canine Follies and Fair, 64
Capital Children's Museum, 64
Caputo, Philip, 26
Carousels, Coney Island & Cotton Candy, 16-19
Carroll, Lewis, 115
Carrot festival, 73-74, 85
Carson City (NV) Chamber of Commerce, 84
Cartoon art, 46
Caterpillars, 83-84
Catoggio, Michael, 23
Celebrity auctions, 116
Celebrity sports contests, 59-60
Charleston, WV, 127
Chase, James E., 41
Chase's Annual Events, 6
Chemical Bank, 124
Cherry Pit Spitting Contest, 121
Chesapeake Bay, 27-29
Chicago, IL, 96, 114
Chicken Pluckin' Contest, 121
Chicken soup, 6-7
Children's bookstores, 123
Children's programs
 aviation, 40
 bubble gum festival, 76
 Carousels, Coney Island & Cotton Candy, 17
 children's theater, 108

costs, 44
Detroit, MI, 25
films, 121
food programs, 48
get-well kits, 114
Halloween, 121
ice cream anniversary, 6
nutrition, 48–49
popcorn festival, 71–72
puppetry, 25
S.E.A.R.C.H. contest, 123
summer reading clubs, 42–44, 113, 124
train series, 42–43, 44
Winter Bear Party, 113
World's Largest Games, 67–68
Children's theater, 108
Childs, Fred, 24
Chili cook-offs, 56–59
Chinese New Year Festival, 82–83, 85
Chocolate Lovers Weekend, 120
Christie, Agatha, 32, 35–37
Christmas
  Christmas trees, 92
  music, 119
  Old English feasts, 115
  Shoe Tree of the Stars, 116
  Wizard of Oz, 80–82
City University of New York, 118
Clancy, Ambrose, 27
Clark County (NV) Library District, 49–50, 56–58, 124
Clemens, Samuel, 77–80
Clowns, 45
Colleges and universities
  contests, 121
  film programs, 118
  fliers and brochures, 107–108
  health programs, 115
  Jazztime, 14–16
  library directory, 120
  newsletters, 101
  Old English feasts, 115
  women's conferences, 118
Collen Center (NY), 107–108
Colorado State University, 115
Columbia, MO, 76, 122–23
Columbia (MO) Public Library, 120
Columbus Day, 116
Comedy. *See* Humor
Committees, 3–4, 5, 23, 52, 53
Community calendars. *See* Calendars of events
Community colleges, 115. *See also* Colleges and universities
Community forums, 23
Contests. *See also* Games; Quizzes
  cherry pit spitting, 121
  chicken pluckin', 121
  chili cook-offs, 56–59
  crossword puzzles, 121
  frog-jumping, 68
  hog-calling, 69
  ice cream, 11–14, 120
  interest in, 3

jigsaw puzzles, 121
kites, 40
marbles tournament, 121
milk drinking, 121
paper airplanes, 37–39
popcorn, 70–71
Sauntering Day, 121
Scrambled Legs, 121
S.E.A.R.C.H., 123
tobacco spitting, 121
turtle derby, 68–69
ugliest umbrella, 121
whistling, 84
World's Largest Games, 66–68
Cooking. *See* Food festivals; Food programs; Recipes
Cooperative programs
  Albany, NY, 23–25
  biggest ice cream sundae, 11–14
  Detroit, MI, 25–26
  Hemingway seminar, 26–27
  initiation of, 2
  Key West, FL, 26–27
  train series, 41
  Vanderbilt Parkway races, 20–23
  Virginia Beach Library, 27–29
  World's Largest Games, 68
Costs. *See* Budgets; Funding sources
Council Bluffs, IA, 127
Cover to Cover Booksellers, 123–124
Cradle of Aviation Museum, 39
Crawford, Ralston, 15
Cretekos, Stacy, 48
Crossword puzzles, 121. *See also* Games
Cruise parties, 61–63
Culinary programs. *See* Food festivals; Food programs; Recipes
Cultural Center of Detroit, 25–26
Cummings, Al, 123

Dance, Jim, 80, 81
Dance programs
  Chinese New Year Festival, 83
  ethnic festivals, 116
  Jazztime, 14–16
Daniel Boone Regional Library, 76–77, 120, 122–123
Dankner, Jackie, 70
Dan's Papers, 120–121
Dartmouth (MA) Public Libraries, 121, 127
Dayton, OH, 101
DeBenedetti, John, 73
Detroit, MI, 25–26, 80–82
Detroit (MI) Historical Museum, 25
Detroit (MI) Institute of Arts, 25
Detroit (MI) Public Library, 25, 50, 80–82, 114, 116–117, 124
Dewey, Ed, 48
Dewey, Gertrude, 48
Diets, 49
Dietz, Norman, 87–89
Dietz, Sandra, 87–89

Different Drummer Books, 123
Dinners as fund raisers, 53–56
Displays and exhibits
  Albany, NY, 24
  aviation, 39
  baseball, 50
  bookstores, 123
  Carousels, Coney Island & Cotton Candy, 17, 18, 19
  cartoon art, 46
  Christmas in Oz, 81
  Detroit, MI, 25
  hair programs, 50
  inventions, 119
  Italian festival, 116
  Jazztime, 15
  mystery programs, 31
  placement of, 4
Doblin, Alfred, 15
Dogs, 64
Domingo, Iolani, 127
Donaldson, Scott, 27
Donations, 52. *See also* Fund raising
Dracula, 90
Dreager, Nadine, 127
Dumas (AR) Cultural Commission, 127
Durant, Keith, 42, 44
Durum Forum, 75–76
Dutelle, Tom, 51
Dutilly, Suzanne, 126

East Brunswick (NJ) Public Library, 59–60, 114
East Meadow (NY) Public Library
  aviation programs, 39–40
  birthday celebrations, 6, 51, 122
  Carousels, Coney Island & Cotton Candy, 16–19
  Chinese New Year Festival, 82–83
  Frankenstein Frolics, 6
  health programs, 6–7, 115
  ice cream anniversary, 6
  kite fly-off, 6
  Lunch'n Books, 4–5
  movies and movie palaces, 2–3
  mystery programs, 31–37
  newsletters, 101–102
  summer reading clubs, 113
  Sweet Sixteen Birthday, 6
Eau Claire, MI, 121
Edmonton (AB) Public Library, 127
Educator's Guide to Free Films, 119
Elements of Style, The (Strunk and White), 98
Elephant's birthday party, 9–11
Elmira, NY, 78–79
Elmira College, 78
Ephron, Nora, 118
Ethnic programs, 46–48, 116–117
Exercise, 49
Exhibits. *See* Displays and exhibits

Fairs. *See* Festivals
Families, 49

Festivals
    Chinese New Year, 82–83, 85
    Christmas in Oz, 80–82, 85
    Huck Finn Days, 77–80, 85
    interest in, 3
    International Whistle-Off, 84, 85
    Woollybear Festival, 83–84, 85
Fetty, Vivian, 42
Field trips, 29, 83
Film programs
    Albany, NY, 24
    aviation, 39, 40
    Carousels, Coney Island & Cotton Candy, 17, 18
    Chinese New Year Festival, 82, 83
    creative approaches, 1
    ethnic festivals, 116
    food programs, 48
    free films, 119
    hair programs, 50
    Hemingway series, 27
    Hooray for the Bay!, 29
    humanities, 118–119
    humor, 45
    male roles, 50
    mysteries, 31–33, 118
    noontime scheduling, 118
    60's movies, 118
    train series, 41–42, 44
    women's roles, 49–50, 118
Fines moratorium, 114
Finn, Huckleberry, 77–80
Fishkin, Shelley F., 78
Fleischman, Barbara, 53
Fliers and brochures
    Carousels, Coney Island & Cotton Candy, 19
    Hooray for the Bay!, 28
    Huck Finn Days, 79
    Jazztime, 15–16
    mailing, 105
    reproduction, 104
    samples, 105–109
    Sherlock Holmes programs, 88, 90
    suggestions, 104–105
    Theatre in the Works, 88, 89
    train series, 43–44
    Winefest, 61
Flight programs, 37–41
Florida Endowment for the Humanities, 27
Flushing, NY, 120
Food festivals
    brussels sprouts, 72–73, 85
    bubble gum, 76–77, 85
    carrots, 73–74, 85
    garlic, 74–75, 85
    pasta, 75–76, 85
    popcorn, 70–72, 85
Food programs
    children's activities, 48
    chili cook-offs, 56–59
    Chinese New Year Festival, 82–83

cookbooks, 48
cooking programs, 114–115
dinners as fund raisers, 53–56
film programs, 48
food fairs, 114
hamburgers, 124
lobsters, 115
Old English feasts, 115
Taste of America, 46–48
Taste of Chicago, 114
Taste of Hartford, 114
Football, 60
Forbes, Malcolm, Jr., 39
Ford, Henry, 21
Forgiveness Week, 114
Fort Collins, CO, 115
Foster, Faith, 25
Foundation Center, 4, 8
Foundation Directory, 8
Fram, Joel, 123
Frankenstein Frolics, 6, 32
Freeport (NY) Memorial Library, 121
Friends of the Albany County Public Library, 54–55
Friends of the Atascadero California Library, 115
Friends of the Bryant Library, 115
Friends of the Buffalo and Erie County (NY) Public Library, 114
Friends of the Dartmouth (MA) Public Libraries, 121
Friends of the Detroit (MI) Public Library, 116–117
Friends of the East Brunswick (NJ) Public Library, 114
Friends of the J.V. Fletcher Library, 119
Friends of the Monroe County Library, 26–27
Friends of the Virginia Beach Library, 27
Frog-jumping contests, 68
Fund raising
    Capital Canine Follies and Fair, 64
    celebrity sports contests, 59–60
    chili cook-offs, 56–59
    community considerations, 3
    costs, 60
    cruise parties, 61–63
    dinners, 53–56
    Jello Jump, 63–64
    lawn mower race, 63
    museums, 62–63
    planning, 52
    promotion, 52–53
    public television stations, 60–62
    thank yous, 53
Funding sources. *See also* Humanities state grants; National Endowment for the Arts; National Endowment for the Humanities
    Albany, NY, 23

ethnic festivals, 116
film programs, 50
Hemingway seminar, 27
Hooray for the Bay!, 29
options for, 4, 8
Spokane Public Library, 41
women's roles, 117

Games. *See also* Contests; Quizzes
    Game of Love, 51
    interest in, 3
    mystery programs, 31
    popcorn, 70–71
    World's Largest Games, 66–68, 85
Garden City, NY, 51
Gardening, 1
Garlic festival, 74–75, 85
Gensel, John Garcia, 14
Gillette, WY, 45
Gilroy, CA, 74–75
Gimmicks, 5–7. *See also* Contests; Games; Quizzes
Glazer, Frederic J., 127
Goddard, Dick, 84
Goldberger, Paul, 24
Goodrich, Kelly, 127
Grant writing, 4, 8. *See also* Funding sources; Humanities state grants; National Endowment for the Arts; National Endowment for the Humanities
GRANTS Database, 8
Grantsmanship Center, 4, 8
Graphic designers, 94
Graphics
    importance of, 3
    logos, 94–97
    resources, 111–112
    suppliers, 112
    tools for, 109–110
Great Neck (NY) Public Library, 116
Greer, Nancy, 43
Gregory-Pindell, Cheryl, 23
Grella, George, 31
Griffith, Richard, 15
Griswold, Denny, 86
"Guiding Light" stars, 59–60
Guinness Book of World Records, 11, 13, 14, 66–67
Gum. *See* Bubble gum

Hair, 50
Half Hollows Hills Community Library (Huntington, NY), 20–23
Halloween, 31, 108–109, 121
Hamburg, NY, 124
Hamburgers, 124
Hannibal, MO, 77–78
Hartford, CT, 78, 92, 114, 119
Harwell, Ernie, 25, 50
Health fairs, 49, 115

Health programs, 6-7, 45, 48-49, 115
Heckscher, August, 21
Heiskell, Andrew, 53
Helig, John, 21
Hemingway, Ernest, 26-27
Hemingway, Patrick, 26
Herbs, 1
Hernandez, Francisco, 84
Hewett, Marie, 30
Hewitt, Holly, 78
High schools, 121
Hilton, Jim, 11-14
Hiltonsmith, Warren, 3
Historic preservation, 21
Hobos, 41, 42
Hog-calling contest, 69
Hogs, 70
Holbrook, Hal, 77
Holidays. *See* Christmas; Halloween; Valentine's Day
Holistic medicine, 49. *See also* Health programs
Holmes, Sherlock, 31-35, 88, 90
Holtville, CA, 73-74
Honolulu, HI, 103
Hooray for the Bay!, 27-29
Hospitals, 6-7
Hotchkiss, Jack, 24
Hotels, 120
Houston (TX) Public Library, 124
Huck Finn Days, 77-80, 85
Hudgins, Chris, 50
Hudson River Museum, 39, 62-63, 96, 103-104, 109, 127
Humanities state grants, 27, 29, 41, 50, 117, 122. *See also* National Endowment for the Humanities
Humor, 45-46, 64
Hunsberger, Charles, 57
Huntington, NY, 20-23
Hyatt Hotel, 120

Ice cream, 6, 11-14, 120
Illinois Restaurant Association, 114
Image, 2, 93-94, 111
Indiana Committee for the Humanities, 50, 117
Indianapolis, IN, 114-115
Indianapolis-Marion County (IN) Public Library, 117-118, 126
Insight, 103
International Chili Society, 57-59
International Typeface Corporation, 107
International Whistle-Off, 85
International Wizard of Oz Club, 80, 81, 85
Inventions, 119
Italian festival, 116

J.B. Speed Art Museum, 103
J.V. Fletcher Library (MA), 119
James, Laurie, 15
Japanese festival, 116
Jasen, David, 14-15

Jaycees, 63-64, 75
Jazz, 14-16, 25. *See also* Music programs
Jello Jump, 63-64
Jigsaw puzzles, 67, 121. *See also* Games; Quizzes
John Cotton Dana Library Public Relations award, 19
Johnston, Elisa, 103
Jones, Spike, 84
Jugglers, 46

Ka 'Elele, 103
Kael, Pauline, 118
Kaiser, William, 39
Kangas, Robert, 81
Karamzin, Sharon, 59, 60
Katz, Bernard, 25
Katz, Bob, 117
Kaufelt, David, 27
Kaufelt, Lynn, 27
Kazoos, 45-46
Keene State College (NH), 121
Kennedy, William, 24
Kern, Jerome, 122
Kert, Bernice, 27
Kewanee, IL, 70
Key West, FL, 26-27
Kites, 6, 39-40
Koch, Ed, 53
Kovier, Carol Dratch, 117
Krueger, Gerry, 43, 44, 96
Kusmotono, Shifu Tonny, 82

Lake Havasu City (AZ) Chamber of Commerce, 122
Langdon, Ida, 78
Langdon, Jervis, 78
Langdon, Olivia, 78
Langhans, Rufus, 21
Langlykke, Peter, 62, 63, 127
Laramie, WY, 54-56
Las Vegas, NV, 49-50, 56-58
Latshaw, Patricia H., 126
Laughter. *See* Humor
Lawn mower race, 63
Lazar, Jon, 31
Lerner, Gerda, 118
Leung, Zen, 82, 83
Lewis, Fran, 117
Lewis, Sinclair, 122
Lewis Carroll Society of North America, 115
Liebman, Arthur, 31-32, 88, 90
Liebman, Joyce, 31-32, 88, 90
Liebold, Louise, 102
Lincoln Center, 122
Lincoln Library (IL), 95, 124
Lions Club, 60, 63
Literary programs, 4, 8. *See also* names of authors, such as Hemingway, Ernest
Lobster Fly-In, 115
Local history, 24
Logos, 94-97
London Bridge, 122

Long Island Motor Parkway, 20-23
Long Island University, 14-16
Lord, Betty Bao, 83
Los Angeles (CA) County Fair, 121
Louisville, KY, 103
Love, 51
Love Your Library, 119
Loveless, Jim, 106
Lowenberg, Bill, 24
Lowery, Fred, 84
Lunchtime programs, 4-5, 113-114, 118, 124
Luxeder, Marty, 64

McEneny, Jack, 24
MacEoin, Dorothy Aukofer, 103
Mackinac Island, MI, 121
Macy's department store, 66-68
Magic, 119
Mailing, 100
Mailing lists, 87-90, 100
Maleska, Eugene T., 121
Manchester, CT, 78
Manheimer, Ron, 41
Marbles Tournament, 121
Margulies, Walter, 94
Martial arts, 82, 83
Martin, David, 27
Marx, Stan, 115
Mass media. *See* Newspapers; Radio; Television
Mates, Julian, 14-16
Maxham, Tim, 13
Medeiros, Rosemary, 127
Media. *See* Cable television; Newspapers; Public television; Radio; Television
Memphis in May International Festival, 95
Men's roles, 50
Mental health, 49
Miami Herald, 26-27
Michigan City (IN) Public Library, 50
Milk drinking contest, 121
Miller, Ali Fujino, 39, 126
Miller, Joni K., 124
Miller, Robert, 21
Miller, Sally, 20-23
Milltown (NJ) Public Library, 59-60
Milwaukee (WI) Public Library, 118
Mimeographing, 98
Minnesota Historical Society, 126
Minot, ND, 75-76
Monroe County (FL) Library, 26-27
Montclair (NJ) Public Library, 115-116
Moon, William Least Heat, 123
Moore, Billy, 29
Morris, Mrs. Marty, 73
Mount Sinai Hospital, 6-7
Moveable Feast, 26-27
Movies. *See* Film programs
Museums
aviation, 37-40
baseball, 50

brochures, 109
calendars of events, 103–104
cruise parties, 62–63
Detroit, MI, 25
dinners, 56
hair programs, 50
logos, 96
marine sciences, 29
mystery programs, 30–31
newsletters, 103
Music programs
   Chinese New Year Festival, 82–83
   Christmas, 119
   composers' birthdays, 122
   Detroit, MI, 25
   folksingers, 41
   Huck Finn Days, 77
   jazz, 14–16, 25
   noontime programs, 113–114
   sing-alongs, 46
   women's composers, 118
   World's Largest Games, 68
   young adult programs, 117
Musical chairs, 64
Mutschler, Charles, 41, 44
Mystery programs, 30–37, 88, 90, 118

Nassau Community College, 51, 115
Nassau County (NY) Parks and Recreation Department, 113–114
National Air and Space Museum, 37, 39
National Endowment for the Arts, 4, 8, 27
National Endowment for the Humanities, 23, 116, 119
National Library Week, 42
National Radio Heritage Association, 120
Naylor, David, 2
Neely, Martina, 59
Neely, William, 59
New Orleans (LA) Public Library, 115
New York City, 9–11, 58–59, 66–68, 97, 107–108
New York Council for the Humanities, 122
New York Giants, 60
New York Public Library, 53–54, 96
New York Public Library for the Performing Arts, 122
New York State Council on the Arts, 17
New York State Museum, 50
News releases
   for fund raising, 53
   rules for, 90–91
   sample, 91
   timing of, 4, 87
   train series, 44

Newsletters
   benefits, 97
   distribution, 100
   first announcement of events, 4
   follow-up story, 5
   format, 98
   Jazztime promotion, 15
   logos, 96
   paper and inks, 99–100
   photographs, 98
   proofreading, 100
   reproduction, 98–100
   samples, 101–103
   Seattle Museum of Flight, 38, 39
   writing, 98
Newspapers
   feature stories, 11, 13, 44, 53, 57
   importance of in promotion, 87
   photographs submitted to, 19
Night of 100 Dinners, 53–56
Ninomiya, Y., 39
Noontime programs, 4–5, 113–114, 118, 124
North Vancouver (BC) District Public Library, 127
Nutrition programs, 48–49

Oaks, L. Robert, 2
O'Brien, Timothy, 26, 27
Ohoopee (GA) Regional Library, 118–119
Oliver, Susan, 39
Olympia, WA, 126
On Writing Well (Zinsser), 98
Onondaga County (NY) Public Library, 115
Oregon City (OR) Public Library, 121
Orient, Long Island, 87–89
Oryx Press, 8
Osborne, Lynn, 50
Overmyer, Don, 103

Paper airplanes, 37–39
Paper companies, 112
Pardee, Alan, 103
Parties. *See* Birthday celebrations; Christmas; Cruise parties; Halloween; Valentine's Day
Pastaville USA, 75–76, 85
Patafio, John J., Jr., 87
Patchogue-Medford (NY) Library, 114
Pawtucket (RI) Public Library, 116
Peck, Pat, 62
Pendray, G. Edward, 94
Percival, John, 14, 119
Pereira, John, 40
Perry, William, 78
Perspectives, 101
Philadelphia Zoo, 113
Phillips, Harvey, 119
Phillips, Utah, 41, 44
Phoenix, AZ, 115

Photographs
   following events, 5
   importance of, 53, 87
   in newsletters, 98
   submitted to newspapers, 19
   with news releases, 90–91
Picnic, 122
Plainedge (NY) Public Library, 114
Planning
   Carousels, Coney Island & Cotton Candy, 16–17
   fund raising, 52
   steps in, 3–4
Plays. *See* Theater programs
Playwrights Horizons, 97, 105–106
Plimpton, George, 26
Plymouth (MA) Public Library, 120
Poets & Writers, 4, 8, 17
Police department, 4
Polish American festival, 116–117
Pollock, Donald, 31
Ponomarev, Valery, 15
Popcorn festivals and programs, 70–72, 85, 121
Popcorn Institute, 96
Port Washington (NY) Public Library, 116, 118
Posters. *See* Fliers and brochures
PR News, 86, 110
Preservation programs, 21
Press kits, 4, 91
Press releases. *See* News releases
Printing, 98–99
Programs. *See also* Children's programs; Contests; Cooperative programs; Festivals; Film programs; Fund raising; Games; Promotion; Special events; Young adult programs
   basic tips, 5
   costs, 43–44
   follow-up activities, 5
   gimmicks, 5–7
   last-minute changes, 4–5
   quotations concerning, 126–127
   scheduling, 4, 18–19
   thank-yous, 5
   titles of, 5–6, 124
Promotion. *See also* Fliers and brochures; Graphics; News releases; Newsletters; Press kits; Public service announcements; Radio; Television
   Albany, NY, 24–25
   approach to, 86–87
   aviation programs, 40
   biggest ice cream sundae, 13
   Bronx Zoo, 11
   Carousels, Coney Island & Cotton Candy, 18–19
   chili cook-offs, 57–58
   costs, 43–44
   food programs, 48
   fund raising, 52–53
   garlic festival, 75

Hooray for the Bay!, 28
Huck Finn Days, 79
image, 2, 93–94, 111
importance of, 3
Jazztime, 15–16
mailing lists, 87–90
Night of 100 dinners, 53, 55
options for, 4
periodicals, 110
photographs and, 5, 19, 53, 87, 90–91, 98
popcorn festival, 72
quotations concerning, 126–127
resources, 110–111
Sherlock Holmes programs, 88, 90
Theatre in the Works, 87–89
timing of, 18–19
train series, 43–44
Winefest, 61
Proofreading, 100
Providence (RI) Public Library, 119
PSAs. *See* Public service announcements
Public relations, 86. *See also* Promotion
Public relations award, 19
Public Relations Journal, 4, 94, 110
Public Relations Quarterly, 110
Public service announcements, 80, 81, 91–92
Public television. *See also* Cable television; Television
biggest ice cream sundae, 13
fund raising, 60–62
Huck Finn Days, 78
logos, 95
popcorn festival, 70–71
Publicity. *See* Promotion
Puppetry, 25
Puzzles, 67, 121. *See also* Games

Queens Botanical Gardens, 58–59
Queens College (NY), 107–108, 118
Quimby, John, 48
Quizzes. *See also* Contests; Games
Agatha Christie, 35–37
hobos, 42
humor self-test, 45
popcorn, 70
railroad slang, 42, 44
Sherlock Holmes, 32–35
tournaments of trivia, 121

R.J. Reynolds Industries, 122
Races
automobile, 20–23
caterpillar, 84
Huck Finn Days, 78, 79
lawn mowers, 63
popcorn, 70
turtle derby, 68–69
Radio. *See also* Television
Huck Finn Days, 78
interviews, 44, 92–93
old-time radio programs, 31, 120

public service announcements, 91–92
remote broadcasting, 93
Railroads, 41–44
Raleigh, MS, 121
Rattiner, Dan, 120–121
Rawls, Mac, 29
Reading lists. *See* Booklists
Reading programs
Albany Public Library, 92
costs, 44
for teenagers, 117
Here Come the Bears!, 113
Rustle Up Some Readin', 124
train theme, 42–44
Recipes
Belgian cheese pie, 73
carrot-stuffed chicken rolls with apricot sauce, 74
chicle gum, 77
chili, 59
grilled angler with garlic beurre rouge, 75
Mulligan Stew, 42
pizza-pleaser popcorn, 72
Record-setting events
biggest ice cream sundae, 11–14
World's Largest Games, 66–69
Recreation centers, 11–14
Recreation departments, 113
Redding, CT, 78
Redenbacher, Orville, 71
Reed, Kelly Scott, 103
Rhue, Ben, 40
Richardson, John, 123
Robertson, Bill, 27
Robertson, Crawford, 21
Robertson, George, 21
Rochester, NY, 30–31
Rogers, Haydon, 20
Rogers, Will, 74
Roop, Ophelia Georgiev, 126
Rosenblum, Bonnie, 62
Roslyn, NY, 115, 119–120
Rosten, Norman, 17–18
Rothenberg, Marion, 102
Rothstein, Cathy, 62, 95
Rowley, William, 24
Roy, Wendy Metcalf, 127
Rubber stamp art, 124–125
Runte, Alfred, 41

Sackner, Marvin, 6
St. Albans, VT, 11–14
St. Louis, MO, 60–62, 70–71, 95
St. Louis (MO) Public Library, 106
St. Paul, MN, 126
Salt Lake City (UT) Public Library, 108–109, 126
San Francisco, CA, 123
Santa Cruz (CA) Beach Boardwalk, 72–73, 95
Sarah Lawrence College, 118
Sauk Centre, MN, 122
Sauntering Day, 121
Scanlon, Doc, 24

Schaefer, William, 68
Scheduling, 4, 18–19
Schluckebier, Debbie, 76
Schubel, J. R., 29
Schwantes, Carlos, 41
Science 85 magazine, 37
Scribner, Charles, Jr., 26
Sea programs, 27–29
Seattle (WA) Museum of Flight, 37–39, 126
Shiverdecker, Darlene, 121
Shortz, Will, 121
Simpson, Susan, 54
Singing. *See* Music programs
Slide shows
Albany, NY, 24
aviation, 39
Bi-Folkal Productions, Inc., 120
Carousels, Coney Island & Cotton Candy, 19
from special events programs, 19
Hooray for the Bay!, 29
train series, 41, 42
typography, 107
Vanderbilt Parkway races, 23
Sloan, Sonny, 53
Small Business Administration, 119
Smith, Elinor, 39
Smith, Erick, 27
Smith, Harold, Jr., 127
Smith, Paul, 27
Smithsonian Institution, 17, 40, 102–103
Snelling, Richard, 13
Soap opera stars, 59–60
Society for Creative Anachronism, 115, 122
South Dartmouth, MA, 127
Spampinato, Clemente, 116
Special events
approach to, 2
Bronx Zoo, 9–11
professional staffing, 2
promotion, 11, 13, 15–16, 18–19
rationale for, 2
scheduling, 18–19
sponsorship, 1–2
Special Events Report, 2, 8
Speiser, Bruno, 18
Spokane (WA) Public Library, 41–46, 96
Sports. *See* names of specific sports, such as Baseball
Spring Hill, FL, 121
Springfield, IL, 124
Stamford (CT) Arts Council, 101
Stanton, Vera, 126
State University at Stony Brook (NY), 121
Stepanek, Gael, 15
Stone, Beverly, 75
Stone, Robert, 26
Strong Museum (NY), 30–31
Strunk, William, Jr., 98
Suffolk County, NY, 113
Syracuse, NY, 115

Talma, Sheila Kirven, 117
Tamura, Mike, 103
Tap dancing, 66–67
Taste of America, 46–48
Taste of Chicago, 114
Taste of Hartford, 114
Teddy bears, 113
Teenagers. *See* Young adult programs
Television. *See also* Cable television; Public television
  coverage of special events, 31–32
  Hemingway seminar, 27
  interviews, 92–93
  public service announcements, 91–92
  train series, 44
  Woollybear Festival, 84
Testani, Giovanna, 15
Theater in the Park, 120
Theater programs
  children's theater, 108
  Chinese New Year Festival, 82
  Christmas in Oz, 80
  Huck Finn Days, 78
  Jazztime, 14–16
  Vanderbilt Parkway races, 21, 23
Theatre in the Works, 87–89
Thematic programs. *See* specific themes, such as Women's roles
Theodore, Lee, 14
Thompson, Lowry, 124
Ticket sales, 52, 53
Tiffany, Louis, 21
Timberland Regional Library, 126
Tobacco spitting contest, 121
Trains, 41–44
Travel programs, 124
Trebbi, Jean, 27
Trivia quizzes. *See* Quizzes

Tubalation, 119
Tucson (AZ) Museum of Art, 56
Tucson (AZ) Public Library, 113, 116, 127
Turtle derby, 68–69
Twain, Mark, 77–80
Twelve Mile, IN, 63
Typesetting, 99
Typography, 99, 106–107

U & lc, 106–107, 112
Union Pacific Railroad, 42, 44
Universities. *See* Colleges and universities
University of California, Berkeley, 115
University of Maryland, 120
Used book sales. *See* Book sales

Valentine's Day, 51, 117
Valparaiso, IN, 71–72
Van Sickle, Jim, 31–32
Vanderbilt, William K., 21
Vanderbilt Parkway, 20–23
Verdon, Gwen, 14
Vermilion, OH, 83–84
Vidalia, GA, 118–119
Vigilotta, Joan, 123
Virginia Beach (VA) Library, 27–29
Virginia Foundation for the Humanities, 29
Volunteers, 11–14, 64

Wade, Roland, 58
Wadsworth Atheneum, 92
Walsh, Ed, 126
Washington, D.C., 64, 102–103
Washington State Commission for the Humanities, 41
Water programs, 27–29

Webb, George, 29
Webb, Jane, 29
West, Jim, 59
West Florida Library System, 114
West Virginia Library Commission, 118, 127
Westbury (NY) Recreation Department, 113, 126
Westchester (IN) Public Library, 50
Westford, MA, 119
Whistling contests, 84, 85
White, Bill, 70
White, E. B., 98
Wildwood by the Sea, NJ, 121
Winefest, 60–61
Winston-Salem, NC, 122
Winter parties, 120–121
Wiseman, Bob, 57
Wizard of Oz, 80–82, 85
Wolbier, Joan, 103
Wolfe, Joel, 48
Wolfe, Lisa, 42, 96
Women's roles, 49–50, 117–118
Wong, Janis, 83
Woollybear Festival, 83–84, 85
World's Largest Games, 66–68, 85
Wright State University, 101

Yonkers, NY, 39, 62–63, 96, 103–104, 127
Yosemite National Park, 115
Young adult programs, 117
Yuin, Gloria, 83

Zielinski, John, 106
Zinsser, William, 98
Zoos, 9–11, 113

KRAUSKOPF LIBRARY STACKS
021.7 L622
Liebold, Louise Con/Fireworks, brass ban

3 1896 00031 8414

021.7 L622 88-1339
Liebold, Louise Condak.
Fireworks, brass bands, and
elephants

NOV 15   8457

WD